VOLUME NINETY NINE

ADVANCES IN
COMPUTERS

VOLUME NINETY NINE

Advances in
COMPUTERS

Edited by

ATIF MEMON
College Park, MD, USA

AMSTERDAM • BOSTON • HEIDELBERG • LONDON
NEW YORK • OXFORD • PARIS • SAN DIEGO
SAN FRANCISCO • SINGAPORE • SYDNEY • TOKYO
Academic Press is an imprint of Elsevier

Academic Press is an imprint of Elsevier
225 Wyman Street, Waltham, MA 02451, USA
525 B Street, Suite 1800, San Diego, CA 92101-4495, USA
125 London Wall, London, EC2Y 5AS, UK
The Boulevard, Langford Lane, Kidlington, Oxford OX5 1GB, UK

First edition 2015

Notices
Knowledge and best practice in this field are constantly changing. As new research and experience broaden our understanding, changes in research methods, professional practices, or medical treatment may become necessary.

Practitioners and researchers must always rely on their own experience and knowledge in evaluating and using any information, methods, compounds, or experiments described herein. In using such information or methods they should be mindful of their own safety and the safety of others, including parties for whom they have a professional responsibility.

To the fullest extent of the law, neither the Publisher nor the authors, contributors, or editors, assume any liability for any injury and/or damage to persons or property as a matter of products liability, negligence or otherwise, or from any use or operation of any methods, products, instructions, or ideas contained in the material herein.

ISBN: 978-0-12-802131-6
ISSN: 0065-2458

For information on all Academic Press publications
visit our web site at store.elsevier.com

Working together
to grow libraries in
developing countries

www.elsevier.com • www.bookaid.org

CONTENTS

4. Recent Advances in Automatic Black-Box Testing   157

Leonardo Mariani, Mauro Pezzè, and Daniele Zuddas

5. Inroads in Testing Access Control   195

Tejeddine Mouelhi, Donia El Kateb, and Yves Le Traon

PREFACE

This volume of *Advances in Computers* is the 99th in this series. This series, which has been continuously published since 1960, presents in each volume four to seven chapters describing new developments in software, hardware, or uses of computers.

This 99th volume is the first in a mini-series of volumes based on the theme "Advances in Software Testing." The need for such a thematic mini-series came up when I was teaching my graduate class "Fundamentals of Software Testing," in which students were asked to study and report on recent (years 2010–2015) advances in various topics surrounding software testing. They failed to find up-to-date survey papers on almost all topics. In this mini-series, I have invited leaders in their respective fields of software testing to write about recent advances.

Volume 99 focuses on five important topics. Chapter 1, entitled "Combinatorial Testing: Theory and Practice," by Kuhn *et al.*, reviews the theory and application of the method of combinatorial testing, focusing particularly on research since 2010, with a brief background providing the rationale and development of combinatorial methods for software testing. They discuss significant advances that have occurred in algorithm performance, and the critical area of constraint representation and processing. In addition to these foundational topics, they take a look at advances in specialized areas including test suite prioritization, sequence testing, fault localization, the relationship between combinatorial testing and structural coverage, and approaches to very large testing problems.

In Chapter 2, entitled "Constraint-Based Testing: An Emerging Trend in Software Testing," Gotlieb discusses constraint-based testing. The general idea behind this testing paradigm is to use a constraint solver to calculate the test inputs to be used for testing a software system so that the fault-revealing capabilities of the testing process can be improved. The incredible progress achieved in the last years on the development of powerful constraint solvers has fostered the emergence of effective and efficient constraint-based testing techniques. This chapter reviews in detail the main achievements reached in the field by illustrating them on simple examples.

In Chapter 3, Masri discusses "Automated Fault Localization: Advances and Challenges." Following a program failure, the main concern of the developer is to identify what caused it in order to repair the code that induced it. The first activity is termed fault localization, whereas the second is referred to as fault repair. Even though both activities are very important, this chapter will only focus on automated fault localization research. First, it presents the background that provides the bases for the main existing fault localization techniques. Second, it describes early research and relevant shortcomings. And finally, it presents the latest major advances in this area of research.

In Chapter 4, "Recent Advances in Automatic Black-Box Testing," Mariani *et al.* discuss research in black-box testing. In the last few years, research in this area has focused mostly on the automation of black-box approaches to improve applicability and scalability. This chapter surveys the recent advances in automatic black-box testing, covering contributions from 2010 to 2014, presenting the main research results and discussing the research trends.

Finally, in Chapter 5, "Inroads in Testing Access Control," Mouelhi *et al.* discuss access control, which forms a significant part of computer security. This chapter pursues the goal of describing the landscape in the research area of access control testing. It provides an outline of the different existing research over the literature according to the taxonomy reflecting the different phases of common software testing processes (generation, selection, prioritization, quality assessment, regression). It also provides an outline of some existing initiatives that support usage control besides access control by testing obligation policies. Finally, the authors point out future research directions that emerge from the current research study.

I hope that you find these articles of interest. If you have any suggestions of topics for future chapters, or if you wish to be considered as an author for a chapter, I can be reached at atif@cs.umd.edu.

PROF. ATIF M. MEMON, PH.D.
College Park, MD, USA

CHAPTER ONE

Combinatorial Testing: Theory and Practice

D. Richard Kuhn*, Renee Bryce[†], Feng Duan[‡], Laleh Sh. Ghandehari[‡], Yu Lei[‡], Raghu N. Kacker*

*National Institute of Standards and Technology, Gaithersburg, Maryland, USA
†Department of Computer Science & Engineering, University of North Texas, Denton, Texas, USA
‡Department of Computer Science & Engineering, University of Texas at Arlington, Arlington, Texas, USA

Contents

Advances in Computers, Volume 99
ISSN 0065-2458
http://dx.doi.org/10.1016/bs.adcom.2015.05.003

2015 Published by Elsevier Inc.

Abstract

Combinatorial testing has rapidly gained favor among software testers in the past decade as improved algorithms have become available and practical success has been demonstrated. This chapter reviews the theory and application of this method, focusing particularly on research since 2010, with a brief background providing the rationale and development of combinatorial methods for software testing. Significant advances have occurred in algorithm performance, and the critical area of constraint representation and processing. In addition to these foundational topics, we take a look at advances in specialized areas including test suite prioritization, sequence testing, fault localization, the relationship between combinatorial testing and structural coverage, and approaches to very large testing problems.

1. INTRODUCTION

An interesting phenomenon often occurs with large software systems. After successful use for a long period of time, the software is installed in a new location, with a different user base, and a new set of bugs appear. Typically, the reason is not surprising—the change in usage has resulted in a different set of inputs, and some of these input combinations trigger failures that have escaped previous testing and extensive use. Such failures are known as *interaction failures*, because they are only exposed when two or more input values interact to cause the program to reach an incorrect result.

For example, a pump may be observed to fail only when pressure is below a particular level and volume exceeds a certain amount, a 2-way interaction between pressure and volume. Figure 1 illustrates how such a 2-way interaction may happen in code. Note that the failure will only be triggered when both *pressure* <10 and *volume* >300 are true. Either one of the conditions, without the other, will not be a problem.

```
if (pressure < 10) {
    // do something
    if (volume > 300)  {
        faulty code
    }
    else {
        good code
    }
}
else {
    // do something else
}
```

Figure 1 2-Way interaction failure triggered only when two conditions are true.

1.1 Empirical Data on Failures

The example above focuses on a 2-way interaction failure. *Pairwise testing*, using tests that cover all 2-way combinations of parameter values, has long been accepted as a way of detecting such interaction failures [1–4]. However, higher-order *t*-way interactions may also cause failures. For instance, consider a failure that is triggered by unusual combinations of three or four sensor values. For thorough checking, it may be necessary to test 3-way and 4-way combinations of values. The question arises as to whether testing all 4-way combinations is enough to detect all errors. What is the distribution of interaction failures beyond 2-way in real systems? Surprisingly, this question had not been studied when NIST began investigating interaction failures in 1999 [5]. Results of this and subsequent studies showed that across a variety of domains, all failures were triggered by a maximum of 4-way to 6-way interactions [6–8]. As shown in Fig. 2, the detection rate increases rapidly with interaction strength (the interaction level *t* in *t*-way combinations is often referred to as *strength*). With the NASA application, for example, 67% of the failures were triggered by only a single parameter value, 93% by 2-way combinations, and 98% by 3-way combinations. The detection rate curves for the other applications studied are similar, reaching 100% detection with 4-way to 6-way interactions. Studies by other researchers [8–10] have been consistent with these results.

The empirical data show that most failures are triggered by a single parameter value or interactions between a small number of parameters, generally two to six, a relationship known as the *interaction rule*. An example of a single-value fault might be a buffer overflow that occurs when the length of

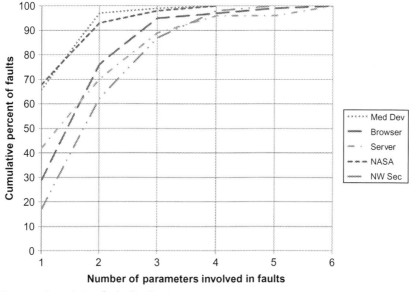

Figure 2 Cumulative fault distribution.

an input string exceeds a particular limit. Only a single condition must be true to trigger the fault: *input length > buffer size*. A 2-way fault is more complex, because two particular input values are needed to trigger the fault, as in the example above. More generally, a *t*-way fault involves *t* such conditions. We refer to the distribution of *t*-way faults as the *fault profile*.

A question naturally arises as to why the fault profiles of different applications are somewhat similar. While there is no definitive answer as yet, one clue can be seen in Fig. 3. Figure 3A shows the distribution of conditions in branching statements (e.g., *if*, *while*) in four large avionics software modules [11]. Nearly all are single conditions or 2-way, with a rapidly declining proportion involving 3-way or more complex sets of conditions. This curve is superimposed on the fault profiles presented above in Fig. 3B. Note that it closely matches the profile for the NASA database application. The data for this application were from initial testing results, while the other curves are for fielded products. Thus, the distribution of faults in this initial testing is quite close to the distribution of conditions documented in the FAA report. (It is not clear why the distribution of faults for the medical device software is as shown, as no information was available on the level of testing or usage for these products.) The fault profiles may reflect the profile of *t*-way conditions in their application software, but as faults are discovered and removed, the

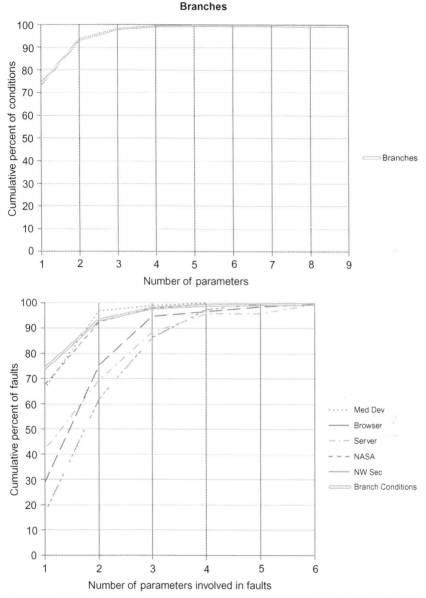

Figure 3 (A) Distribution of conditions in branching statements. (B) Fault distribution of different application domains.

more complex 3–way, 4–way, and beyond, faults comprise a larger proportion of the total. Testing and extensive usage thus tend to push the curves down and to the right.

1.2 Implications for Testing

The fault profiles reported above suggest that testing which covers a high proportion of 4–way to 6–way combinations can provide strong assurance. If we know that t or fewer variables are involved in failures and we can test all t-way combinations, then we can have reasonably high confidence that the application will function correctly. As shown above, the distribution of faults varies among applications, but two important facts are apparent: a consistently high level of fault detection has been observed for 4–way and higher strength combinations, and no interaction fault discovered so far, in thousands of failure reports, has involved more than six variables. Thus, the impossibility of exhaustive testing of all possible inputs is not a barrier to high assurance testing. That is, even though we cannot test all possible combinations of input values, failures involving more than six variables are extremely unlikely because they have not been seen in practice, so testing all possible combinations would provide little or no benefit beyond testing 4–way to 6–way combinations.

As with all testing, it is necessary to select a subset of values for variables with a large number of values, and test effectiveness is also dependent on the values selected, but testing t-way combinations has been shown to be highly effective in practice. This approach is known as *combinatorial testing* (CT), an extension of the established field of statistical Design of Experiments (DoE). Matrices known as *covering arrays* (CAs) cover all t-way combinations of variable values, up to a specified level of t (typically $t \leq 6$), making it possible to efficiently test all such t-way interactions.

Consider the example in Table 1 that shows four configurations to consider when testing a web application. The tester wants to test their web app on three types of devices (called parameters), three web browsers, three PHP

Table 1 Sample Input for a Combinatorial Test Suite That Has Four Parameters Which Have Three Possible Values Each

Device	Web Browser	PHP Version	Network Connection
PC	Safari	5.6.6	WiFi
Tablet	Firefox	5.5.22	3G
Smart phone	Chrome	5.6.5	4G

Table 2 Sample Combinatorial Test Suite for the Input 3^4 from Table 1

Test No.	Device	Web Browser	PHP Version	Network Connection
1	PC	Safari	5.5.22	3G
2	PC	Firefox	5.6.5	4G
3	PC	Chrome	5.6.6	WiFi
4	Tablet	Safari	5.6.5	WiFi
5	Tablet	Firefox	5.6.6	3G
6	Tablet	Chrome	5.5.22	4G
7	Smart phone	Safari	5.6.6	4G
8	Smart phone	Firefox	5.5.22	WiFi
9	Smart phone	Chrome	5.6.5	3G

versions, and three network connections. Each parameter has three options (called values). To exhaustively test, every combination requires $3*3*3*3 = 81$ possible combinations.

We use the ACTS tool described in Section 3.3 to generate a 2-way combinatorial test suite. This requires only nine test cases (configurations) in order to test all pairs of parameter-value combinations as shown in Table 2. A pair is a combination of values for two different parameters. For instance, Test Case 1 covers six pairs: (PC, Safari), (PC, PHP version 5.5.22), (PC, 3G), (Safari, PHP version 5.5.22), (Safari, 3G), (PHP version 5.5.22, 3G).

The effectiveness of any software testing technique depends on whether test settings corresponding to the actual faults are included in the test sets. When test sets do not include settings corresponding to actual faults, the faults may not be detected. Conversely, we can be confident that the software works correctly for t-way combinations contained in passing tests. When the tests are derived from t-way CAs, we know that 100% of the t-way combinations have been tested.

2. COVERING ARRAYS

CT is an adaptation of the "DoE" methods to test software and systems. CT and DoE are dynamic testing and learning methods in the sense that a system of interest is exercised (run) for a set of different test cases and the behavior or response of the system for those test cases is investigated. Historically, CT evolved from attempts to improve performance of software-based systems starting in the 1980s [12]. DoE refers to a methodology for conducting controlled experiments in which a system is exercised (worked in action) in a purposeful (designed) manner for chosen test settings of various input variables called *factors*. In DoE, many factors each having multiple test settings are investigated at the same time and the DoE plans satisfy relevant combinatorial properties. The corresponding values of one or more output variables (called responses) are measured. A statistical model (at least one) for the system response is associated with each DoE test plan. The DoE test plan and the responses values are used to estimate the unknown parameters of the model. The estimated model so obtained represents statistical information for improving the performance of a class of similar systems [13–17].

2.1 History of DoE

Conventional DoE methods were developed starting in the 1920s by British geneticist Ronald Fisher and his contemporaries and their followers, to improve agricultural production [18,19]. Later DoE was adapted for experiments with animals, medical research, and then to improve manufacturing processes, all subject to unavoidable variation. DoE continues to be a gold standard for research in life sciences, medical technologies, and drug discovery. Recently, the US Office of the Secretary of Defense promulgated more effective use of DoE in Defense Operational Test and Evaluation [20]. The objective in conventional DoE is to improve the mean response over replications. A Japanese engineer, Taguchi, promulgated (starting in the late 1960s Japan and 1980s USA) a variation of DoE methods for industrial experiments whose objective is to determine test settings at which the variation due to uncontrolled factors was least [21–25]. Taguchi promoted use of mathematical objects called orthogonal arrays (OAs) as templates for industrial experiments. OAs were largely mathematical curiosities before Taguchi stated using them for industrial experiments to develop robust products and processes.

The concept of OAs was formally defined by Rao [26] as generalization of Latin squares [27]. The matrix shown in Table 3 is an OA referred to as OA(8, $2^4 \times 4^1$, 2). The first parameter (which is 8) indicates the number of rows and the second parameter (which is $2^4 \times 4^1$) indicates that there are five columns of which four have two distinct elements each, denoted here by {0, 1}, and one column has four distinct elements, denoted here by {0, 1, 2, 3}. The third parameter (which is 2) indicates that this OA has strength 2, which means that every set of two columns contains all possible

Table 3 Orthogonal Array OA(8, $2^4 \times 4^1$, 2)

	1	2	3	4	5
1	0	0	0	0	0
2	1	1	1	1	0
3	0	0	1	1	1
4	1	1	0	0	1
5	0	1	0	1	2
6	1	0	1	0	2
7	0	1	1	0	3
8	1	0	0	1	3

pairs of elements exactly the same number of times. Thus, every pair of the first four columns contains the four possible pairs of elements {00, 01, 10, 11} exactly twice, and every pair of columns involving the fifth column contains the eight possible pairs of elements {00, 01, 02, 03, 10, 11, 12, 13} exactly once. In an OA of strength t, every set of t-columns contains all possible t-tuples of elements exactly the same number of times.

A fixed-value OA denoted by $OA(N, v^k, t)$ is an $N \times k$ matrix of elements from a set of v symbols {0, 1, ..., $(v-1)$} such that every set of t-columns contains each possible t-tuple of elements the same number of times. The positive integer t is the strength of the OA. In the context of an OA, elements such as 0, 1, 2, ..., $(v-1)$ used in Table 3 are symbols rather than numbers. The combinatorial property of an OA is not affected by the symbols that are used for the elements. Every set of three columns of a fixed-value OA of strength 2 represents a Latin square (one column representing the rows, one column representing the columns, and the third column representing the symbols). A mixed-value OA is an extension of fixed-value OA where $k = k_1 + k_2 + \cdots + k_n$; k_1 columns have v_1 distinct elements, k_2 columns have v_2 distinct elements, ..., and k_n columns have v_n distinct elements, where $v_1, v_2, ..., v_k$ are different. Mathematics of OAs and extensive references can be found in Ref. [28]. Sloane maintains an electronic library of known OAs [29].

Consider an industrial DoE which has five factors A, B, C, D, and E and one response Y. Suppose A, B, C, and D have two test values each, denoted by {A_0, A_1}, {B_0, B_1}, {C_0, C_1}, and {D_0, D_1}, respectively, and the factor E has four test values, denoted by {E_0, E_1, E_2, E_3}. The combinatorial test

Table 4 DoE Plan Based on OA(8, $2^4 \times 4^1$, 2)

Test Cases	A	B	C	D	E	Response
1	A_0	B_0	C_0	D_0	E_0	y_1
2	A_1	B_1	C_1	D_1	E_0	y_2
3	A_0	B_0	C_1	D_1	E_1	y_3
4	A_1	B_1	C_0	D_0	E_1	y_4
5	A_0	B_1	C_0	D_1	E_2	y_5
6	A_1	B_0	C_1	D_0	E_2	y_6
7	A_0	B_1	C_1	D_0	E_3	y_7
8	A_1	B_0	C_0	D_1	E_3	y_8

structure of this DoE is the exponential expression $2^4 \times 4^1$ which indicates that there are five factors of which four have two test settings each and one has four test settings. The number of possible test cases is $2^4 \times 4^1 = 64$. The OA(8, $2^4 \times 4^1$, 2) can be used to set up an experiment to evaluate the change in response when the test value of each factor is changed. The factors A, B, C, D, and E are associated with the columns of OA(8, $2^4 \times 4^1$, 2) and the test values are associated with the entries of the columns. Then the rows of OA(8, $2^4 \times 4^1$, 2) specify 8 of the 64 possible test cases shown in Table 4.

The last column of Table 4 displays the values y_1, y_2, ..., y_8, of the response Y for the eight test cases. The combinatorial properties of an OA enable estimation of the parameters of a statistical model associated with a DoE plan based on the OA. The estimated parameters and the estimated statistical model identify test settings of the five factors at which the system may have improved performance.

2.2 From DoE to CAs

Along with the advent of computers and telecommunication systems in the 1980s, independent verification and validation of software and hardware–software systems became important. Taguchi inspired the use of OAs for testing software systems. Software engineers in various companies (especially Fujitsu in Japan and the descendent organizations of the AT&T Bell System in the United States) started to investigate use of DoE methods for testing software and hardware–software systems. The earliest papers include the following: Refs. [1–3,30,31]. The limitations of OAs for independent verification and validation of software-based systems became clear soon after they were used. (i) Often, an OA matching the required combinatorial test structure does not exist; for example, a nontrivial OA of strength 2 matching the test structure $2^4 \times 3^1$ (four factors with two distinct settings and one with three settings) is mathematically impossible. (ii) Frequently, OA-based test suites included invalid test cases which are impossible (or meaningless) to execute; for example, in testing jointly various operating systems and browsers Linux cannot be combined with Microsoft Internet Explorer. (iii) Available OA tables were limited to at most strength three, while for testing software systems, test suites of strength larger than three may be required. (iv) In testing software systems, hundreds of factors may be involved, but available OA tables had fewer columns. Tatsumi [2,3] and Dalal and Mallows [4] provided the insight that in testing software, combinatorial balancing property of OAs (that each t-tuple should appear the same number of times) was not required (because parameters of statistical model were not being estimated). In testing software systems, space filling was needed, that is, each t-tuple of interest of the test settings must be covered at least once. Therefore, mathematical objects called CAs are better suited than OAs as templates for generating test suites for software testing.

The concept of CAs was formally defined by an AT&T mathematician Sloane [32]. Additional developments on CAs can be found in the following recent papers: Refs. [33,34]. A fixed-value CA denoted by $CA(N, v^k, t)$ is an $N \times k$ matrix of elements from a set of v symbols $\{0, 1, \ldots, (v-1)\}$ such that every set of t-columns contains each possible t-tuple of elements at least once. The positive integer t is the strength of the CA. A fixed-value CA may also be denoted by $CA(N, k, v, t)$. A mixed-value CA is an extension of fixed-value CA where $k = k_1 + k_2 + \cdots + k_n$; k_1 columns have v_1 distinct elements, k_2 columns have v_2 distinct elements, ..., and k_n columns have v_n distinct elements. The six rows of rows of Table 5 form a covering array

Table 5 Covering Array $CA(6, 2^4 \times 3^1, 2)$

	1	2	3	4	5
1	0	0	0	0	0
2	1	1	1	1	0
3	0	0	1	1	1
4	1	1	0	0	1
5	0	1	0	1	2
6	1	0	1	0	2

CA(6, $2^4 \times 3^1$, 2). In these six rows, each set of two columns contains each possible pair of symbols at least once. The combinatorial property of CAs is more relaxed (less stringent) than that of OAs: a CA need not be balanced in the sense that not all t-tuples need to appear the same number of times. All OAs are CAs but not all CAs are OAs. (An OA of index one in which every t-tuple appears exactly once is the best possible CA.) Thus, the concept of CAs is a generalization of OAs. CAs have a number of advantages over OAs for testing software systems. (i) CAs can be constructed for any combinatorial test structure of unequal numbers of test settings. (ii) If for a combinatorial test structure an OA exists, then a CA of the same or less number of test cases can be obtained. (iii) CAs can be constructed for any required strength (t-way) testing, while OAs are generally limited to strength 2 and 3. (iv) In generating test suites based on CAs, invalid combinations can be deliberately excluded. (v) CA for very large number of factors can be constructed.

For a given number of factors k, the size of a combinatorial t-way test suite based on a CA (number of rows of CA) increases exponentially with the number of test settings v of each factor. Therefore, in CT it is advisable to limit the number of distinct discrete test settings of each factor to less than 10; preferred values are 2–4. The discrete test settings are generally determined by equivalence partitioning and boundary value analysis of the domain of possible values for each factor.

The size of combinatorial t-way test suite also increases rapidly as t increases. For example, consider the combinatorial test structure example $3^3 4^4 5^2$ from Ref. [35]. The number of possible test cases is $3^3 4^4 5^2 = 172{,}800$. Exhaustive testing may not be practical. The sizes (number of test cases) of t-way test suites (determined using ACTS/IPOG) for $t = 2, 3, 4, 5,$ and 6 are, respectively, 29, 137, 625, 2532, and 9168. This highlights the important question of how the strength t should be set? A reasonable choice of the strength t requires experience with the type of system under test (SUT) being tested. The available knowledge about the SUT and the nature of possible faults to be detected is used in the specification of test factors, test setting, and the strength t. In one testing experiment involving 128 binary factors (each having two distinct test settings), CAs of strength t for $t = 2, \ldots, 10$ were needed. The sizes of required CAs determined by Torres-Jimenez [36] are, respectively, $N = 11, 37, 112, 252, 1231, 2462, 17{,}544, 90{,}300,$ and $316{,}940$. When the available knowledge about the SUT is severely limited, the choice of t is difficult. The choice of t requires a trade-off between the cost of testing (determined by the size of test suite) and the potential benefits of higher strength testing.

2.3 Combinatorial Coverage

A recent technical report from the University of Cambridge estimates the global cost of debugging software has risen to $312 billion annually. The authors suggest that software developers spend approximately 50% of their programming time on average finding and fixing bugs [37]. While there are many types of defects that contribute to project costs and many ways to test for different types of defects, one type of defect that we examine in this chapter is that of interaction faults. Tests based on CAs can be highly effective as they systematically cover t-way combinations of values. CAs include these combinations in a very compact form, but as long as all of the combinations are covered, it does not matter whether they come from CAs or a less efficient test set, possibly generated randomly. Test quality is obviously of central importance for software assurance, but there are few good measures available. A very basic, minimal foundation is that every requirement has been addressed by at least one test. If source code is available, then coverage measures such as statement or branch coverage may also be useful. Mutation testing is also a popular approach to evaluating test set adequacy. Combinatorial methods offer an additional tool for measuring test set quality.

Any test with n variables contains $C(n,t)$ t-way combinations, and any collection of tests will contain a set of combinations, though many are duplicated. If the test set is large enough, it may provide full t-way coverage, even if not originally constructed as a CA. *Combinatorial coverage*, i.e., the coverage of t-way combinations in a test set, is thus a useful measure of test set quality [38,39]. Note that such a coverage measure is independent of other measures of test quality, such as the code coverage induced by a particular set of tests. It is also directly related to fault detection. Combinatorial coverage is a measure of the input space that is tested.

The level of input space coverage also provides some measure of the degree of risk that remains after testing. Combinatorial coverage provides a direct measure of the proportion of input combinations for which the system has been shown to work correctly, which can be used in gauging the residual risk after testing.

2.3.1 Measures of Combinatorial Coverage

Combinatorial coverage measures include the following (definitions and examples from [35]):

Variable-value configuration: For a set of t variables, a variable-value configuration is a set of t valid values, one for each of the variables, i.e., the variable-value configuration is a particular setting of the variables.

Example. Given four binary variables a, b, c, and d, for a selection of three variables a, c, and d the set $\{a=0,\ c=1,\ d=0\}$ is a variable-value configuration, and the set $\{a=1,\ c=1,\ d=0\}$ is a different variable-value configuration.

Simple t-way combination coverage: For a given test set for n variables, simple t-way combination coverage is the proportion of t-way combinations of n variables for which all valid variable-value configurations are fully covered.

Example. Table 6 shows four binary variables, a, b, c, and d, where each row represents a test. Of the six possible 2-way variable combinations, ab, ac, ad, bc, bd, cd, only bd and cd have all four binary values covered, so simple 2-way coverage for the four tests in Table 6 is $2/6=33.3\%$. There are four 3-way variable combinations, abc, abd, acd, bcd, each with eight possible configurations: 000, 001, 010, 011, 100, 101, 110, 111. Of the four combinations, none has all eight configurations covered, so simple 3-way coverage for this test set is 0%. As shown later, test sets may provide strong coverage for some measures even if simple combinatorial coverage is low.

It is also useful to measure the number of t-way combinations covered out of all possible settings of t variables.

Total variable-value configuration coverage: For a given combination of t variables, total variable-value configuration coverage is the proportion of all t-way variable-value configurations that are covered by at least one test case in a test set. This measure may also be referred to as total t-way coverage.

An example helps to clarify these definitions. For the array in Table 6, there are $C(4,2)=6$ possible variable combinations and $2^2 \times C(4,2) = 24$ possible variable-value configurations. Of these, 19 variable-value configurations are covered and the only ones missing are $ab=11$, $ac=11$, $ad=10$, $bc=01$, $bc=10$, so the total variable-value configuration coverage is $19/24=79\%$. But only two, bd and cd, out of six, are covered with all four value pairs. So for simple t-way coverage, we have only 33% (2/6) coverage, but 79% (19/24) for total variable-value configuration coverage. Although

Table 6 Test Array with Four Binary Components

a	b	c	d
0	0	0	0
0	1	1	0
1	0	0	1
0	1	1	1

the example in Table 6 uses variables with the same number of values, this is not essential for the measurement, and the same approach can be used to compute coverage for test sets in which parameters have differing numbers of values.

Figure 4 shows a graph of the 2-way (red (dark gray in the print version)/solid) and 3-way (blue (black in the print version)/dashed) coverage data for the tests in Table 6. Coverage is given as the Y axis, with the percentage of combinations reaching a particular coverage level as the X axis. For example, the 2-way line (red (dark gray in the print version)) reaches $Y=1.0$ at $X=0.33$, reflecting the fact that 2/6 of the six combinations have all four binary values of two variables covered. Similarly, $Y=0.5$ at $X=0.833$ because one out of the six combinations has two of the four binary values covered. The area under the curve for 2-way combinations is approximately 79% of the total area of the graph, reflecting the total variable–value configuration coverage, designated S_t. Two additional quantities are also useful. $\Phi_t=$ the proportion of full t-way coverage; in the example above, $\Phi_2=0.33$. $M_t=$ minimum coverage for level t; in the example, $M_2=0.50$. It is easy to show that $S_t \geq \Phi_t + M_t - \Phi_t M_t$ [39].

In addition to analyzing the combination coverage of individual test suites, lower bounds for coverage have been established for a number of test criteria, including base choice [40] and modified condition decision coverage (MCDC) [11]. For example, simple all-values testing provides the expression

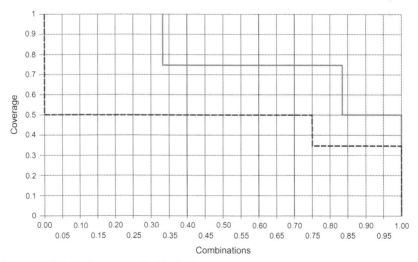

Figure 4 Graph of coverage for Table 1 tests.

Table 7 Base-Choice Tests for 2^4 Configuration

	a	b	c	d
Base	0	0	0	0
Test 2	1	0	0	0
Test 3	0	1	0	0
Test 4	0	0	1	0
Test 5	0	0	0	1

$$S_t \geq M_t = \frac{1}{v^{t-1}}$$

With base-choice testing [40], every parameter value must be covered at least once and in a test where other values are held constant. This process works by specifying one or more values for each parameter as base choices, which may be arbitrary, or "special interest" values, such as values more frequently used. Where parameters $p_1 \ldots p_n$ have v_i values each, the number of tests required is at least $1 + \Sigma_{i=1,n}(v_i - 1)$, or $1 + n(v-1)$ if all n parameters have the same number of values v. An example is shown below in Table 7, with four binary parameters.

It can be shown that the minimum combination coverage for base choice is $M_t = \frac{1 + t(v-1)}{v^t}$, and consequently also $S_t \geq \frac{1 + t(v-1)}{v^t}$. A variety of results for other strategies are given in Ref. [39].

2.3.2 Using Combinatorial Coverage

Figure 5 illustrates the application of combinatorial coverage analysis to a set of 7489 tests developed for spacecraft software [41], using conventional test design methods (not designed as a CA) to verify normal operation and a variety of fault scenarios. The system includes 82 variables, with the configuration shown in Table 8 of $1^3 2^{75} 4^2 6^2$ (three 1–value, 75 binary, two 4–value, and two 6–value). Figure 5 shows combinatorial coverage for this system (red (gray in the print version) = 2–way, blue (black in the print version) = 3–way, green (dark gray in the print version) = 4–way, orange (light gray in the print version) = 5–way). Pairwise coverage is with 82% of the 2–way combinations covering 100% of possible variable-value configurations covered and about 98% of the 2–way combinations have at least 75% of possible variable-value configurations covered (long horizontal portion of red (gray in the print version) line).

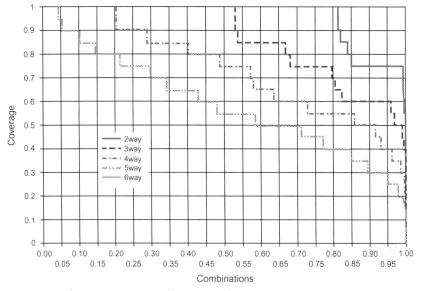

Figure 5 Configuration coverage for spacecraft example.

Table 8 Total *t*-Way Coverage for Fig. 5 Configuration

Interaction	Combinations	Settings	Coverage
2–Way	3321	14761	94.0
3–Way	88560	828135	83.1
4–Way	1749060	34364130	68.8
5–Way	27285336	603068813	53.6

3. ALGORITHMS FOR CT

As mentioned in previous sections, CT for the purpose of software testing stems from a rich history of DoE, including designs such as OAs [12]. This previous work has had a strong influence on algorithms to generate combinatorial test suites. In this section, we discuss challenges to generating combinatorial test suites, categories of algorithms that have been popular in literature, and automated tools for this purpose.

Numerous algorithms exist to generate CAs or mixed-level CAs to represent combinatorial test suites. This is an NP-hard problem, meaning no efficient exact method exists. Further complications arise when constraints are required in many practical applications. That is, events may need to run in a particular sequence or that one event may disable the option to run other events. Testers may have test cases that they have already run, called seeds, and want credit for the combinations covered in those test cases rather than generating new tests to cover those interactions again. For some inputs, the best reported test suites or sizes are available [42–44], while others, particularly those of mixed-level CAs or inputs with seeds or constraints, are not collected and shared. In this section, we briefly review different types of algorithms that generate combinatorial test suites.

3.1 Categories of Algorithms

Four categories of algorithms have been popular for the purpose of generating combinatorial test suites. These include
- algebraic techniques,
- greedy algorithms,
- heuristic search,
- constraint satisfaction problem algorithms.

Software testers need to choose the technique that best applies to their domain. For instance, if a tester has seven parameters that have five options each, an algebraic technique will give the best-known solution [43]. On the other hand, if a system has a varying number of options for each parameter and constraints among parameters, algebraic techniques are often less effective in terms of producing a smaller test suite. Constraint satisfaction problem algorithms have also been used, but mainly on small inputs. Table 9 summarizes trade-offs among these algorithm classes.

If a system has parameters with different numbers of options, this requires a mixed-level CA for the solution. Greedy algorithms and heuristic search are often the best algorithms for the scenario of mixed-level inputs. For instance, consider the input $4^{15}3^{17}2^{29}$. The greedy DDA produces a test

Table 9 Covering Array Algorithm Characteristics

	Algebraic	Greedy	Heuristic Search
Size of test suites	Accurate on special cases, but not as general as needed	Reasonably accurate	Most accurate (if given enough time)
Time to generate tests	Yes	Yes	Often time consuming (for good results)
Seeding/ constraints	Difficult to accommodate seeds/constraints	Yes	Yes

suite of size 35, the greedy IPO reports a test suite of size 36, and the AETG algorithm reports a test suite of size 41 [45]. Of course, there is still variation in the results among these three greedy algorithms in which each outperforms the others on different inputs.

On the other hand, the best-known result for input $5^1 3^8 2^2$ is 15 test cases as achieved by a heuristic search technique, simulated annealing [46]. Testers must consider the tradeoff in time when selecting a greedy or heuristic search algorithm. Heuristic search algorithms may take much longer to find a "good" solution. This issue of time to generate test suites becomes more exaggerated as the t-way strength of coverage for a test suite increases. For instance, Cohen et $al.$ report several results that show the dramatic difference in test suite size and time to generate 2-way combinatorial test suites using implementations of TCG, AETG, and simulated annealing [47]. For the input $5^1 3^8 2^2$, the size/execution time (in seconds) for TCG is 18/6, AETG is 20/58, and simulated annealing is 15/214. The results are more dramatic as the size of the inputs increase. For the input 10^{20}, the size/ execution time (in seconds) for TCG is 213/1333, AETG is 198/6001, and simulated annealing is 183/10,833.

Constraints between parameters/options are common in software systems. Addressing constraints is a challenging issue. We give a brief overview here, but refer the reader to Section 5 for a more detailed discussion. Consider Fig. 6 below that shows four scenarios for constraints using the input $3^1 2^3$:

1. *Original scenario without constraints*: This scenario has no constraints. There are 30 pairs to cover and this may be done in as few as six test cases.

2. *Scenario with constraints that results in a smaller test suite*: This scenario has three constraints, including that f0:0 may not be combined with f1:3, f2:5, or f3:7. These constraints leave 27 pairs left to cover. In this case, we are able to cover all of the pairs while respecting the constraints in as few as five test cases.

3. *Scenario with constraints that results in a larger test suite*: This scenario also has three constraints: f0:0 may not be combined with f1:3; f1:3 may not be combined with f2:5; and f2:5 may not be combined with f3:7. Due to these constraints, the fewest number of test cases to cover all pairs with respect to the constraints is seven test cases.

4. *No feasible solution*: The final scenario shows that the tester specified constraints in which it is not possible to construct a solution. If we must select an option for each parameter in order to generate a test case, you will notice that the constraints prohibit us from assigning a value

Scenario 1: Original input size of solution is 6.

f0	f1	f2	f3
0	3	5	7
1	4	6	8
2			

30 pairs to cover

(0,3)(0,4)(0,5)(0,6)(0,7)(0,8)
(1,3)(1,4)(1,5)(1,6)(1,7)(1,8)
(2,3)(2,4)(2,5)(2,6)(2,7)(2,8)
(3,5)(3,6)(3,7)(3,8)
(4,5)(4,6)(4,7)(4,8)
(5,7)(5,8)
(6,7)(6,8)

Scenario 2: 3 constraints result in 27 pairs to cover and a solution of size 5

(0,3)(0,4)(0,5)(0,6)(0,7)(0,8)
(1,3)(1,4)(1,5)(1,6)(1,7)(1,8)
(2,3)(2,4)(2,5)(2,6)(2,7)(2,8)
(3,5)(3,6)(3,7)(3,8)
(4,5)(4,6)(4,7)(4,8)
(5,7)(5,8)
(6,7)(6,8)

Scenario 3: 3 constraints result in 27 pairs to cover and a solution of size 7

(0,3)(0,4)(0,5)(0,6)(0,7)(0,8)
(1,3)(1,4)(1,5)(1,6)(1,7)(1,8)
(2,3)(2,4)(2,5)(2,6)(2,7)(2,8)
(3,5)(3,6)(3,7)(3,8)
(4,5)(4,6)(4,7)(4,8)
(5,7)(5,8)
(6,7)(6,8)

Scenario 4: 6 constraints result in 18 pairs to cover and there is no feasible solution

(0,3)(0,4)(0,5)(0,6)(0,7)(0,8)
(1,3)(1,4)(1,5)(1,6)(1,7)(1,8)
(2,3)(2,4)(2,5)(2,6)(2,7) (2,8)
(3,5)(3,6)(3,7)(3,8)
(4,5)(4,6)(4,7)(4,8)
(5,7)(5,8)
(6,7)(6,8)

Figure 6 Different scenarios with constraints.

to each parameter and covering all pairs. For instance, you will notice that f0:0 may not be combined with f1:3, so we would have to select f0:0 and f1:4 for the first two values of this test case. However, we are unable to select a value that respects the constraints for f2 since f2:5 may not be combined with f1:3 and f2:6 may not be combined with f1:4. This same scenario repeats if we include f0:1 and f1:3 in a test case. Greedy algorithms and heuristic search algorithms may address constraints. On the other hand, algebraic techniques may have difficulty addressing constraints. Section 5 discusses constraints in more depth.

3.2 Algorithms for Higher Strength Combinatorial Test Suites

Algorithms for higher strength combinatorial tests face the challenge that the number of t-tuples to cover increases exponentially as t increases. For instance, Table 10 below shows four sample inputs and the number of t-tuples to cover for $t = 2 \ldots k$. For instance, the input 3^{13} has 702 2-tuples, 7722 3-tuples, 47,915 4-tuples, and goes up to 1,594,323 13-tuples! This poses challenges for algorithms, particularly in terms of time to generate test suites and the amount of memory used for computations.

The categories of algorithms to generate test suites for higher strength combinatorial test suites include the same as those mentioned previously

Table 10 Higher Strength Covering Array Examples

	$10^1 9^1 8^1 7^1 6^1 5^1 4^1 3^1 2^1 1^1$	10^4	3^{13}	11^{16}
$t=2$	1320	600	702	14,520
$t=3$	18,150	4000	7722	745,360
$t=4$	157,773	10,000	57,915	26,646,620
$t=5$	902,055	–	312,741	703,470,768
$t=6$	3,416,930	–	1,250,954	1,301,758,600
...	...	–	...	...
$t=k$	3,628,800	10,000	1,594,323	45,949,729,863,572,200

Table 11 IPOG Test Size and Runtime for 5^{10} Input

t-Way	2	3	4	5	6
Size	48	308	1843	10,119	50,920
Time	0.11	0.56	6.38	63.8	791.35

in this section: algebraic techniques, greedy algorithms, heuristic search algorithms, and CSP algorithms. While the trade-offs of these algorithms are the same as those mentioned earlier in this section for $t=2$, the amount of time and memory usage for higher strength coverage often require special consideration. For instance, Table 11 shows the size of the test suites and execution time for $t=2$ through $t=6$ coverage of the input 5^{10} using the IPOG algorithm [48]. The result for $t=2$ strength coverage results in a test suite of size 48 in 0.11 s while the algorithm produces 50,920 test cases for $t=6$ in 791.35 s.

The major challenges faced by algorithms to generate combinatorial test suites include the time to generate test suites, the size of the test suites, and ability to address seeding and constraints. Numerous algorithms exist to generate combinatorial test suites, with popular categories of algorithms including algebraic, greedy heuristic, and heuristic search algorithms. Testers must consider their particular domain and testing environment when selecting an algorithm to generate CAs. Further, testers may seek guidance by visiting website that maintains the best-known reported solutions or sizes for many inputs [42–44].

3.3 Example Tools

A variety of tools can be found on the website *pairwise.org*, including both commercial and open source. Two of the most widely used CA generators are Microsoft PICT [48,49] and NIST ACTS [50]. In this section, we review ACTS. Tools may vary in features [51–55], and test environments are beginning to make it possible to integrate tools in ways that testers find most useful. One of the most well-developed such frameworks is CITlab [56], which is integrated with the Eclipse editor and provides a means of defining domain-specific languages and connecting other Eclipse plugins.

ACTS is a freely distributed set of research tools for software testing downloadable from an NIST website [50]. The IPOG algorithm in ACTS generates combinatorial t-way test suites for arbitrary combinatorial test structures and any strength t with support of constraints (to exclude invalid combinations). CCM (for Combinatorial Coverage Measurement) is a research tool in ACTS for determining combinatorial coverage of a test suite which may not have been developed from a combinatorial viewpoint.

(1) IPOG excludes those combinations of the test settings which are invalid according to the user-specified constraints. (2) IPOG tool supports two test generation modes: scratch and extend. The former builds a test suite from the scratch, whereas the latter allows a test suite to be built by extending a previously constructed test suite which can save earlier effort in the testing process. (3) IPOG tool supports construction of variable-strength test suites. For example, of the 10 test factors all could be covered with strength 2 and a particular subset of 4 out of 10 factors (which are known to be interrelated) could be covered with higher strength 4. (4) IPOG tool verifies whether the test suite supplied by a user covers all t-way combinations. (5) IPOG tool allows the user to specify expected output for each test case in terms of the number of output parameters and their values. (6) IPOG tool supports three interfaces: a Graphical User Interface (GUI), a Command Line Interface (CLI), and an Application Programming Interface (API). The GUI allows a user to perform most operations through menu selections and button clicks. The CLI can be more efficient when the user knows the exact options that are needed for specific tasks. The CLI is also very useful for scripting. The API is designed to facilitate integration of ACTS with other tools (see Fig. 7 below).

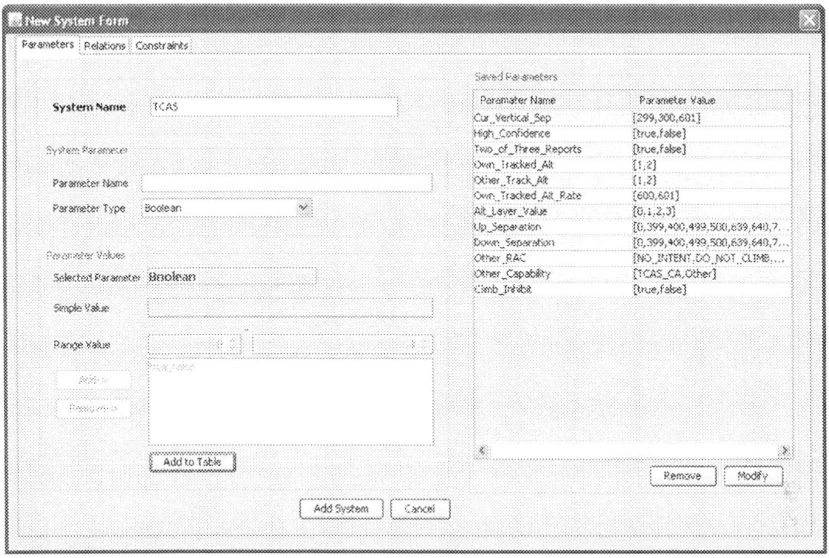

Figure 7 ACTS/IPOG user interface.

3.4 ACTS/CCM

CCM [39] measures the combinatorial coverage of a test set, including the measures discussed in Section 2.3. It accepts a comma-separated values (CSV) format file where each row represents a test and each column represents a parameter. CSV files can be exported from any spreadsheet program. Constraints can be specified at the beginning of the file, in the same syntax used for ACTS/IPOG; each line will be considered a separate constraint. The invalid combinations will be shown if there are constraints specified. If any coverage measurement has been specified, the invalid combinations will be generated. For continuous-valued parameters, a user can specify equivalence classes by indicating the number of value classes and boundaries between the classes. Boundaries may include decimal values. Where the boundary between two classes c_1 and c_2 is x, the system places input values less than x into c_1 and values greater than or equal to x in c_2. CCM outputs a graphic display of combinatorial coverage, as shown in Section 2.3, and complete statistics on tests, number of t-way combinations and combination settings needed for full coverage; number of t-way combination settings covered, and invalid combinations as determined by constraints. CCM was developed by NIST and the Centro Nacional de Metrologia, Mexico. The user interface is shown in Fig. 8.

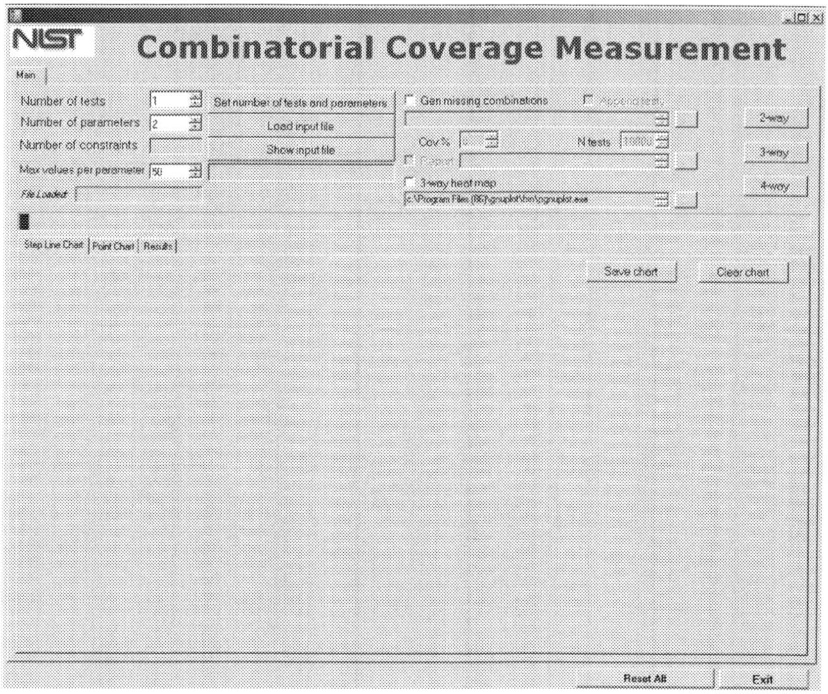

Figure 8 ACTS/CCM user interface.

4. INPUT PARTITIONING AND REPRESENTATION

CA algorithms can produce highly compact matrices of t-way value combinations, but how does a tester decide what values to use? Input space partitioning is a critical step in any software test approach, and traditional input modeling and partitioning methods are equally effective for CT, but some aspects of combinatorial methods introduce differences from this step in conventional approaches.

4.1 Combinatorial Issues in Input Model Development

When applied to developing input models for a CA tool, some issues become particularly important—three general classes of combination anomalies known as *missing combinations, infeasible combinations,* and *ineffectual combinations* [57]. The efficiency of CT stems partly from the fact that an individual test covers $C(n,t)$ combinations, so a CA can compress a large number of combinations into a reasonably small set of tests. Combination anomalies add complications to the generation of CAs.

Missing combinations are those that may be required to trigger a failure, but which are not included in the test array. A t-way CA will of course include all t-way combinations, and some $(t+1)$-way combinations, but not all (or it would be a $(t+1)$-way CA). If there are some combinations that engineering judgment leads testers to believe are significant, they may be included specifically, to supplement the CA.

Infeasible combinations are extremely common and are addressed by constraints. These are combinations which will never occur when the application is in use, perhaps because they are physically impossible. These combinations cannot be handled by simply removing tests that contain them, because many other, potentially necessary, combinations would be removed at the same time. Thus constraints are used to prevent the production of infeasible combinations in the CA. For example, if parameter B must have the value "100" whenever parameter A = 100, then a constraint such as "A = 100 → B = 100" can be included in constraints processed by the CA generator. Section 4.3, below, discusses this process in detail.

Ineffectual combinations may occur when the presence of another combination causes them to be ignored by the application [57,58]. A common scenario is when an error value causes the application to stop, so other combinations in the same test are not included in processing. This situation is often handled by separating tests for error processing from other tests [59]. Ineffectual combinations may also result when there are dependencies among combinations, which may be handled with constraints, as with infeasible combinations.

It is important to keep in mind that the anomalies discussed above can occur with any test method. For example, a test that triggers an error may terminate the application, so other possible interactions caused by values in the failing tests will never be discovered. It is simply that most methods do not consider parameter interaction to the same degree of granularity as CT. Using combinatorial methods helps to expose anomalies that may reduce the effectiveness of other methods.

4.2 Size Considerations with CAs

Key cost factors are the number of values per parameter, the interaction strength, and the number of parameters. The number of tests produced increases with $v^t \log n$, so the number of values per parameter is a critical consideration. Guidance for combinatorial methods usually recommends keeping the number of values per parameter to a limit of roughly 10. The number of parameters is much less significant for this approach, as the test set size increases with $\log n$, for n parameters, and current tools make it possible to generate CAs for systems with a few hundred parameters, at least for lower strength arrays. For larger systems, random test generation may be used. If there are no constraints among variables, random generation makes it possible to probabilistically cover t-way combinations to any desired level [60]. In the more common case where there are constraints, a large test set may be generated randomly and then its combinatorial coverage measured while ensuring maintenance of the constraints [39].

4.3 Modeling Environment Conditions and State

When we perform input parameter modeling, it is important to consider environment conditions that often affect the behavior of a system. There are two types of environment condition, i.e., static and dynamic conditions. Static conditions are set before a system is put into execution and do not change over time. Examples of static conditions include the hardware or software platform, system configurations, and environment variables. For instance, a web application may behave differently depending on whether it is running on a desktop machine or a mobile device like a smart phone. In this case, the runtime platform can be modeled as a parameter in the input model and the different types of platform the web application is designed to run can be modeled as different values of the parameter. As another example, many software applications allow the user to customize their behavior using a configuration file. Each configuration option can be modeled as a parameter in the input model and the different choices for a configuration option can be modeled as different values of the corresponding parameter.

Dynamic conditions capture the state of the environment that changes as a system runs. For example, many systems use a database to manage their data. The same operation may behave differently depending on the state of the database. Thus, it is important to model the state of the database as a factor that could affect the system behavior. This can be accomplished by identifying a set of abstract parameters that capture some important characteristics of the database. As another example, in an object-oriented system, the behavior of a method often depends on the state of the object on which the method is invoked. Consider that a class manages a *set* of objects that does not allow duplicates. The class provides a method named *insert* that can be used to add an object into the set. This method would behave differently depending on whether the object already exists in the set. Thus, it is important to model the state of the set, which can be accomplished by identifying an abstract parameter that indicates whether the object to be added already exists in the set.

4.4 Types of Constraints for Input Parameter Model

After parameters and values are identified, another important part of input parameter modeling is to identify potential constraints that may exist between different parameters and values. Constraints are restrictions that must be satisfied by each test; otherwise, a test may be rejected by the SUT and thus would not serve the purpose. Similar to identification of parameters and values, constraints can be identified from various sources of information, e.g., requirement document, and domain knowledge.

Different types of constraint can be classified based on different dimensions. A constraint can be an environment or system constraint, depending on whether it is imposed by the runtime environment a system is designed to run or by the system itself. A constraint can be a first-order or higher-order constraint, depending on whether the constraint needs to be evaluated against individual tests or sets of tests. A constraint can be a temporal or nontemporal constraint, depending on whether the constraint specifies properties related to time. In the following, we discuss these different types of constraints in more detail.

4.4.1 Environment Constraints Versus System Constraints

Environment constraints are imposed by the runtime environment of the SUT. For example, tester may want to ensure a web application executes correctly in different web browsers running on different operating systems. In this scenario, tests are combinations of web browsers and operation systems. Safari 6.0 or later cannot be executed on Windows. If the web browser is Safari 6.0 or later, the operating system cannot be Windows. Therefore, no test should contain the combination of {Safari6, Windows}. In general, combinations that violate environment constraints could never occur at runtime and must be excluded from a test set.

System constraints are imposed by the semantics of the SUT. For example, a hotel reservation system may impose a constraint that the number of guests in a room must be no more than the number of available beds. Note that invalid combinations which do not satisfy system constraints may still be rendered to the SUT at runtime. If this happens, these invalid combinations should be properly rejected by the SUT. Therefore, it is important to test these combinations for the purpose of robustness testing, i.e., making sure that the SUT is robust when invalid combinations are presented. In order to avoid potential mask effects, robustness testing often requires that each test contains only one invalid combination.

The key difference between environment constraints and system constraints is that environment constraints must be satisfied by all the tests whereas tests that do not satisfy system constraints may be generated for robustness testing.

4.4.2 First-Order Constraints Versus Higher-Order Constraints

First-order constraints are constraints that restrict parameter values in an individual test. For example, in a debit account transaction, the amount of money to withdraw from an account should be no more than either the balance of the account or the withdrawal limit of the account. In general, first-order constraints can be expressed using first-order logic expressions. Satisfaction of first-order constraints can be evaluated based on individual tests.

Higher-order constraints are constraints that impose certain restrictions on test sets or even sets of test sets, instead of on individual tests. Higher-order constraints can be more complex to understand and more expensive to evaluate. Constraints encountered in practice are typically no higher than second-order constraints. Many systems impose structural constraints, i.e., restrictions on the structure of test data. Structural constraints are typically higher-order constraints. For example, when we test software applications that access a database, we often need to populate some tables in the database as part of the effort to set up the test environment. These tables typically need to satisfy some structural constraints in order to ensure validity of the data that are stored in these tables. One common example is referential integrity, which requires that every data object referenced in one table must exist in some other table. Referential integrity is a second-order constraint, as it must be evaluated against a set of data objects, instead of individual data objects.

We note that most existing constraint solvers only handle first-order constraints. In order to handle higher-order constraints, a constraint solver customized for a particular domain is typically required. For example, a customized constraint solver may be developed to handle structural constraints that are commonly encountered in database testing.

4.4.3 Temporal Constraints Versus Nontemporal Constraints

Temporal constraints impose restrictions on the temporal behavior exercised by a system. There are two types of temporal constraints, sequencing constraints and real-time constraints. Sequencing constraints specify the possible orders in which a sequence of actions or events is allowed to take place.

For example, a sequencing constraint may specify that a ready signal must be received before any operation is performed on a device.

Real-time constraints specify temporal properties with an explicit reference to time. For example, a real-time constraint may specify that an event must take place 5 ms before another event takes place. This is in contrast with sequencing constraints, which specifies temporal properties using relative timing, i.e., without an explicit reference to time. That is, a sequencing constraint may specify that an event E must happen before another event E', but it does not specify how much time event E should occur before E'.

Nontemporal constraints are properties that are not related to time. Existing work on CT has been mainly focused on nontemporal constraints. This is partly because temporal constraints involve the extra dimension of time and are thus more difficult to handle.

5. CONSTRAINTS HANDLING IN CA ALGORITHMS

In practice, CA algorithms must be able to process constraints imposed by real-world considerations. The way in which constraints are represented can have significant impacts on algorithm and tool performance.

5.1 Representations of Constraints

Constraints identified in an input parameter model must be specified in a way that allows them to be automatically processed. One common approach to specifying constraints is representing them as a set of forbidden tuples, i.e., combinations that are not allowed to appear in any test. A test is valid if and only if it does not contain any forbidden tuple. For example, Fig. 9 shows a system consisting of three Boolean parameters A, B, C and two user-specified forbidden tuples $\{A=0, C=0\}$ and $\{B=0, C=1\}$. Test $\{A=0, B=0, C=0\}$ is invalid since it contains forbidden tuple $\{A=0, C=0\}$. Test $\{A=0, B=0, C=1\}$ is invalid since it contains forbidden tuple

Parameters:	Tests:
A={0,1}, B={0,1}, C={0,1}	{A=0, B=0, C=0} (Invalid)
Forbidden tuples:	{A=0, B=0, C=1} (Invalid)
{A=0, C=0}, {B=0, C=1}	{A=0, B=1, C=1} (Valid)
	...

Figure 9 Example of invalid and valid tests.

{B=0, C=1}. Test {A=0, B=1, C=1} is valid since it does not contain any forbidden tuple. When there are a large number of forbidden tuples, it can be difficult for the user to enumerate them.

Alternatively, constraints can be specified using logic expressions. A logical expression describes a condition that must be satisfied by all the tests. A test is valid if and only if it satisfies all the logic expressions. Consider the system in Fig. 9, where the forbidden tuples can be represented by two logic expressions, (A=0) => (C!=0) and (B=0) => (C!=1). For complicated systems, logical expressions are more concise than explicit enumeration of forbidden tuples.

5.2 Major Approaches to Constraint Handling

Due to the existence of constraints, some parameter values cannot be combined in the same test. In this case, a conflict is said to exist between these parameter values. There are four general approaches [61] to constraint handling for constructing CAs, including *abstract parameters*, *submodels*, *avoid*, and *replace*. These approaches employ different strategies to deal with potential conflicts between parameters.

The *abstract parameters* and *submodels* approaches remove conflicts from the input parameter model by means of model transformation prior to actual test generation. The *avoid* approach makes sure that only conflict-free tests are selected by checking validity of each test during actual test generation. The *replace* approach removes conflicts from a test set that has already been generated by replacing invalid tests with valid ones.

5.2.1 The Abstract Parameters Approach

In the *abstract parameters* approach, the original input parameter model that contains conflicts is transformed to one without conflicts prior to actual test generation. The main idea is to use one or more abstract parameters to represent valid subcombinations of input parameters. First, conflicting parameters, i.e., parameters that contain one or more conflicts, are identified. Second, abstract parameters are introduced to replace these conflicting parameters. Each abstract parameter is used to represent a group of conflicting parameters. The values of an abstract parameter represent valid combinations of the corresponding conflicting parameters that satisfy the given coverage goal.

For example, assume that there exists a constraint, A > B, between two parameters A and B of the system shown in Fig. 10. For 2-way testing, a new input parameter model can be created by replacing these two parameters

Parameters:	Abstract parameter for 2-way testing:
A={1,2,3}, B={1,2,3}, C={1,2} **Constraints:** A>B	AB = {(A=2, B=1), (A=3, B=1), (A=3, B=2)}

Figure 10 Example of abstract parameters.

with a new abstract parameter AB whose domain consists of all the 2-way valid combinations of parameters A and B, i.e., (A=2, B=1), (A=3, B=1), and (A=3, B=2). A test generation algorithm that does not support constraints can be applied to this new model to create a 2-way test set for this example.

The *abstract parameters* approach may lead to overrepresentation of some subcombinations. Consider the example in Fig. 10, the number of 2-way tests for abstract parameter AB and parameter C would be $3 \times 2 = 6$, where any valid combination between parameters A and B will occur twice. In fact, five tests are enough to satisfy 2-way coverage, where one of the three subcombinations between A and B only occurs once while each of the others two subcombinations occurs twice. As a result, for systems with wide ranged parameters, it may create a test set that is unnecessarily large.

5.2.2 The Submodels Approach

Similar to the *abstract parameters* approach, the *submodels* approach removes conflicts by transforming the original input parameter model. In this approach, an input parameter model containing conflicts is rewritten into two or more smaller conflict-free models. A test set is generated for each smaller model and the final test set is the union of all the test sets for the smaller models.

The key notion in the *submodels* approach is called split parameter. A split parameter is a parameter that is involved in a conflict and that has the least number of values. After a split parameter is identified, the input parameter model is split into a number of submodels, one for each value of the split parameter. Next, for each submodel, two-parameter conflicts involving the value of the split parameter are eliminated by removing values of the other parameters involved in the conflicts. Note that conflicts involving more than two parameters can be reduced to conflicts involving two parameters.

Submodel 1	Submodel 2	Submodel 3
A={2,3}	A={3}	A={}
B={1}	B={2}	B={3}
C={1,2}	C={1,2}	C={1,2}

Figure 11 Example of submodels.

Again, consider the example in Fig. 10. Parameters A and B are involved in the conflicts. Suppose that parameter B is used as the split parameter. The input parameter model is split into three submodels, one for each value of B. Then conflicts are eliminated in these three submodels, which are shown in Fig. 11.

Note that if conflicts still exist in the submodels that do not involve the split parameter, the process is applied recursively. When all submodels are conflict-free, some submodels can be merged. A merge is possible if two submodels differ only in one parameter.

When no further merges can be done, tests are generated for each submodel. The final test set is the union of the tests generated for each submodel. Consider the example in Fig. 11 and generate 2-way tests. For submodel 1, there will be $2 \times 2 = 4$ tests; for submodel 2, there will be 2 tests; for submodel 3, there will be 0 tests. The union of these six tests is the final test set.

Similar to the *abstract parameters* approach, this approach may create test sets that are unnecessarily large. This is because parameter values that are not involved in any conflict will be included in every submodel, which may create overlapping tests that do not contribute to test coverage. In Fig. 11, suppose that {A=3, B=1, C=2} from submodel 1 is the last test (of the six possible tests) to be included in the final test set. This test does not contribute to coverage, since all the 2-way combinations covered by this test have been covered by other tests. That is, {A=3, B=1} has already been covered by test {A=3, B=1, C=1} from submodel 1, {B=1, C=2} has already been covered by test {A=2, B=1, C=2} from submodel 1, and {A=3, C=2} has already been covered by test {A=3, B=2, C=2} from submodel 2.

5.2.3 The Avoid Approach

The *avoid* approach does not perform any transformation on the input parameter model. Instead, it tries to avoid conflicts when tests are actually generated. The key idea is to avoid generating invalid tests, i.e., tests that do not satisfy all the constraints. This is accomplished by checking the validity of each candidate test and discarding tests that do not pass the check. More discussion on how to perform validity check is provided in Section 5.3.

Compared to the *abstract parameters* and *submodels* approaches, the *avoid* approach often produces a smaller test set. This approach, however, is mainly applicable to greedy methods, which construct a test set one value at a time. That is, greedy methods consider a test set to be a matrix of values and a test set is built by choosing each value one at a time. The *avoid* approach cannot be directly applied to algebraic methods, which construct a test set based on some mathematic formulas without the notion of selecting a test over multiple candidates.

5.2.4 The Replace Approach

The *replace* approach allows conflicting tests, i.e., tests that contain conflicts, to be created in a test set. Conflicting tests are then removed from the test set by replacing them with conflict-free tests while preserving test coverage of the test set. Note that conflicting tests cannot be simply discarded. This is because some combinations that do not have a conflict may be covered by these conflicting tests only. In this case, new conflict-free tests must be created to cover these combinations in order to preserve test coverage.

One approach to replacing an invalid test is to make multiple clones of the invalid test, each of which changes one or more of the parameter values to remove the conflicts from the test. The number of clones is chosen according to the strength of coverage and the number of conflicting parameters, in order to make sure that test coverage is preserved. If multiple conflicts exist in the same test, conflicts are removed one at a time via cloning, until all conflicts are eliminated.

Table 12 shows how to apply the *replace* approach to build a 2-way test set for the system in Fig. 10. Since it is 2-way coverage and any conflict only involves two parameters, two clones are created for each of the conflicting tests. For each pair of clones, the value of the first parameter involved in the conflict is changed in the first clone and the value of the second parameter involved in the conflict is changed in the second clone. For example, T1 consists of a conflict {A = 1, B = 1}. This conflict is removed by replacing T1 with T1a in which the value of A is changed from 1 to 2. Finally, after removing the invalid and duplicate tests, a test set consisting of T1a, T2a, T4, T5a, and T7 is found.

Table 12 Application of the Replace Approach to the System in Fig. 10

Tests Ignoring Constraints	Parameters			Tests Cloned	Parameters			Tests Replaced	Parameters		
	A	B	C		A	B	C		A	B	C
T1	**1**	**1**	2	T1a	*	1	2	T1a	2	1	2
T2	**1**	**2**	1	T1b	1	*	2	T1b	1	–	2
T3	**1**	**3**	2	T2a	*	2	1	T2a	3	2	1
T4	2	1	1	T2b	1	*	1	T2b	1	–	1
T5	**2**	**2**	2	T3a	*	3	2	T3a	–	3	2
T6	**2**	**3**	1	T3b	1	*	2	T3b	1	–	2
T7	3	1	2	T4	2	1	1	T4	2	1	1
T8	3	2	1	T5a	*	2	2	T5a	3	2	2
T9	**3**	**3**	2	T5b	2	*	2	T5b	2	1	2
				T6a	*	3	1	T6a	–	3	1
				T6b	2	*	1	T6b	2	1	1
				T7	3	1	2	T7	3	1	2
				T8	3	2	1	T8	3	2	1
				T9a	*	3	2	T9a	–	3	2
				T9b	3	*	2	T9b	3	1	2

Conflicts in each test are indicated in bold. "*" indicates a value that needs to be changed; "–" indicates that no value can be assigned.

Similar to the *abstract parameters* and *submodels* approaches, the *replace* approach may create test sets that are unnecessarily large. The reason is that clones are often overlapping. Thus, some combinations are covered more than once. This may create redundant tests that can be removed without compromising test coverage.

Note that the three approaches, i.e., *abstract parameters*, *submodels*, and *replace*, may create unnecessarily large test sets. Test sets generated by these approaches can be reduced by removing redundant tests, i.e., tests that can be removed without compromising test coverage. This can be accomplished by processing the tests one by one and discarding tests that do not cover new combinations.

5.3 Validity Checking for the Avoid Approach

A key step in the *avoid* approach is to perform validity checking, i.e., checking whether all the constraints are satisfied for a given test. In general, there are two ways to check the validity of a test, including constraint solving and forbidden tuples.

The way in which validity checking is performed is independent from the way in which constraints are specified. Constraints specified using forbidden tuples can be converted into a set of logic expressions, which can be handled using a constraint solver. Similarly, a set of forbidden tuples can be derived from constraints specified using logic expressions and can be handled using a forbidden tuple-based approach.

5.3.1 Constraint Solving-Based Validity Checking

In this approach, a constraint solver is typically employed to perform validity checking. The main idea is to encode the problem of validity checking as a constraint satisfaction problem. Each time when a parameter value is to be assigned in a test, it must pass a check performed by the constraint solver to ensure all the constraints are satisfied.

The main challenge of this approach is dealing with the fact that the constraint solving process can be time consuming, especially when constraints are complex. In particular, existing constraint solvers are designed to check satisfaction of individual formulae. That is, they typically do not exploit information from the solving history to speed up constraint solving that may be performed in the future.

Several approaches have been reported aiming to optimize the use of constraint solvers in the context of CT [62,63]. For example, an algorithm called IPOG-C [62] is developed that tries to reduce the number of calls to the constraint solver. In particular, algorithm IPOG-C reduces the number of validity checks on target combinations by leveraging the fact that if a test is determined to be valid, then all the combinations covered by this test would be valid and thus do not have to be explicitly checked. In case that a call to the constraint solver cannot be avoided, algorithm IPOG-C tries to simplify the solving process as much as possible. It divides constraints into non-intersecting groups to reduce the number of constraints that have to be checked during a validity check.

5.3.2 Forbidden Tuples-Based Validity Checking

An alternative approach to performing validity checking is to ensure that no forbidden tuple is contained in the test. As discussed above, forbidden tuples can be used to verify if a (complete) test is valid or not. However, a partial test that contains no forbidden tuples may be invalid. Consider the example shown in Fig. 12. A partial test $\{A=0, B=0\}$ is invalid even when it

Parameters:	Partial tests:
A={0,1}, B={0,1}, C={0,1}	{A=0, B=0} (Invalid)
Forbidden tuples:	{A=0, B=1} (Valid)
{A=0, C=0}, {B=0, C=1}	...

Figure 12 Example of invalid and valid partial tests.

includes no forbidden tuples, because we cannot later assign a valid value for parameter C to make a complete test.

Generally speaking, we cannot directly use forbidden tuples to check a partial test's validity. This is because user-specified forbidden tuples may imply more other forbidden tuples that are not explicitly specified. A partial test that covers no explicit forbidden tuple may cover some implicit forbidden tuples. In Fig. 12, $\{A=0, B=0\}$ is an implicit forbidden tuple, making the partial test $\{A=0, B=0\}$ invalid.

It is not practical for the user to specify all implicit forbidden tuples in a system. Thus, it is desired to automatically derive all implicit forbidden tuples from a set of forbidden tuples given by the user. This would allow the validity of a partial test to be determined in the same way as for a complete test, i.e., by ensuring the partial test does not contain any implicit or explicit forbidden tuple. However, the number of forbidden tuples can be large, making this approach very inefficient.

The concept of minimum forbidden tuple [64] is proposed to address this challenge. Intuitively, a minimum forbidden tuple (MFT) is a forbidden tuple of minimum size. It is shown that if a tuple is invalid, it must cover at least one MFT. Thus, a partial test is valid if and only if it covers no MFT. This makes it possible to use MFTs to perform validity checks on both complete and partial tests. The number of MFTs is typically much smaller than the number of all possible forbidden tuples. Thus, the cost of managing forbidden tuples, in terms of both storage and lookup cost, can be significantly reduced.

The MFT generation algorithm iteratively applies two processes, i.e., derive and simplify, on the set of forbidden tuples until it converges.

(*Derive*) Given a parameter P having n values as its domain, and n forbidden tuples each of which contains a different value of parameter P, a new forbidden tuple can be constructed by combining all values in these n forbidden tuples, excluding the values of parameter P.

(*Simplify*) A tuple within the set of forbidden tuples can be removed if it covers any other forbidden tuple in the set.

The MFTs generation algorithm starts from the set of explicit forbidden tuples. It iteratively derives new forbidden tuples and simplifies the set of forbidden tuples, until no new forbidden tuples can be derived. The final set of forbidden tuples consists of all MFTs which explicitly indicate all the constraints implied by user-specified forbidden tuples and parameter domains. We use an example shown in Fig. 13 to describe how it works. In steps 1 and 2, three new forbidden tuples are derived using parameter A and B. There are no new forbidden tuples that can be derived using parameter C, so we move to the simplify process, as in step 3, but no tuples can be removed at this time. The next iteration then starts with the three new forbidden tuples which are marked with "*". In step 4, we derive a

Parameters: A={0,1,2}, B={0,1,2}, C={0,1,2}			
Step 1	{ A=0, B=0 } { A=0, B=1 } { A=1, C=0 } { A=2, C=0 } { B=2, C=0 }	(derive using A)	{ B=0, C=0 } { B=1, C=0 }
Step 2	{ A=0, B=0 } { A=0, B=1 } { A=1, C=0 } { A=2, C=0 } { B=2, C=0 }	(derive using B)	{ A=0, C=0 }
Step 3	(simplify)		
Step 4	{ A=0, B=0 } { A=0, B=1 } { A=1, C=0 } { A=2, C=0 } { B=2, C=0 } { B=0, C=0 }* { B=1, C=0 }* { A=0, C=0 }*	(derive using A)	{ C=0 }
Step 5	{ A=1, C=0 } { A=2, C=0 } { B=2, C=0 } { B=0, C=0 } { B=1, C=0 } { A=0, C=0 }	(simplify)	
Step 6	{ A=0, B=0 } { A=0, B=1 } { C=0 }	Finished	

Figure 13 Example of MFT generation process.

new tuple $\{C=0\}$ using parameter A. There are no new forbidden tuples can be derived using parameter B and C, so we move to the simplify process, as in step 5, six forbidden tuples covering $\{C=0\}$ are removed. Now there are only three forbidden tuples remaining in the set and no new tuples can be derived from them. They are MFTs and can be used to perform validity checking.

6. CASE STUDIES

CT has found extensive use in software development, and a variety of examples for diverse industries can be found in the proceedings of the International Workshops on CT [65]. The two highlighted in this section illustrate quite different aspects of this method in practice. The first, on the Document Object Model (DOM), is an interesting validation of the interaction rule and its implications. Tests covering 4-way combinations detected all faults found in complex real-world software that had previously been detected with exhaustive testing of discretized values [66–68]. The second example below is, to our knowledge, the largest published study on industrial use of CT, a 2.5-year investigation of the method to aerospace software that demonstrated significant cost savings and improved test coverage [69].

6.1 Document Object Model

The DOM [66,67] is a World Wide Web Consortium (W3C) standard for representing and interacting with documents through web browsers. DOM makes it easier for developers to incorporate nonsequential access in websites by providing conventions for updating the content, structure, and style of documents dynamically. Implemented in browsers, DOM components typically include tens of thousands of lines of source code. Due to its importance for Internet applications worldwide, NIST developed the DOM Conformance Test Suites, to assist developers in ensuring interoperability and predictable behavior of website components. The conformance tests are comprehensive, providing exhaustive testing (all possible combinations) of discretized values for 35 DOM events, a total of more than 36,000 tests. Multiple commercially produced DOM implementations were tested.

Since the DOM test suite was designed for exhaustive testing, it provided a unique opportunity to evaluate one of the major advantages of CT—the empirical interaction rule that faults involve a small number of factors interacting, so covering all t-way faults, for small value of t, can be nearly as effective as exhaustive testing. Five new DOM test suites were created, covering

Table 13 Comparison of *t*-Way with Exhaustive Test Set Size

t-Way	Tests	Pct Original (%)	Test Results	
			Pass	Fail
2–Way	702	1.92	202	27
3–Way	1342	3.67	786	27
4–Way	1818	4.96	437	72
5–Way	2742	7.49	908	72
6–Way	4227	11.54	1803	72

2-way through 6-way combinations, to compare the effectiveness of *t*-way CT with the original exhaustive test suite [68]. According to the interaction rule, testing all *t*-way combinations, for a suitable value of *t*, should be as effective as exhaustive testing of discretized values. Results, shown in Table 13, were consistent with the rule. At $t = 4$, the combinatorial test suite detected all DOM faults discovered in exhaustive testing.

Several interesting observations can be made about these results. Notice that 2-way tests detected only 37.5% of the faults, pairwise testing is clearly inadequate for this application, and even 3-way tests detected no additional faults. However, with 4-way CAs, all faults found in exhaustive testing were discovered, with less than 5% of the original test set size. This is an enormous savings, particularly for a user-interface-related application such as DOM, where human involvement is required to verify test results involving images on a screen. We can also observe another aspect of these results consistent with the observations made in the introduction to this chapter. While the distribution of 1-way and 2-way faults was broad (e.g., under 20% to more than 90% for 1-way), a very narrow distribution was observed for 4-way to 6-way faults. In other words, empirical data suggest that results could be quite varied for 1-way, 2-way, and even 3-way CAs. On the other hand, when we reach *t*-way strengths of 4-way and beyond, fault detection should be both stronger and more consistent across applications. The DOM testing results are an example of such a situation.

6.2 Lockheed Martin

Lockheed Martin is one of the world's largest aerospace firms. In 2005, the company began investigating application of pairwise testing to improve test effectiveness and reduce costs [69,70]. This work led to discussions with

NIST and subsequently a Co-operative Research and Development Agreement (CRADA) to evaluate the cost/benefit trade-offs and areas of suitable application for CT of complex industrial software [71]. (One of the ways in which NIST conducts joint research with US industry is through CRADAs, which allow federal laboratories to work with US industry and provide flexibility in structuring projects, intellectual property rights, and in protecting industry proprietary information and research results.)

The pilot project objectives included: investigating CT across multiple application areas, including system, software, and hardware testing; estimating possible improvements in fault detection with combinatorial methods; and quantifying possible reductions in test cost and overall lifecycle cost through earlier fault detection. The ACTS tool was used, supplemented with other tools that provided complementary capabilities, including Air Academy Associates: SPC XL, DOE KISS, DOE PRO XL, DFSS MASTER; Phadke & Associates: rdExpert; and Hexawise's web-based Hexawise tool.

A diverse set of eight pilot projects were included in the evaluation, spanning a cross-section of the company's mission areas:

- F-16 Ventral Fin Redesign Flight Test Program—system-level problem analysis, comparing with historical results [70]
- Electronic Warfare (EW) system testing—evaluating and extending existing tests
- Navigation Accuracy, EW performance, Sensor information, and Radar detection—generating test cases for subsystems
- Electromagnetic Effects (EMI) Engineering—CT tests were compared with tests developed using conventional methods
- Digital System Command testing—file function testing with multiple parameters
- Flight Vehicle Mission Effectiveness (ME)—comparing CT with tests generated from a statistical analysis tool
- Flight Vehicle engine failure modes—CT tests were compared with tests developed using conventional methods
- Flight Vehicle engine upgrade—combinations of flight mode factors were compared with existing tests

Pilot projects found CT effective for reducing the number of tests and for improving test coverage [71]. While there was some variation among projects, the company estimated that CT would reduce testing cost by roughly 20%, while providing 20–50% better test coverage. In some cases, significant but previously undiscovered bugs were found. As a result of this experience,

Lockheed Martin established a process to encourage adoption of combinatorial methods in company projects, documented lessons learned, and developed recommendations for the testing community at large.

7. ADVANCED TOPICS IN CT

As CT has evolved in practice, new opportunities and challenges have been identified. This section reviews research in a number of specialized topics that are increasingly finding use for solving test and assurance problems.

7.1 Test Suite Prioritization

Test suite prioritization by combinatorial-based coverage has been studied from two perspectives. The first generates combinatorial test suites using inputs that contain weights on the parameter values. The second takes an existing test suite and reorders the test cases by combinatorial-based interaction coverage.

7.1.1 Generation of Prioritized Test Suites by Combinatorial-Based Coverage

Test suites that are generated by combinatorial-based coverage use an ℓ-biased covering array, defined as:

A ℓ-biased covering array is a covering array $CA(N; 2, k, v)$ in which the first rows form tests whose utility is as large as possible according to some criterion. That is, no $CA(N; 2, k, v)$ has rows that provide larger utility according to the chosen criterion.

We refer to an ℓ-biased covering array as a prioritized combinatorial test suite. To generate a prioritized combinatorial test suite, a tester must carefully assign weights to parameters and their values. The weights are assigned a value between 0 (low priority) to 1 (high priority). A test then computes the weights of pairs by multiplying their weights. For instance, assume we have a pair with weights 0.2 and 0.1. The total weight is then $0.2*0.1 = 0.02$. The goal of the algorithm is then to cover as much "weight" among pairs as soon as possible rather than simply covering pairs. As discussed in the section on Algorithms, there are many possible categories of algorithms that are able to generate covering arrays and they may certainly be modified to cover weight as needed for ℓ-biased covering arrays. Bryce et al. give one example that uses a greedy algorithm [72].

7.1.2 Prioritization of Existing Test Suites by Combinatorial-Based Coverage

Test suite prioritization by combinatorial-based coverage has been applied to event-driven systems, focusing on combinations of parameter values on or across windows. In this section, we briefly discuss this test suite prioritization problem and then give an example.

The Test Suite Prioritization problem is defined by Rothermel *et al.* [73]:

Given T, a test suite, Π, the set of all test suites obtained by permuting the tests of T, and f, a function from Π to the set of real numbers, the problem is to find $\pi \in \Pi$ such that $\forall \pi' \in \Pi, f(\pi) \geq f(\pi')$. In this definition, Π refers to the possible prioritizations of T and f is a function applied to evaluate the orderings.

Example. Consider the case of test suite prioritization for a web application in which the source of the test cases is a set of user sessions. Figure 14 shows that users connect a website where their actions (POST/GET requests) are recorded by a webserver. A tool converts these user visits to a test case. Given that there are a large number of test cases, we then prioritize these test cases according to a criterion. In the case of combinatorial-based coverage criteria for GUI and web applications, intrawindow and interwindow interactions have been proposed and empirically studied.

For instance, consider the example input shown below where we have three webpages that have the parameters and values as shown in Table 14. We will prioritize by interwindow combinatorial-based coverage. That is, combinations of parameter -values between pages.

Next consider the three test cases shown in (Table 15). Each test case includes sequences in which a user visits pages and specifies values for parameters on the pages.

Give the input and test cases, Table 16 shows the interwindow pairs that are covered in these test cases. In this scenario, we select Test Case 1 as the

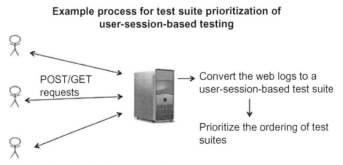

Example process for test suite prioritization of user-session-based testing

POST/GET requests

Convert the web logs to a user-session-based test suite

Prioritize the ordering of test suites

Figure 14 Test suite prioritization example.

Table 14 Example Web Interface Parameter Values

Page	Values for Parameter 1	Values for Parameter 2	Values for Parameter 3
Page 1	0,1,2,3	4,5	
Page 2	6	7,8	9
Page 3	10,11	12	

Table 15 Test Cases for Web Pages

Test	Test Case
1	0,4,6,8,11
2	0,6,10
3	4,6,8,11

Table 16 Pairwise Coverage of Tests

Test	Covered Pairs	No. of Pairs Covered
1	(0,6)(0,8)(0,11)(4,6)(4,8)(4,11)(6,11)(8,11)	8
2	(0,6)(0,10)(6,10)	3
3	(4,6)(4,8)(4,11)(6,11)(8,11)	5

first test case since it covers eight pairs while the other test cases cover fewer pairs. We mark these pairs in Test Case 1 as covered and then select the next case such that it covers the most remaining "uncovered pairs." In this case, we select Test Case 2 since it covers two new pairs, but Test Case 3 does not cover any new pairs.

Empirical studies have shown that prioritization by combinatorial-based coverage has been valuable for improving the rate of fault reduction in several studies. For instance, Bryce *et al.* studied seven systems and observed a trend that test suite prioritization by combinatorial-based coverage often improved the rate of fault detection for GUI and web applications [72]. A tool, CPUT, is freely available for testers to repeat this process with their own web logs. CPUT converts Apache web logs to user-session-based test suites and prioritizes those test suites by combinatorial-based coverage [74].

Test suite prioritization by combinatorial-based criteria has been investigated from two viewpoints: (1) generate test suites from scratch by incorporating the weights of t-tuples into the test generation process and (2) reorder existing test suites by a combinatorial-based coverage criterion.

Existing work in this area is quite promising in regard to the ability to improve fault-detection effectiveness. It is simple to incorporate weights into algorithms that generate combinatorial test suites, but testers must take care in assigning weights. If a tester has existing test suites, they may also prioritize by combinatorial-based coverage. Testers may use and extend the CPUT tool to apply test suite prioritization for user-session-based testing in their own domains [74].

7.2 Sequence Covering Arrays

Event sequences are important in many aspects of software testing [75–80]. For example, a typical e-commerce web system presents a variety of controls to the user, such as buttons, text entry fields, selection lists, including many with suboptions such as pull-down menus. It should be possible for the user to engage these controls in any order with the system working correctly irrespective of the order used. Another example (in fact, the application for which the methods described here were developed) is the process of plugging in various peripherals. If the developer has made assumptions about the order in which peripherals are connected and controls engaged, then a user who violates this expected sequence may encounter errors. Applications should work correctly regardless of the sequence of events selected by the user, or else indicate that a different order is required.

In many cases, the key factor in triggering a failure is whether a particular event has occurred prior to a second event, regardless of whether other events have occurred between these two. For example, the system may fail if a pump has been started before a particular valve has been opened at some point, even though other events may have occurred in between. Sequence covering arrays were developed to locate faults of this type, using combinatorial methods to increase efficiency [81]. Tests based on these arrays ensure that every t events from a set of n ($n > t$) will be tested in every possible t-way order, possibly with interleaving events among each subset of t events.

Definition. A sequence covering array, SCA(N, S, t), is an $N \times S$ matrix where entries are from a finite set S of s symbols, such that every t-way permutation of symbols from S occurs in at least one row and each row is a permutation of the s symbols [82]. The t symbols in the permutation are not required to be adjacent. That is, for every t-way arrangement of symbols x_1, x_2, ..., x_t, the regular expression.$^*x_1.^*x_2.^*x_t.^*$ matches at least one row in the array.

Sequence covering arrays were introduced in Ref. [82] for software testing but were later shown to be equivalent to t-scrambling sets [83,84].

Margalit [85] provides closer bounds, and additional results and algorithms were presented in Refs. [86,87].

7.2.1 Example

We may have a component of a factory automation system that uses certain devices interacting with a control program. We want to test the events defined in Table 17. There are $6! = 720$ possible sequences for these six events, and the system should respond correctly and safely no matter the order in which they occur. Operators may be instructed to use a particular order, but mistakes are inevitable and should not result in injury to users or compromise the operation. Because setup, connections, and operation of this component are manual, each test can take a considerable amount of time. It is not uncommon for system-level tests such as this to take hours to execute, monitor, and complete. We want to test this system as thoroughly as possible, but time and budget constraints do not allow for testing all possible sequences, so we will test all three-event sequences.

With six events, a, b, c, d, e, and f, one subset of three is $\{b, d, e\}$, which can be arranged in six permutations: $[b\,d\,e]$, $[b\,e\,d]$, $[d\,b\,e]$, $[d\,e\,b]$, $[e\,b\,d]$, $[e\,d\,b]$. A test that covers the permutation $[d\,b\,e]$ is $[a\,d\,c\,f\,b\,e]$; another is $[a\,d\,c\,b\,e\,f]$. With only 10 tests, we can test all three-event sequences, shown in Table 18. In other words, any sequence of three events taken from $a\ldots f$ arranged in any order can be found in at least one test in Table 18 (possibly with interleaved events).

Returning to the example set of events $\{b, d, e\}$, with six permutations: $[b\,d\,e]$ is in Test 5, $[b\,e\,d]$ is in Test 4, $[d\,b\,e]$ is in Test 8, $[d\,e\,b]$ is in Test 3, $[e\,b\,d]$ is in Test 7, and $[e\,d\,b]$ is in Test 2.

With 10 events, the number of permutations is 10! or 3,628,800 sequences for exhaustive testing. In that case, a 3-way sequence covering

Table 17 Example System Events

Event	Description
a	Connect air flow meter
b	Connect pressure gauge
c	Connect satellite link
d	Connect pressure readout
e	Engage drive motor
f	Engage steering control

Table 18 All 3-Event Sequences of 6 Events

Test	Sequence
1	*a b c d e f*
2	*f e d c b a*
3	*d e f a b c*
4	*c b a f e d*
5	*b f a d c e*
6	*e c d a f b*
7	*a e f c b d*
8	*d b c f e a*
9	*c e a d b f*
10	*f b d a e c*

Table 19 2-Way Sequence Covering Array

Test	Sequence
1	*a b c d e*
2	*e d c b a*

array requires only 14 tests to cover all 3–way sequences, and 72 tests are all that is needed for 4–way sequences.

7.2.2 Generating Sequence Covering Arrays

Any 2-way sequence covering problem requires only two tests. A 2-way sequence covering array can always be constructed by listing the events in some order for one test and in reverse order for the second test. See Table 19 for an example.

Sequence covering arrays are related to covering arrays in covering *t*-way combinations, but there are significant limitations in producing SCAs from covering arrays [87]. Consequently, specialized algorithms have been developed for SCAs and are a continuing subject of research. For *t*-way sequence covering, $t > 2$, greedy methods are efficient and produce arrays with number of tests proportional to log *n*, for *n* events [81]. An improved greedy algorithm was developed by Erdem *et al.* [86], producing fewer tests, and further results by Chee *et al.* developed algorithms producing significantly smaller arrays than either Ref. [82] or [86], and results are provided up to strength 5.

Event sequences are encountered frequently in testing, and combinatorial methods are effective in reducing the testing burden, especially for applications that require human involvement for test setup or system configuration. Since the test array size grows only logarithmically with the number of events, *t*-way sequence coverage is practical in many applications. Areas for future research in sequence covering arrays include algorithms to provide smaller test arrays, or in shorter time; measures of fault detection in practical application; and handling of constraints. Constraints are a particularly challenging issue with SCAs [81,85] since even a small limitation on *t*-way sequences can severely limit the possible arrangements in the sequence covering array. Variations such as multiple occurrences of an event and missing events are also possible, so an additional question is how sequence covering arrays compare with other methods of event sequence testing, such as those based on finite automata or other approaches that are frequently used in protocol testing.

7.3 Fault Localization

After executing a combinatorial test set, the execution status, i.e., pass or fail, of each test is obtained. When one or more tests fail, the next task is fault localization, i.e. identifying faults that cause the failure. The problem of fault localization can be divided into two subproblems: (1) Identifying failure-inducing combinations. A combination is failure-inducing if its existence in a test causes the test to fail. (2) Identifying actual faults in the source code. A fault is a code defect that can be an incorrect, extra, or missing statement.

7.3.1 Identifying Failure-Inducing Combinations

One naïve approach to identifying failure-inducing combinations is to execute all possible tests and then identify combinations that only appear in failed tests. This approach is, however, not practical as it requires exhaustive testing. In the literature, several approaches have been reported that try to identify failure-inducing combinations by executing only a small set of tests. These approaches are essentially approximate solutions. That is, failure-inducing combinations identified by these approaches are likely, but not guaranteed, to be failure-inducing.

Existing approaches on identifying failure-inducing combinations can be largely classified into two groups. The first group of approaches takes as input a single test as well as its execution status and tries to identify failure-inducing combinations in the test. A simple solution involves checking every possible combination, one at a time, contained in the failed test. This solution is expensive due to the fact that the number of combinations contained in a test is an exponential function of the size of the test. Two efficient algorithms called FIC and FIC_BS are reported to quickly locate a failure-inducing combination by checking only a small number of possible combinations [10]. These two algorithms, however, make certain assumptions that may not be satisfied in practice. In particular, they assume that no new inducing combination is introduced when a value is changed to create a new test.

The second group of approaches takes as input a set of tests as well as their execution statuses and tries to identify failure-inducing combinations that may appear in any of these tests. This group could further divided into two subgroups. The approaches in the first subgroup identify failure-inducing combinations without adding any new test to the initial test set. For example, a machine learning-based approach was reported that uses a technique called classification tree to identify failure-inducing combinations [88]. Based on the execution result of a test set, this approach builds a classification tree that encodes information needed to predict status of a test execution. A score is assigned to each combination that is likely to cause an execution to fail. If the combination's score is greater than a predefined threshold, the combination is marked as inducing.

The approaches in the second subgroup generate and execute additional tests to identify failure-inducing combinations. These approaches first identify suspicious combinations with respect to the initial test set. Suspicious combinations are combinations that appear in failed tests but not in passed tests. These combinations are candidates that may be failure-inducing. Then, a small set of new tests is generated to refine the set of suspicious combinations.

One approach called AIFL [89] first identifies all the suspicious combinations in a test set. Next, it uses a strategy called OFOT (One Factor One Time) to systematically change one value of the failed test at a time. Therefore, k new tests are generated for each failed test of size k. These new tests are executed to refine the suspicious combination set. In particular, if a suspicious combination appears in any new test that passes, then this combination is removed from the suspicious set. This process can be repeated until a stable point is reached where the suspicious set does not change in two consecutive iterations [90].

Another approach implemented in a tool called BEN [91] ranks suspicious combinations, after they are identified, based on three notions of suspiciousness, including suspiciousness of component, combination, and environment. A component represents a parameter value. Suspiciousness of combination is computed based on suspiciousness of components that appear in the combination. Suspiciousness of environment with respect to a combination is computed based on suspiciousness of components that appear in the same test but not in the combination. The higher the suspiciousness of a combination and the lower the suspiciousness of its environment, the higher this combination is ranked.

The ranking of suspicious combinations allows the next step to focus on the most suspicious combinations. New tests are generated for a given number of top-ranked suspicious combinations to refine the set of suspicious combinations. A new test is generated for a top-ranked suspicious combination in a way such that it includes this suspicious combination while minimizing the suspiciousness of environment for this combination. If the new test fails, it is likely that this suspicious combination is a failure-inducing combination. Otherwise, this suspicious combination is not suspicious anymore and is removed from the suspicious set. The process of ranking and refinement is repeated until a stable point is reached, e.g., the set of suspicious combination does not change in two consecutive iterations.

7.3.2 Identifying Faults in the Source Code

The problem of how to identify faults in the source code is one of the most studied problems in software engineering. Many approaches have been reported and can be applied after CT [92,93]. For example, spectrum-based approaches try to identify faults by analyzing the spectrums of passed and failed test executions. The key idea behind spectrum-based approaches is that faults are more likely to be exercised in failed test executions than in passed executions, which is independent from the way tests are generated. Thus, it is possible to apply spectrum-based approaches after CT.

The BEN approach introduced in the previous section is later extended to locate faults in the source code [94]. The main idea of the BEN approach consists of leveraging the notion of failure-inducing combination to generate a group of tests that are very similar but produce different outcomes. Similar tests are likely to exercise similar execution traces. Different outcomes produced by similar tests are more likely due to existence of faults. In contrast, different outcomes produced by tests that are significantly different are more likely due to program logic.

Given a failure-inducing combination, BEN generates a group of tests that includes one failed test and several passed tests. The failed test is referred to as a core member and contains the failure-inducing combination, while the suspiciousness of environment with respect to this combination is minimized. The passed tests are referred to as derived members and are derived from the core member by changing only one value of the core member. In other words, derived members differ from the core member in only one value but produce a different outcome.

For each statement, a suspiciousness value is computed by comparing the execution trace of the core member and each of the derived members. A statement is highly suspicious if it is only exercised in failed tests but not in passed tests. Statements are ranked based on a nonascending order of their suspiciousness values. The higher a statement is ranked, the more likely it is considered to be faulty.

7.4 Relationship Between CT and Structural Coverage

Before an application is purchased or accepted, and especially when a system fails, one of the first questions that will be asked is "How well was it tested?" A variety of measures have been developed to answer this question, based on the extent and manner in which components of the system have been exercised. Code coverage is one component to the answer for this question, so it is natural to consider how CT relates to code coverage. Do higher strength covering arrays produce greater code coverage? If so, at what rate does code coverage increase with increasing values of t? Additionally, what impact does the input model have on the relationship between covering array strength and coverage? We briefly review some of the more widely used measures and then consider results relating t-way testing to these measures.

- Statement coverage is the proportion of source statements exercised by the test set. Statement coverage is a relatively weak criterion, but provides a level of confidence that some basic testing has been done.
- Decision or branch coverage is a measure of branches that have been evaluated to both *true* and *false* in testing. When branches contain multiple conditions, branch coverage can be 100% without instantiating all conditions to true/false.
- Condition coverage measures the proportion of conditions within decision expressions that have been evaluated to both true and false. Note that 100% condition coverage does not guarantee 100% decision coverage. For example, "`if (A||B) {do something} else {do something else}`" is tested with [0 1], [1 0], then A and B will both have been evaluated to

0 and 1, but the *else* branch will not be taken because neither test leaves both A and B false.

- MCDC requires that every condition in a decision in the program has taken on all possible outcomes at least once, each condition has been shown to independently affect the decision outcome, and that each entry and exit point have been traversed at least once [11].

Since *t*-way testing has been shown effective in detecting faults, we might expect it to generate a high level of code coverage as well. Although there are only a few studies regarding this question, results indicate that tests based on covering arrays can produce good code coverage, but the degree of coverage is heavily dependent on the input model used.

7.4.1 Basic Structural Coverage

Czerwonka [49] studied branch and statement coverage generated by covering arrays of tests for $t = 1$ to $t = 5$, including questions of how the minimum, maximum, and range of coverage varied with increasing strength. Also considered was whether *t*-way tests produced statistically significant differences in coverage as compared with basic test criteria such as all values, and if any improvements in coverage with increasing *t* were the result of combinatorial effects or simply larger test suites. Four relatively small command line utilities were used in this study, with 100 different test suites for each level of *t*.

Consistent with early work on CT, results in Ref. [49] showed that code coverage does increase as covering array strength increases, as intuition would predict. Additional interesting findings included:

- Statement and branch coverage generated by the test suites at $t = 2$ and beyond were not extremely high, ranging from 64% to 76% for statement and 54% to 68% for branch.
- As covering array strength increased, the difference between minimum and maximum code coverage became narrower; thus, higher strength test arrays produced better coverage and were also more stable in the level of coverage produced.
- Both statement and branch coverage increased significantly at $t = 2$ as compared with all values ($t = 1$), but increases diminished rapidly with additional increases in *t*.
- The relationship between test suite size and covering array strength varied among the programs tested. For some, it appeared that improved coverage was not simply the result of additional tests at higher *t* levels, but in some other cases, test suite size, coupled with greater input combination diversity, was responsible for the improvement.

- The low levels of coverage may have been the result of factor and levels chosen for the covering arrays not sufficiently modeling the possible inputs for each program.

7.4.2 Effects of Input Model

The last point noted above may also explain the significant difference in coverage success shown in a different study that investigated the effectiveness of CT for achieving MCDC coverage. Bartholomew [95,96] applied combinatorial methods in producing MCDC-adequate test suites for a component of software defined radio system, showing that tests based on covering arrays could produce 100% MCDC coverage. Recall that MCDC subsumes branch coverage, which in turn subsumes statement coverage, so full MCDC coverage means that statement and branch coverage were 100% as well. A key feature in the application of MCDC is that tests are constructed based on requirements. Achieving structural coverage is viewed as a check that the test set is adequate, i.e., the MCDC source coverage is not the goal in itself, only a metric for evaluating the adequacy of the test set.

In this study, a module of 579 lines was instrumented for branch and condition coverage and then tested with the objective of achieving MCDC requirements specified by the Federal Aviation Administration. Initial tests obtained results similar to those in Ref. [49], with approximately 75% statement coverage, 71% branch coverage, and 68% MCDC coverage. However, full branch coverage, and therefore statement coverage also, was obtained after "a brief period of iterative test case generation" [95], which required about 4 h. MCDC, a substantially more complex criterion, was more difficult. In a few cases, obtaining complete MCDC coverage required construction of code stubs to force a particular sequence of tests, with specific combinations, to be executed. This process required two additional iterations, and a total of 16 additional hours. Complete test cases, based on covering arrays, were generated with a model checker, using the process described in Ref. [35]. This iterative process is consistent with the traditional use of the MCDC criterion as a check on test adequacy, as described previously. The integrated use of covering array-based tests, with a model checker to determine expected results for each test, was found to be extremely successful in reducing testing costs for MCDC. A NASA report [97] indicates that achieving MCDC coverage often requires seven times the initial cost of code development, so the results reported in Ref. [95] suggest the potential for significant cost savings if replicated on larger systems.

7.5 Testing Very Large Systems

Thus far in this chapter, we have discussed primarily combinations of input values, but the same combinatorial ideas can be used with configurations and software product lines. Such uses are increasingly common, as mobile applications and other types of software with extensive configuration options have proliferated. These systems are often referred to as *highly configurable software* [98]. Software product lines [99–103] are a particularly interesting type of configurable system, where components may be assembled according to a user's feature specification, resulting in potentially millions of possible instantiations. Since a product line with 50 features that can be included or excluded will have 2^{50}, or roughly 10^{15}, possible instantiations, only a small proportion of these possible configurations will ever be built. Since it is naturally impossible to test even a fraction of this number of configurations, combinatorial methods have been used to make testing more tractable. Instead of testing all configurations, it may be practical to test all 2-way, 3-way, or higher strength interactions among features. One of the most significant differences with SPL testing is simply the number of variables that must be considered. For example, an SPL may have hundreds of features that can be selected, with many more constraints than in other testing problems. One SPL is reported with 6000 features [99]. Several techniques have been devised to deal with this scale of test design.

One of the key problems with applying CT for a large number of variables is that covering array algorithms are often limited in the number of input variables that can be handled, and may be severely impacted by the presence of constraints. To process constraints, covering array generators often use Satisfiability Modulo Theory (SMT) constraint solvers. An alternative is to "flatten" the model to boolean values and then use boolean satisfiability (SAT) solvers.

A model can be "flattened" by systematically replacing variable values with boolean variables that represent a variable-value combination, with constraints to ensure that only one of the values (per variable) in the original model is selected. The process is straightforward: for each variable p_i with values $v_1, v_2, \ldots, v_k$, create k boolean variables that represent the selection of one of the k values for p_i. Then establish constraints as follows. We represent p_i set to value v_j as p_{ij}; thus, boolean variables are $p_{i1} \ldots p_{ik}$.

- One constraint, $p_{i1} + p_{i2} + \cdots + p_{ik}$, ensures that at least one of the k values is selected
- One constraint for each pair of values to ensure that at most one of the k values is selected (where $\bar{x}$ represents x negated): $(\bar{p}_{i1} + \bar{p}_{i2})$, $(\bar{p}_{i1} + \bar{p}_{i3}), \ldots, (\bar{p}_{ik-1} + \bar{p}_{ik})$

Table 20 Application Configurations

Parameter	Values
Operating system	XP, OS X, RHEL
Browser	IE, Firefox, Opera
Protocol	IPv4, IPv6
CPU	Intel, AMD
DBMS	MySQL, Sybase, Oracle

For example, constraints can be flattened for the configuration in Table 2. In this example, if we have a Linux system to test, there should be no tests containing IE as the browser, since this combination will not be seen in practice. Thus, there must be a constraint such as "Linux $\rightarrow$!IE" (Table 20).

Using the process described previously, we arrive at the following constraint set to prevent more than one operating system to be selected in the flattened model.

XP $\vee$ OX $\vee$ or RHEL	(1)
!XP $\vee$!OSX	(2a)
!XP $\vee$!RHEL	(2b)
!OSX $\vee$!RHEL	(2c)

Constraint (1) ensures that at least one of the options is selected, and constraints 2a, 2b, and 2c prevent more than one from being selected at the same time. Thus, this set of constraints preserves the original semantics that these are mutually exclusive options. Note that a large number of these constraints may be generated—for k options, we will need one constraint like (1) above to ensure at least one option is selected, and $C(k,2)$ constraints to ensure at most one is selected. However, modern SAT solvers have become extremely efficient, so this approach may work well. In some cases, it may be preferable to use the original model with an SMT solver, and in others a flattened model with SAT solver may perform better. The trade-offs between these two approaches are an area of ongoing research [104].

8. FUTURE DIRECTIONS

Combinatorial testing (CT) has evolved into an accepted practice in software engineering. As it has entered mainstream use, research interest has become more specialized and application oriented. Progress continues to be made in covering array generation algorithms, often with the aim of applying combinatorial methods to a broader range of testing problems, particularly those with larger inputs and complicated constraints. Concurrently, researchers are improving combinatorial test design methods by focusing on input model analysis and tools to assist in this phase of test design. CT continues to expand into domains such as software product lines and mobile applications. Here, we review current and upcoming developments in these areas and suggest potential impacts for practical testing. Finally, we briefly discuss harder problems in the field for which broadly effective solutions are not fully perfected.

8.1 Algorithms

While conventional algorithms produce very compact arrays for many inputs, improvements are being achieved. One recent trend in covering array algorithms is the use of reduction strategies on existing arrays. That is, a t-way covering array with N tests is systematically reduced to fewer than N tests using a variety of mathematical transformations. The near-term impacts of algorithm improvements in array construction include extending the applicability of combinatorial methods. For applications such as modeling and simulation, where a single test may run for hours, reducing covering array size by even a few tests is of great value.

These methods have recently improved upon the best-known sizes of some covering array configurations [37,105] and active research continues in this area. Similar transformations can also be done where there are constraints, and if the existing test suite was not designed as a covering array [55], using reductions that preserve the combinatorial coverage of the original test suite. An extension of this strategy [106] includes the option of allowing a subset of parameters to have values freely assigned, i.e., new tests can be generated rather than requiring them to be selected from the original test set. Other work shows that heuristic search can in some cases compete with greedy methods in speed and practicality for covering array construction [107]. Additionally, greedy algorithms can be improved using graph-coloring methods [108], to improve on a covering array generation phase that is optimal for $t = 2$ but does not retain optimal properties at $t > 2$.

A somewhat different aspect of applying combinatorial methods in test suite reduction is the use of interaction coverage as a criterion for reducing a test suite [109]. This may be particularly valuable for regression testing.

Various test reduction strategies have been applied in the past, but sometimes result in deteriorating fault-detection effectiveness. Since combination coverage is effective in fault detection, retaining high combinatorial coverage in a reduced test set can preserve effectiveness using fewer tests. Yet another practical consideration is the setup time between tests. Many testing problems, especially for system integration or other large system tests, require changes to the SUT configuration with each test. Minimizing this time, while retaining high combination coverage, can thus be an effective strategy [54].

8.2 Input Modeling

A second major research trend involves the integration of combinatorial methods in the development environment and addressing practical problems particular to various domains. The first step in any testing effort is to understand and define the input model, that is, the set of parameters and values that will be included in tests, along with any constraints on values or sequencing. This phase is an issue for any testing approach, not just combinatorial, but the unique aspects of CT have led researchers to tailor conventional methods. Test environments tailored to CT are being developed [56,110] to work with popular frameworks such as Eclipse. These environments will allow for validating the consistency and other meta-properties of constraint sets [53].

Software product lines are increasingly used and their enormous range of possible configurations provides a natural domain for CT. An extensive survey [111] shows the variety of ways in which t-way testing is now being applied in SPL testing and evaluation. Because of the large number of parameters in many SPLs, methods are being devised to extend the range of practical application for covering array generators. Software product lines often have hundreds, or even thousands, of variables. Conventional covering array algorithms are resource-limited in both time and storage to a few hundred. One approach is flattening of the input models, as described in Section 7.5 [104]. Such methods are an active area of research.

Two current lines of research for improving definition of the input model are classification trees and UML models. UML sequence diagrams can be used as inputs to rule-based tools that extract an input model that can be used with a covering array generator [112]. Input variables and values are extracted from UML message specifications and guard conditions, providing partial automation of the process to reduce effort for test designers.

Classification trees fit well with t-way testing, because they allow easy analysis and definition of test parameters in a tree structure [113]. Leaf nodes of the tree can be treated as category partitions and used directly in generating covering arrays. Robust tools based on classification trees, UML diagrams, and related concepts can help make combinatorial methods easier to use for test developers.

8.3 Harder Problems

CT will continue to find new domains of application, but some research problems remain to be solved. Two broad areas in particular are likely to receive attention from researchers because of their practical significance in industrial applications.

Very large systems: As with many areas of software engineering, *scalability* is essential. Fortunately, current combinatorial methods and covering array generators can address the vast majority of testing requirements. As noted earlier in the chapter, however, development approaches such as software product lines may involve thousands of parameters, with large numbers of constraints. Current covering array algorithms do not scale to such large problems, and existing constraint solvers are also insufficient for an extremely large number of constraints and variables.

Test development time: Case studies and experience reports show that combinatorial methods can provide better testing at lower cost, but these methods can require significant expertise and do not necessarily speed up the testing process. As such, if time-to-market is the primary concern, conventional test methods are likely to be preferred by developers. Application domains where CT has seen the most rapid acceptance so far are those with very high assurance requirements, such as aerospace/defense, finance, and manufacturing. Reducing the time required for using combinatorial methods is a significant challenge.

Research and practice have shown that CT is highly effective across a range of testing problems, and this range of applicability continues to expand for new domains and technologies. The current high level of research interest in the field suggests that it may continue to advance, providing stronger testing at reduced cost for developers.

CONCLUSIONS

CT has gained acceptance as a method to reduce cost and increase the effectiveness of software testing in many industries. The key insight underlying this method is that not every parameter contributes to every failure and most failures are caused by interactions between relatively few parameters. Empirical data indicate that software failures are triggered by only a few variables interacting (generally six or fewer). This finding has important implications for testing because it suggests that testing up to t-way combinations of parameters for small values of t can provide highly effective fault detection.

Industrial use has validated this conclusion. CT has seen tremendous growth in both industrial usage and research in the past 10 years. From an average of less than 10 papers a year prior to 2005, the field has grown to include an annual conference (since 2012) [65] and 100 or more papers a year in conferences and journals. Efficient covering array generation algorithms have been developed, and sophisticated tools have incorporated covering array algorithms with the capacity to process constraints that may be encountered in practical applications. As with any technology, extensions and new applications are being discovered, and the challenges introduced by these new uses are being addressed.

Disclaimer: Certain commercial products are identified in this document, but such identification does not imply recommendation by the US National Institute for Standards and Technology, nor does it imply that the products identified are necessarily the best available for the purpose.

REFERENCES

[1] R. Mandl, Orthogonal Latin squares: an application of experiment design to compiler testing, Commun. ACM 28 (1985) 1054–1058.

[2] K. Tatsumi, Test-case design support system, in: Proceedings of International Conference on Quality Control, Tokyo, 1987, pp. 615–620.

[3] K. Tatsumi, S. Watanabe, Y. Takeuchi, H. Shimokawa, Conceptual support for test case design, in: Proceedings of 11th IEEE Computer Software and Applications Conference, 1987, pp. 285–290.

[4] S.R. Dalal, C.L. Mallows, Factor-covering designs for testing software, Technometrics 40 (1998) 234–243.

[5] D.R. Wallace, D.R. Kuhn, Failure modes in medical device software: an analysis of 15 years of recall data, Int. J. Reliab. Qual. Saf. Eng. 8 (4) (2001) 351–371.

[6] D.R. Kuhn, M.J. Reilly, An investigation of the applicability of design of experiments to software testing, in: 27th NASA/IEEE Software Engineering Workshop, NASA Goddard Space Flight Center, December 4–6, 2002.

[7] D.R. Kuhn, D.R. Wallace, A. Gallo, Software fault interactions and implications for software testing, IEEE Trans. Softw. Eng. 30 (6) (2004) 418–421.

[8] K.Z. Bell, M.A. Vouk, On effectiveness of pairwise methodology for testing network-centric software, in: Proceedings of the ITI Third IEEE International Conference on Information & Communications Technology, Cairo, Egypt, December, 2005, pp. 221–235.

[9] K.Z. Bell, Optimizing effectiveness and efficiency of software testing: a hybrid approach, PhD Dissertation, North Carolina State University, 2006.

[10] Z. Zhang, J. Zhang, Characterizing failure-causing parameter interactions by adaptive testing, in: Proceeding of ACM International Symposium on Software Testing and Analysis (ISSTA), 2011, pp. 331–341.

[11] J.J. Chilenski, An investigation of three forms of the modified condition decision coverage (MCDC) criterion, 2001, Report DOT/FAA/AR-01/18, April, 214 pp.

[12] R.N. Kacker, D. Richard Kuhn, Y. Lei, J.F. Lawrence, Combinatorial testing for software: an adaptation of design of experiments, Measurement 46 (2013) 3745–3752.

[13] W.G. Cochran, G.M. Cox, Experimental Designs, Wiley, New York, 1950.

[14] O. Kempthorne, Design and Analysis of Experiments, Wiley, New York, 1952.

[15] G.W. Snedecor, W.G. Cochran, Statistical Methods, Iowa State University Press, Ames, Iowa, 1967.

[16] G.E.P. Box, W.G. Hunter, J.S. Hunter, Statistics for Experimenters, Wiley, New York, 1978.

[17] D.C. Montgomery, Design and Analysis of Experiments, fourth ed., Wiley, New York, 2004.

[18] R.A. Fisher, Statistical Methods for Research Workers, Oliver and Boyd, Edinburgh, 1925.

[19] R.A. Fisher, The Design of Experiments, Oliver and Boyd, Edinburgh, 1935.

[20] C. McQueary, Using design of experiments for operational test and evaluation, Memo, Office of the Secretary of Defense. www.dote.osd.mil/pub/policies/2009/200905UsingDoEforOTE_MOA.pdf, May 2009.

[21] G. Taguchi, Introduction to Quality Engineering, UNIPUB Kraus International, White Plains, New York, 1986.

[22] G. Taguchi, System of Experimental Design, vols. 1 and 2, UNIPUB Kraus International, White Plains, New York, 1987. (English translations of the third ed. of Jikken Keikakuho (Japanese) published in 1977 and 1978 by Maruzen).

[23] G. Taguchi, Taguchi on Robust Technology Development, ASME Press, New York, 1993.

[24] R.N. Kackar, Off-line quality control, parameter design and the Taguchi method, J. Qual. Technol. 17 (1985) 176–209.

[25] M.S. Phadke, Quality Engineering Using Robust Design, Prentice Hall, Englewood Cliffs, New Jersey, 1989.

[26] C.R. Rao, Factorial experiments derivable from combinatorial arrangements of arrays, J. R. Stat. Soc. (Suppl.) 9 (1947) 128–139.

[27] D. Raghavarao, Constructions and Combinatorial Problems in Design of Experiments, Dover, New York, 1971.

[28] A.S. Hedayat, N.J.A. Sloan, J. Stufken, Orthogonal Arrays: Theory and Applications, Springer, New York, 1999.

[29] N.J.A. Sloane, Webpage. http://www2.research.att.com/~njas/oadir/.

[30] S. Sato, H. Shimokawa, Methods for setting software test parameters using the design of experiments method (in Japanese), in: Proceedings of 4th Symposium on Quality Control in Software, Japanese Union of Scientists and Engineers (JUSE), 1984, pp. 1–8.

[31] H. Shimokawa, Method of generating software test cases using the experimental design (in Japanese), 1985, Report on Software Engineering SIG, Information Processing Society of Japan, No. 1984-SE-040.

[32] N.J.A. Sloane, Covering arrays and intersecting codes, J. Comb. Des. 1 (1993) 51–63.

[33] J.F. Lawrence, R.N. Kacker, Y. Lei, D.R. Kuhn, M. Forbes, A survey of binary covering arrays, Electron. J. Comb. 18 (2011) P84.

[34] J. Torres-Jimenez, E. Rodriguez-Tello, New bounds for binary covering arrays using simulated annealing, Inform. Sci. 185 (2012) 137–152.
[35] D. Richard Kuhn, R.N. Kacker, Y. Lei, Practical combinatorial testing, NIST Special Publication 800-142. http://csrc.nist.gov/groups/SNS/acts/documents/SP800-142-101006.pdf, 2010.
[36] P. Kitsos, D.E. Simos, J. Torres-Jimenez, A.G. Voyiatzis, Exciting FPGA Cryptographic Trojans using Combinatorial Testing, Technical Report, SBA-Research, Vienna Austria, 2015.
[37] T. Britton, L. Jeng, G. Carver, P. Cheak, T. Katzenellenbogen, Reversible debugging software, Technical report, University of Cambridge, Judge Business School, 2013.
[38] D.R. Kuhn, R.N. Kacker, Y. Lei, Combinatorial measurement tool user guide, Available online at http://csrc.nist.gov/groups/SNS/acts/documents/ComCoverage 110130.pdf, 2011 (accessed 14.05.12).
[39] D.R. Kuhn, I. Dominguez Mendoza, R.N. Kacker, Y. Lei, Combinatorial coverage measurement concepts and applications, in: IEEE Sixth International Conference on Software Testing, Verification and Validation Workshops (ICSTW), 2013, pp. 352–361.
[40] P.E. Ammann, A.J. Offutt, Using formal methods to derive test frames in category-partition testing, in: Proceedings of Ninth Annual Conference Computer Assurance (COMPASS'94), Gaithersburg, MD, IEEE Computer Society Press, 1994, pp. 69–80.
[41] J.R. Maximoff, M.D. Trela, D.R. Kuhn, R. Kacker, A method for analyzing system state-space coverage within a t-wise testing framework, in: IEEE International Systems Conference, April 4–11, San Diego, 2010.
[42] NIST Covering Array Tables, Available online at http://math.nist.gov/coveringarrays/ipof/ipof-results.html (accessed 23.03.15).
[43] C. Colbourn, Covering array tables for t = 2,3,4,5,6. Available online at http://www.public.asu.edu/~ccolbou/src/tabby/catable.html (accessed 23.03.15).
[44] J. Torres-Jimenez, Covering arrays, Available at http://www.tamps.cinvestav.mx/~jtj/# (accessed 23.03.15).
[45] R. Bryce, Algorithms for covering arrays, PhD Dissertation, Arizona State University, 2006.
[46] M.B. Cohen, C.J. Colbourn, P.B. Gibbons, W.B. Mugridge, Constructing test suites for interaction testing, in: Proceedings of the International Conference on Software Engineering (ICSE 2003), May, 2003, pp. 28–48.
[47] M.B. Cohen, C.J. Colbourn, A.C.H. Ling, Constructing strength three covering arrays with augmented annealing, Disc. Math. 308 (2008) 2709–2722.
[48] J. Czerwonka, Pairwise testing in the real world. http://msdn.microsoft.com/en-us/library/cc150619.aspx.
[49] J. Czerwonka, On use of coverage metrics in assessing effectiveness of combinatorial test designs, in: 2013 IEEE Sixth International Conference on Software Testing, Verification and Validation Workshops (ICSTW), 2013, pp. 257–266.
[50] Combinatorial methods in software testing, National Institute of Standards and Technology. http://csrc.nist.gov/acts.
[51] P. Satish, K. Sheeba, K. Rangarajan, Deriving combinatorial test design model from UML activity diagram, in: IEEE Sixth International Conference on Software Testing, Verification and Validation Workshops (ICSTW), 2013, pp. 331–337.
[52] X. Qu, M.B. Cohen, A study in prioritization for higher strength combinatorial testing, in: IEEE Sixth International Conference on Software Testing, Verification and Validation Workshops (ICSTW), 2013, pp. 285–294.
[53] P. Arcaini, A. Gargantini, P. Vavassori, Validation of models and tests for constrained combinatorial interaction testing, in: IEEE Seventh International Conference on

Software Testing, Verification and Validation Workshops (ICSTW), 2014, pp. 98–107.

[54] H. Wu, C. Nie, F.C. Kuo, Test suite prioritization by switching cost, in: IEEE Seventh International Conference on Software Testing, Verification and Validation Workshops (ICSTW), 2014, pp. 133–142.

[55] E. Farchi, I. Segall, R. Tzoref-Brill, A. Zlotnick, Combinatorial testing with order requirements, in: 2014 IEEE Seventh International Conference on Software Testing, Verification and Validation Workshops (ICSTW), 2014, pp. 118–127.

[56] A. Gargantini, P. Vavassori, Citlab: a laboratory for combinatorial interaction testing, in: IEEE Fifth International Conference on Software Testing, Verification and Validation Workshops (IWCTW), 2012, pp. 559–568.

[57] D. Kuhn, R.N. Kacker, Y. Lei, Test parameter analysis (Chapter 5), in: E. Miranda (Ed.), Introduction to Combinatorial Testing, CRC Press, Boca Raton, FL, 2013.

[58] I. Segall, R. Tzoref-Brill, A. Zlotnick, Simplified modeling of combinatorial test spaces, in: IEEE Fifth International Conference on Software Testing, Verification and Validation Workshops (ICSTW), 2012, pp. 573–579.

[59] I. Segall, R. Tzoref-Brill, A. Zlotnick, Common patterns in combinatorial models, in: IEEE Fifth International Conference on Software Testing, Verification and Validation Workshops (ICSTW), 2012, pp. 624–629.

[60] A. Arcuri, L. Briand, Formal analysis of the probability of interaction fault detection using random testing, in: IEEE Transactions on Software Engineering, 18 August, IEEE Computer Society, 2011. http://doi.ieeecomputersociety.org/10.1109/TSE.2011.85.

[61] M. Grindal, J. Offutt, J. Mellin, Handling constraints in the input space when using combination strategies for software testing, Technical report HS-IKI-TR-06-001, School of Humanities and Informatics, University of Skövde, 2006.

[62] L. Yu, Y. Lei, M. Nourozborazjany, R.N. Kacker, D. Richard Kuhn, An efficient algorithm for constraint handling in combinatorial test generation, in: IEEE Sixth International Conference on Software Testing, Verification and Validation Workshops (IWCTW), 2013, pp. 242–251.

[63] M.B. Cohen, M.B. Dwyer, J. Shi, Exploiting constraint solving history to construct interaction test suites, in: Testing: Academic and Industrial Conference Practice and Research Techniques-MUTATION, 2007. TAICPART-MUTATION 2007, 2007, pp. 121–132.

[64] L. Yu, F. Duan, Y. Lei, R.N. Kacker, D. Richard Kuhn, Combinatorial test generation for software product lines using minimum invalid tuples, in: IEEE 15th International Symposium on High-Assurance Systems Engineering (HASE), 2014, pp. 65–72.

[65] IEEE, International workshop on combinatorial testing. http://ieeexplore.ieee.org/xpl/conhome.jsp?reload=true&punumber=1001832.

[66] World Wide Web Consortium, Document object model. http://www.w3.org/DOM/ (accessed 28.03.15).

[67] World Wide Web Consortium, DOM level 3 events specification. http://www.w3.org/TR/DOM-Level-3-Events/ (accessed 08.09.09).

[68] C. Montanez-Rivera, D.R. Kuhn, M. Brady, R.M. Rivello, J. Reyes, M.K. Powers, Evaluation of fault detection effectiveness for combinatorial and exhaustive selection of discretized test inputs, Softw. Qual. Prof. 14 (3) (2012) 12–18.

[69] J. Hagar, R. Kuhn, R. Kacker, T. Wissink, Introducing combinatorial testing in a large organization: pilot project experience report [poster], in: Third International Workshop on Combinatorial Testing (IWCT 2014), in Proceedings of the Seventh IEEE International Conference on Software, Testing, Verification and Validation (ICST 2014), Cleveland, Ohio, March 31–April 4, 2014, p. 153.

[70] A.M. Cunningham, J. Hagar, R.J. Holman, A system analysis study comparing reverse engineered combinatorial testing to expert judgment, in: IEEE Fifth International Conference on Software Testing, Verification and Validation Workshops (IWCTW), 2012, pp. 630–635.

[71] J.D. Hagar, T.L. Wissink, D.R. Kuhn, R.N. Kacker, Introducing combinatorial testing in a large organization, IEEE Comput. 48 (4) (2015) 64–72.

[72] R. Bryce, S. Sampath, A. Memon, Developing a single model and test prioritization strategies for event-driven software, Trans. Softw. Eng. 37 (1) (2011) 48–64.

[73] G. Rothermel, R.H. Untch, C. Chu, M.J. Harrold, Prioritizing test cases for regression testing, IEEE Trans. Softw. Eng. 27 (10) (2001) 929–948.

[74] S. Sampath, R. Bryce, S. Jain, S. Manchester, A tool for combinatorial-based prioritization and reduction of user-session-based test suites, in: Proceedings of the International Conference on Software Maintenance (ICSM)—Tool Demonstration Track, Williamsburg, VA, September 2011, 2011, pp. 574–577.

[75] D.L. Parnas, On the use of transition diagrams in the design of user interface for an interactive computer system, in: Proceedings of the 24th ACM National Conference, 1969, pp. 379–385.

[76] W.E. Howden, G.M. Shi, Linear and structural event sequence analysis, in: International Symposium on Software Testing and Analysis (1996), San Diego California, 1996, pp. 98–106.

[77] S. Chow, Testing software design modeled by finite-state machines, IEEE Trans. Softw. Eng. 4 (3) (1978) 178–187.

[78] J. Offutt, L. Shaoying, A. Abdurazik, P. Ammann, Generating test data from state-based specifications, J. Softw. Test. Verif. Reliab. 13 (1) (2003) 25–53.

[79] B. Sarikaya, Conformance testing: architectures and test sequences, Comput. Netw. ISDN Syst. 17 (2) (1989) 111–126.

[80] X. Yuan, M.B. Cohen, A. Memon, Covering array sampling of input event sequences for automated GUI testing, in: ASE'07: Proceedings of the 22nd IEEE/ACM International Conference on Automated Software Engineering, 2007, pp. 405–408.

[81] D.R. Kuhn, J.M. Higdon, J.F. Lawrence, R.N. Kacker, Y. Lei, Combinatorial methods for event sequence testing, in: IEEE Fifth International Conference on Software Testing, Verification and Validation Workshops (IWCTW), 2012, pp. 601–609. http://csrc.nist.gov/groups/SNS/acts/documents/event-seq101008.pdf.

[82] D.R. Kuhn, J.M. Higdon, J.F. Lawrence, R.N. Kacker, Y. Lei, Combinatorial methods for event sequence testing, CrossTalk J. Defense Software Eng. 25 (2012) 15–18.

[83] B. Dushnik, Concerning a certain set of arrangements, Proc. Am. Math. Soc 1 (1950) 788–796.

[84] J. Spencer, Minimal scrambling sets of simple orders, Acta Math. Acad. Sci. Hungary 22 (1971/1972) 349–353.

[85] O. Margalit, Better bounds for event sequencing testing, in: IEEE Sixth International Conference on Software Testing, Verification and Validation Workshops (ICSTW), 2013, pp. 281–284.

[86] E. Erdem, K. Inoue, J. Oetsch, J. Puehrer, H. Tompits, C. Yilmaz, Answer-set programming as a new approach to event-sequence testing, in: Proceedings of the 2nd International Conference on Advances in System Testing and Validation Lifecycle, Xpert Publishing Services, 2011, pp. 25–34.

[87] Y.M. Chee, C.J. Colbourn, D. Horsley, J. Zhou, Sequence covering arrays, SIAM J. Discret. Math. 27 (4) (2013) 1844–1861.

[88] C. Yilmaz, M.B. Cohen, A. Porter, Covering arrays for efficient fault characterization in complex configuration spaces, in: Proceedings of the 2004 ACM SIGSOFT

International Symposium on Software Testing and Analysis, New York, NY, USA, 2004, pp. 45–54.

[89] L. Shi, C. Nie, B. Xu, A software debugging method based on pairwise testing, in: Proceedings of the 5th International Conference on Computational Science, Berlin, Heidelberg, 2005, pp. 1088–1091.

[90] Z. Wang, B. Xu, L. Chen, L. Xu, Adaptive interaction fault location based on combinatorial testing, in: Proceedings of 10th International Conference on Quality Software (QSIC), 2010, pp. 495–502.

[91] L.S. Ghandehari, Y. Lei, T. Xie, D.R. Kuhn, R. Kacker, Identifying failure-inducing combinations in a combinatorial test set, in: Proceedings of 5th IEEE International Conference on Software Testing, Verification and Validation Workshops IWCTW, 2012, pp. 370–379.

[92] J. Jones, M. Harrold, J. Stasko, Visualization of test information to assist fault localization, in: Proceedings of the 24th International Conference on Software Engineering (ICSE), 2002, pp. 467–477.

[93] M. Renieris, S. Reiss, Fault localization with nearest neighbor queries, in: Proceedings of the International Conference on Automated Software Engineering, 2003, pp. 30–39.

[94] L.S. Ghandehari, Y. Lei, R. Kacker, R. Kuhn, D. Kung, Fault localization based on failure-inducing combinations, in: IEEE International Symposium on Software Reliability Engineering (ISSRE), Pasadena, CA, 2013, pp. 168–177.

[95] R. Bartholomew, An industry proof-of-concept demonstration of automated combinatorial test, in: 8th International Workshop on Automation of Software Test (AST), 2013, pp. 118–124.

[96] R. Bartholomew, R. Collins, Using combinatorial testing to reduce software rework, CrossTalk 23 (2014) 23–26.

[97] Y. Moy, E. Ledinot, H. Delseny, V. Wiels, B. Monate, Testing or formal verification: DO-178C alternatives and industrial experience, IEEE Softw. 30 (3) (2013) 50–57.

[98] M.B. Cohen, M.B. Dwyer, J. Shi, Interaction testing of highly-configurable systems in the presence of constraints, in: Proceedings of the 2007 International Symposium on Software Testing and Analysis, ACM, 2007, pp. 129–139.

[99] C. Henard, M. Papadakis, G. Perrouin, J. Klein, P. Heymans, Y.L. Traon, 2012, Bypassing the combinatorial explosion: using similarity to generate and prioritize t-wise test suites for large software product lines. http://arxiv.org/pdf/1211.5451v1.pdf

[100] J. White, B. Dougherty, D.C. Schmidt, Selecting highly optimal architectural feature sets with filtered cartesian flattening, J. Syst. Softw. 82 (8) (2009) pp. 1268–1284.

[101] J. Lee, S. Kang, D. Lee, J. Lee, S. Kang, D. Lee, A survey on software product line testing, in: Proceedings of the 16th International Software Product Line Conference 1, ACM, 2012, pp. 31–40.

[102] Z. Xu, M.B. Cohen, W. Motycka, G. Rothermel, Continuous test suite augmentation in software product lines, in: Proceedings of the 17th International Software Product Line Conference, ACM, 2013, pp. 52–61.

[103] B.J. Garvin, M.B. Cohen, M.B. Dwyer, Failure avoidance in configurable systems through feature locality, in: J. Caamara, R. Lemos, C. Ghezzi, A. Lopes (Eds.), Assurances for Self-Adaptive Systems, Springer, Berlin, Heidelberg, 2013, pp. 266–296.

[104] C. Henard, M. Papadakis, Y.L. Traon, Flattening or not the combinatorial interaction testing models? in: International Workshop on Combinatorial Testing, IEEE, 2015.

[105] X. Li, Z. Dong, H. Wu, C. Nie, K.Y. Cai, Refining a randomized post-optimization method for covering arrays, in: IEEE Seventh International Conference on Software Testing, Verification and Validation Workshops (ICSTW), 2014, pp. 143–152.

[106] I. Segall, R. Tzoref-Brill, A. Zlotnick, Combining minimization and generation for combinatorial testing, in: IEEE Sixth International Conference on Software Testing, Verification and Validation Workshops (ICSTW), 2015.

[107] J. Petke, M. Cohen, M. Harman, S. Yoo, Practical combinatorial interaction testing: empirical findings on efficiency and early fault detection, IEEE Transactions on Software Engineering (2015), preprint.

[108] L. Yu, F. Duan, Y. Lei, R.N. Kacker, D. Richard Kuhn, Constraint handling in combinatorial test generation using forbidden tuples, in: IEEE Eighth International Conference on Software Testing, Verification and Validation Workshops (ICSTW), 2015.

[109] Q. Mayo, R. Michaels, R. Bryce, Test suite reduction by combinatorial-based coverage of event sequences, in: IEEE Seventh International Conference on Software Testing, Verification and Validation Workshops (ICSTW), 2014, pp. 128–132.

[110] B. Garn, D.E. Simos, Eris: a tool for combinatorial testing of the Linux system call interface, in: IEEE Seventh International Conference on Software Testing, Verification and Validation Workshops (ICSTW), 2014, pp. 58–67.

[111] R. Erick Lopez-Herrejon, S. Fischer, R. Ramler, A. Egyed, A first systematic mapping study on combinatorial interaction testing for software product lines, in: IEEE Seventh International Conference on Software Testing, Verification and Validation Workshops (ICSTW), 2015.

[112] P. Satish, A. Paul, K. Rangarajan, Extracting the combinatorial test parameters and values from UML sequence diagrams, in: IEEE Seventh International Conference on Software Testing, Verification and Validation Workshops (ICSTW), 2014, pp. 88–97.

[113] U. Zeppetzauer, P.M. Kruse, Automating test case design within the classification tree editor, in: IEEE, Federated Conference on Computer Science and Information Systems (FedCSIS), 2014, pp. 1585–1590.

ABOUT THE AUTHORS

Richard Kuhn is a computer scientist in the Computer Security Division of the National Institute of Standards and Technology (NIST). He has authored or coauthored 2 books and more than 100 publications on information security, empirical studies of software failure, and software assurance, and is a senior member of the IEEE. Before joining NIST, he worked as a systems analyst with NCR Corporation and the Johns Hopkins University Applied Physics Laboratory. He received an MS in Computer Science from the University of Maryland, College Park, and an MBA from the College of William & Mary.

Renee Bryce received her BS and MS degrees from Rensselaer Polytechnic Institute and her PhD degree from Arizona State University. She is an Associate Professor at University of North Texas. Her research interests include software testing, particularly combinatorial testing, test suite prioritization, and usability testing. She is an area editor for Software at IEEE Computer. She has served on the program committee of the International Conference on Software Testing Verification and Validation (ICST) and the International Workshop on Combinatorial Testing (IWCT).

Feng Duan is a PhD student in Department of Computer Science and Engineering at the University of Texas at Arlington. He received his BS degree in Computer Science from Fudan University. His research interests include software analysis and testing, particularly combinatorial testing, model-based testing and input parameter modeling.

Laleh Ghandehari is a Computer Science PhD candidate at the University of Texas at Arlington. She received the BS degree from Shahid Beheshti University and the MS degree in Computer Science from Sharif University of Technology. Her research interests include fault localization, software analysis, and software testing. In particular, she focuses on combinatorial testing and fault localization based on combinatorial testing.

Jeff (Yu) Lei is a Professor in Department of Computer Science and Engineering at the University of Texas at Arlington. He received his PhD degree in Computer Science from North Carolina State University, and was a Member of Technical Staff in Fujistu Network Communications, Inc. His research interests are in the area of automated software analysis, testing and verification, with a current focus on combinatorial testing.

Raghu Kacker is a senior researcher in the Applied and Computational Mathematics Division of NIST. He has contributed to design and evaluation of industrial experiments, quality engineering, and evaluation of measurement uncertainty in physical measurements and in outputs of computational models. His current interests include development and use of combinatorial mathematics methods for testing software systems. He has coauthored over 120 refereed publications and 1 book. He has a PhD in statistics (Iowa State University). He is a Fellow of the American Statistical Association and a Fellow of the American Society for Quality. He has also worked in industry (AT&T Bell Telephone Laboratories) and academia (Virginia Tech, Blacksburg, VA).

CHAPTER TWO

Constraint-Based Testing: An Emerging Trend in Software Testing

Arnaud Gotlieb
Simula Research Laboratory, Norway

Contents

Abstract

Constraint-based testing is an emerging trend in software testing research and innovation. The general idea beneath this testing paradigm is to exploit constraint solving and optimization to generate test cases for testing a software system, so that the fault-revealing capabilities of the testing process can be improved. The incredible progresses achieved these last years on the development of powerful constraint solvers

Advances in Computers, Volume 99
ISSN 0065-2458
http://dx.doi.org/10.1016/bs.adcom.2015.05.002

67

have fostered the emergence of effective and efficient constraint-based testing techniques. This chapter reviews in detail the main achievements reached in the field by illustrating them on simple examples and mentioning the main bibliographic references.

1. INTRODUCTION

In business-critical or safety-critical systems, software is often considered as the weakest link of the chain. As a matter of fact, the development of these systems relies more on highly skilled and experienced software engineers, than processes and techniques which guarantee the production of reliable, dependable, and secure software. As a consequence, even if handcrafted software systems are usually of high quality, they are also vulnerable to software defects because their development processes is not immune to human error. In addition, the current complexity and size growth of software, especially in the field of embedded systems, requires the development of automated testing techniques because hand-made test cases are no longer sufficient to validate these systems.

1.1 Software Testing

Among verification and validation approaches which have solid basis, software testing is the most widely used. Software testing requires the actual execution of the software system under test, which brings an immense advantage over other techniques such as software model checking, static analysis, or program proving. Indeed, software testing enables to verify the binary code actually executed, instead of checking only the source code of the system. In particular, software testing does not require to make strong hypothesis on the semantics of programming languages such as binary encoding formats of intermediate data which are almost impossible to verify when optimizing compilers are used and systems are executed on specific machines. Additionally, software testing enables to verify the system under test within its limited-resources execution environment, using the actual linked libraries in a process managed by the operating system.

These elements have placed software testing on top of validation and verification techniques for the industrial world. However, it can be pointed out that software testing suffers from an essential drawback, which relies to its fundamental incompleteness. Quoting the famous saying by Edsger W. Dijkstra, we know that:

Program testing can be used to show the presence of bugs, but never to show their absence!

Indeed, executing the program under test in all possible behaviors is almost always impossible because their number is by far too high. Software testing cannot formally guarantee the correctness of the program with respect to its specification and it cannot guarantee either the total absence of fault. Although often mentioned as the main drawback of software testing, this limitation is well accepted in practice as residual faults in the program are usually well tolerated as soon as they remain infrequent. Actually, reliability models of software systems, even for the most safety-critical ones, do not require the total absence of faults[1].

In fact, software testing suffers more from the cost of its systematic application than from this too theoretical limitation. Each test requires to be formalized in a document with a precise definition of its objective, that is, the explanation of its selection. Test scripts, which have to be treated as any other artifact within the software development chain, must also include a prediction of the expected outcome of the program under test. This latter element is crucial to establish a test verdict, which can be either pass if the expected outcome is similar to the actual outcome, or fail if they are different. Predicting the expected outcome of a program is not easy without a deep understanding of the tested application and sufficient knowledge of the execution platform. Test scripts are usually costly to develop, validate, maintain, and document. This explains why a particularly important challenge in software testing is concerned with the automation of test production, selection, and scheduling. In industrial development of large-scale software systems, the test process represents approximatively half of the overall development process. In order to address this challenge, researchers have dealt with the following problems in software testing, namely:

- **The test data selection problem**. Software testing requires to pick-up input test data for evaluating the correctness of a program under test. Sometimes, test inputs have to be selected within a large input search space. Ideally, one would like to select the inputs which are the most likely to reveal faults in the program, but in practice, as the faults are unknown, one resorts to select test inputs from imperfect testing criteria. The selection is performed by using either a model of the program specifications (*model-based testing or black-box testing*) or from the program under test itself (*code-based testing or white-box testing*), or from models

---

[1] For example, software development standards used in the avionics domain mention that the ultra-critical flight-command system of commercial aircrafts can fail once during 10^9 hours of usage [1]. Note, however, that it corresponds to a probability of 0.1 to observe such a failure over 30 years for a set of 1000 airplanes.

of possible faults (*mutation testing*), or from usage profiles (*statistical testing*). Testing criteria are used to guide the test data selection process, limit the size of test suites, and streamline the testing process. The stumbling block of these techniques involves reaching a sufficient level of confidence in the covering of the behaviors of the program under test. Consequently, validation engineers often have to compromise between the cost of the test and the expected level of reliability of the testing process. This is called the test data selection problem. When existing test suites, generated for testing a previous version of a program under test, are used to test a new version of the program, one wants to find pertinent subsets of test cases to re-execute to check the absence of previously detected faults (*non-regression testing*). In this case, identifying minimal subsets of test cases to re-execute while maintaining the coverage of certain test requirements is a must (*test suite reduction*). Equally important is to find an ideal order in which to re-execute the test cases for detecting regression faults (*test suite prioritization*).

- **The test oracle problem**. Running the program with input test data produces outputs that must be controlled with a procedure called a *test oracle*. Obtaining a complete error-free test oracle, i.e., an oracle which correctly respond to any given input data, is illusory due to the growing complexity of modern software systems. In fact, only a deep knowledge of the system under test enables the writing of useful test oracles. Automating the production of test oracles is thus an issue. Actually, the test oracles used in practice are often restricted to trivial properties that can easily be observed by the developers (for instance to check whether the program crashes or not). This oversimplified treatment of the problem is highly prejudicial to the quality of programs, which may contain a lot of residual bugs. For critical software systems, manual oracles are still in use, meaning that the outcome of the programs are carefully examined by validation engineers. A challenge in this area consists in finding ways to automatically produce these oracles from models, templates or other executable programs.

1.2 Constraint-Based Testing

Unexpectedly, the above-mentioned challenges require to solve hard combinatorial problems. Firstly, the search space originating from an unbounded input space or a large number of different program behaviors can be incredibly huge, sometimes even up to the limit of all available computer resources. Secondly, the test objectives that are required to be covered to ensure a certain level of quality of the program under test can lead to the characterization of very small areas of the input search space. So, selecting test data within those areas becomes like finding a needle in a haystack. For instance, finding an input data such that the execution flow of the program can reach an deeply imbricated line of code or finding a program behavior which provokes a memory leak or exhaust the available memory of the computer are typical concrete examples of hard-to-find test inputs. Despite theoretical limitations of automatic test case generation[2], dealing with these hard combinatorial problems for real-world programs is challenging.

Constraint-based testing was introduced to tackle these problems for various applications, including automatic white-box test inputs generation for imperative programs [3–12] and object-oriented programs [13–18], test pattern generation in hardware design [19–21], model-based test cases generation [22–27], and counter-examples generation [28–31].

The general idea behind constraint-based testing is to exploit constraint solving and optimization to generate test cases for a software system, so that the fault-revealing capabilities of the testing process can be improved. Given a test objective, constraint-based testing extracts a constraint system through the analysis of a program or a model, and solves this constraint system in order to generate test cases satisfying the test objective. For instance, if the generation of a test input that exercises a given path in a numerical program is the test objective. Then by using well-established *symbolic execution techniques*, one can derive a set of constraints over the program input variables, the solving of which leads to the generation of test inputs [32–34] exercising that path. Another example is given by an arithmetical program[3] where a single instruction has been artificially modified for creating a mutated program. The test objective is to find an input able to detect the mutation by comparing the result of the mutated program with the original program [3]. This involves solving two problems at the same time: first, one has to generate an input able to reach the location where the mutation was introduced and second, one has to find an input able to distinguish between the original and the mutated program. Note that program states can be compared either right after the mutated instruction or at the end of the program execution. Here again, constraint solving

---

[2] The problem is known to be undecidable in the general case [2].
[3] A program performing intensive integer computations.

and constraint optimization are crucial to propose effective and efficient automatic test input generation processes. Constraint-based testing typically aims at solving these problems.

Various constraint-solving technologies can be employed in constraint-based testing including linear programming, Boolean satisfiability (SAT-solving), satisfiability modulo theory (SMT-solving), and constraint programming. As for any hard combinatorial problem, there is no silver-bullet approach for all the cases and one often takes advantage of mastering and combining distinct technologies for attacking each problem instance. Going deeply into the comparison of these four technologies would go far beyond the scope of this chapter but we will try to briefly emphasis their strengths and weaknesses in constraint-based testing. Note that performing constraint-based testing does not require a deep knowledge of these technologies as they can be seen as black boxes from the user standpoint. However, effective application of constraint-based testing requires to know how these technologies work and how they differ.

1.3 Constraint-Based Test Input Generation

The most successful application of constraint-based testing takes place in test input generation, which requires to address specifically two problems:

- **Path infeasibility.** An execution path of the program is said to be *infeasible* if there does not exist any test input that can execute it. Path infeasibility is not considered as a fault and it is known, since a long time, that infeasible paths are quite ubiquitous in programs [35]. However, dealing with path infeasibility in automatic test input generation is challenging because detecting infeasibility requires to show that path conditions are contradictory and this demonstration is often difficult. As an example, consider the following path conditions over two integer variables X, Y and try to show infeasibility:

$$X * Y = 6, X < Y - 2, X + Y = 5$$

If one tries to generate a test input which satisfies these path conditions, then one may ended up labeling all the possible values for X and Y. Even if the possible values for X, Y are in finite number (typically if integers are encoded on 64-bits words), this may require an unacceptable amount of time. In this case, constraint reasoning is necessary to show contradictory conditions. On the one hand, showing path infeasibility is often difficult and on the other hand showing path infeasibility is not indispensable for test input generation. In fact, as the final goal is to detect faults in the program under test, wasting time demonstrating that some paths can never be activated could be avoided. Note however that certifying safety-critical programs requires showing that all non-executed statements during the testing phase, are actually infeasible.

- **Paths combinatorial explosion.** When analyzing a program, conditional branching within the program leads to the examination of distinct alternatives, depending on the value of the condition at runtime. In test data generation approaches, a choice is arbitrarily made on this value and the corresponding subpath is explored. If a contradiction is detected during this exploration because of path infeasibility, then the process backtracks and explores alternative subpaths. If the program contains n conditionals and each conditional leads to the exploration of two subpaths, then the program contains at least 2^n paths, among which some are probably infeasible. It means that an exhaustive exploration of all alternatives is impossible as soon as the number of conditionals grows up to more than twenty or thirty. Thus, a standard depth-first search approach for the exploration of paths in a program faces a combinatorial explosion problem.

These two problems have to be dealt with by any automatic test input generation approach. They also make the problem almost impossible to solve in general, so that approaches have to compromise between the completeness of the path exploration and the efficiency of the test input generation process.

1.4 Organization of the Chapter

This chapter has the following structure: Section 2 illustrates constraint-based testing on a motivating example. Section 3 presents some bibliographic notes on this emerging trend in software testing. Section 4 gives the foundations of constraint-based testing and presents distinct constraint-solving techniques for automatic test input generation. Section 5 develops two extensions of constraint-based testing and finally, Section 6 concludes this chapter by drawing some perspectives to constraint-based testing.

2. A MOTIVATING EXAMPLE

The program of Fig. 1 called `divide` intends to solve an ancient simple mathematical problem: A farmer owns a field that is a rectangular

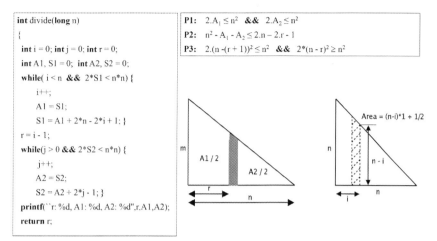

Figure 1 The divide program and three properties to check.

isosceles triangle. He wants to divide it into two areas of the same surface, following a line that is parallel to a side of the triangle. The division can only be performed by whole numbers of feet and there must be a free strip of width at least 1 between the two new fields to plant some trees.

Three properties describe quite naturally the intended behavior of the program:

- (P1) Each area must be less than or equal to the whole area of the triangle divided by 2. Note that the computed areas A1 and A2 correspond to twice the actual areas, in order to avoid divisions and non-integer variables;
- (P2) The splitting error, namely the total area minus the sum of the two new fields, is not bigger than a slice of width one;
- (P3) The theoretical non-integer line of splitting is located in the free area. This is expressed by two inequalities, the area on the right of the free zone is less than or equal to the whole area divided by 2 and this area plus the free zone is bigger than the whole area divided by 2.

Any result computed by the divide program has to satisfy the three properties described above. For this program, they can be seen as a test oracle able to provide a test verdict on any computed result. Among the techniques that can be employed to verify these properties or invalidate them, static analysis, software model checking, program proving, and software testing are the four most popular available techniques. It is worth noticing that, although the divide program is composed of only a few lines of code, it is quite complex to understand and analyze. This situation is not uncommon in practice where it is observed that the difficulty of a program verification task is in not correlated to the size of the program under evaluation. Very large programs can be trivial to process, while programs composed of a couple of lines can be very hard to understand.

Static analysis is appealing for finding the so-called runtime errors or to extract automatically properties on the analyzed program [36]. The general idea is to process the program line by line and compute for each statement, an over-approximated state of the program calculations. These states gather informations related to any possible executions up to the line under consideration. From these over-approximated states, one can infer domain informations and relations on the program variables. Unfortunately, static analysis is unsufficient for the divide program as the properties to be checked are quite complex and cannot easily be automatically inferred[4].

Software model checking is a variant of static analysis where the inferred relations are progressively refined until a counter-example to the properties to be checked is found [37]. Even if this approach revealed itself to be very powerful [38], it is limited by the subset of analyzed execution paths and by the abstract domains used to check the properties.

Program proving using weakest precondition calculus [39] is a powerful technique for proving complex properties. However, it requires the specification of loop invariants for iterative programs. For the divide program, these invariants are difficult to provide automatically because they are similar to properties P1–P3.

The most effective approach to deal with the divide program is software testing where the goal is to find counter-examples to properties P1–P3 through program executions. These counter-examples can be given by test inputs which are submitted to the program in order to produce outputs violating at least one of the given properties. Software testing is powerful enough to reveal the existence of many distinct failures in the divide program, including integer overflows and property violations due to the modular machine arithmetic. Of course, without some guidance in the search of test inputs, the testing process may fail to find these counter-examples, although they actually exist. However, by using constraint-based testing, it is possible to uncover some of these faults. Constraint-based testing of the

---

[4] Property P1–P3 are nonlinear w.r.t. integer variables n and r.

divide program will solve complex constraints by using a constraint solver able to deal with nonlinear constraints over integer variables and constraints which represent the iterative computations of the program. Eventually, constraint-based testing will extract pertinent test inputs for testing the divide program.

Properties P1–P3 for the divide program are actually representative of more general software verification problems, which typically involve nonlinear assignments[5], conditionals, loops, array manipulations, integer, and floating-point computations. Automated program testing tools for real-world programs have to deal with these features, and also additional features such as low-level operations, memory allocation, pointer arithmetic and aliasing, inheritance and polymorphism.

3. BIBLIOGRAPHIC NOTES

Recent advances in program verification has focused on the usage of constraint solvers for code verification but it is in automated testing that the most spectacular advances have been reached. Benefiting from the incredibly level of maturity gained in the past 20 years by constraint solving, including constraint programming, linear programming, and SMT solving, constraint-based testing has emerged has a powerful technique to automatically generate test cases in many different contexts.

The idea of using constraint solving for automating the generation of test cases dates back to the early nineties with the work of Marre [40] and Faivre [41]. Starting from algebraic specifications, the goal in these works was to generate functional test cases by using Constraint Logic Programming [42], an approach which allows the users to develop their own constraint solvers and constraint models.

At the same time, in the context of mutation testing, Offut et al. proposed in [3, 43] to encode the mutation operated on the program as an additional constraint and to explore various control flow paths executing the mutated statement with symbolic execution [32, 33, 44]. Using a dedicated home-made constraint solver, it was then possible to generate a test input which would reach the mutated statement and reveal the different behavior of the mutated program. Taking inspiration of ideas originally proposed by Bicevskis et al. in [45], the constraint solver propagated inequality constraints

---

[5] A typical example is given by the following C instruction $i*=i++$; which has to be interpreted as $i_2 = i_1*(i_1+1)$.

extracted from program statements to reduce the variation domain of input variables. Following a distinct approach based on program executions, meta-heuristics were also explored at the same time for automatic test data generation with the research work of Korel [46], Gupta *et al.* [47], and Tracey *et al.* [48].

In 1998, Gotlieb *et al.* implemented an approach for generating test inputs able to reach a selected location within a C program [4] in a tool called InKa [49, 50]. Unlike Offut's approach, no selection of path was required for that purpose. The proposed technique was based on the usage of the static single assignment form [51], a well-known intermediate representation of programs used in optimizing compilers. A crucial advance of this work concerned the usage of Constraint Logic Programming [42] to implement constraints able to represent control structures of imperative programs such as conditionals and loops [49].

In the early 2000s years, Marinov *et al.* studied the generation of complex inputs for Java programs [13, 14]. By creating dedicated generators for complex data structures, these works led to the design of ad-hoc constraint-solving techniques and heuristics [17]. In 2005, Godefroid, Sen *et al.* [5, 52] on the one hand and Williams *et al.* [6] on the other hand concurrently developed the idea of combining program executions and symbolic execution to automatically generate test inputs. These works initiated the development of powerful test input generators such as PEX [53] and SAGE [54] at Microsoft Research, PathCrawler at CEA [6], CREST [9] at Berkeley, or EXE [7] at Stanford. At the same time, by studying different memory models, Gotlieb *et al.* refined the treatment of complex data structures in constraint-based testing of C programs [11, 55, 56]. On the one hand, benefiting from the tremendous progress achieved in solving constraints from distinct theories in the SMT-solving framework [57], Cadar *et al.* proposed KLEE which showed impressive capabilities for generating test inputs for complex system programs [58]. On the other hand, by combining Abstract Interpretation techniques [59] and constraint programming, Gotlieb proposed Euclide [10] which successfully handled complex properties for a C program used in the civil avionics domain [60]. At the same time, Bardin *et al.* proposed a constraint-based testing tool for binary executables [61, 62].

Of course, the list of references mentioned in this section is not exhaustive and many other techniques and results could have been mentioned. Constraint-based testing is an active research topic which is explored in many different directions within the software testing community.

4. FOUNDATIONS

This section presents the foundations of constraint-based testing and illustrates its main processes through simple examples.

Given a testing goal, constraint-based testing leads to the generation of test inputs which satisfy the goal. Let's illustrate this principle on the simple example program called foo, shown in Fig. 2, previously introduced in [60].

Testing the program of Fig. 2 involves assigning values to the two input signed integer variables x and y and executing the program. Line 4 contains an assertion for checking if the value of z is strictly greater than -2500. A typical test objective for this program is to find test inputs which break the assertion, that is to find values for x and y reaching line 4 and producing a state where $z \leq -2500$. In order to solve this problem, constraint-based testing extracts the following constraint system C, where ite stands for **if–then–else**:

$$C = \{X, Y \in -2^{31}..2^{31} - 1, Z = 0, U = 0, ite(X * Y < 4, U_1 = 5, U_1 = 100),$$
$$ite(U_1 \leq 8, Y_1 = X + U_1, Y_1 = X - U_1), Z_1 = X * Y_1, Z_1 \leq -2500\}$$

Formally speaking, x and X have to be distinguished: x is a program variable implicitly associated to a given cell in the live machine's memory, while X is a logical variable in a constraint system. So, X corresponds to an unknown to be discovered and that cannot be overwritten through the execution of the program. Another difference comes from the renaming of logical variables (e.g., Y, Y_1, ...) that has been performed, following the static single assignment scheme in order to avoid destructive assignment. So, C is a set of constraints which has to be solved in order to find a test input satisfying the test objective. For the foo program of Fig. 2, constraint-based testing can produce $(X = 50, Y = 1)$ as a test input which violates the assertion. Of course, this is not the only solution and other test inputs can also be generated (e.g., $(X = 50, Y = 1000)$), depending on search heuristic or the preferences of the user.

```
int foo(int x, int y)
    int z, u ;
1.  if (x * y < 4) u = 5 ; else u = 100 ;
2.  if (u ≤ 8) y = x + u ; else y = x − u;
3.  z = x * y ;
4.  assert (z > −2500)
```

Figure 2 Constraint-based testing illustrated on a simple example.

The process which extracts the constraint system from the program is called *constraint generation* while the process which intends to solve it is called *constraint solving*. In the rest of this section we discuss both of them for each instruction of a simple imperative language.

4.1 Constraint Generation

A typical approach to generate the constraints associated to a testing goal is to start from a normalized form of the program. Program normalization is a process that breaks complex statements into a sequence of simpler statements by introducing new temporary variables. Normalization also makes explicit numerous treatments that may remain hidden to the developer such as implicit type casting and type conversions. Typical intermediate languages used in normalization are strongly typed and contain only statements that have less than three references. These languages have to be expressive enough to perform memory allocation and deallocation, fixed-size integer and floating-point computations, references manipulations and structure fields assignment and conversion, and complex control structures. Once the program is normalized, variables have to be uniquely numbered, in order to ease their processing as logical variables. The static single assignment form of imperative programs can be used for that purpose. Then, the constraint generation process itself can take place to extract a constraint system from the test objective. Let us now review how to extract and solve the constraints for each program instruction category.

4.1.1 Assignment

When processing an assignment statement such as $v = x \ op \ y$; where op stands for any binary operation, an interpreter generates either a constraint of the form $V = X \ op \ Y$, or a more complex set of constraints such as

$$load(y, Y, M_0), load(x, X, M_0), op(V, Y, X), store(v, V, M_0, M_1)$$

where y, x, v denote memory references, Y, X, V denote logical variables and M_0, M_1 denote memory variables. The choice behind these two approaches depends on the complexity of the test input generation problem. Typically, if the program contains only assignment to integer or floating-point variables, then the former model will be privileged as it avoids useless indirections. If pointers or references are used in the program, then the latter one will be selected to deal with pointer aliasing and indirections. *Load, store,* and *op* maintain relations among references, variables and memory variables, by applying deduction rules to prune the search space of possible memory shapes. They can be quite complex to define and implement if memory models are powerful enough to handle complex statements with pointer arithmetic or type casting.

4.1.2 Conditional

An **if-then-else** statement, or any conditional statement (e.g., **case-of**), can be handled with a special constraint called $ite(D, C_{Then}, C_{Else})$. This constraint maintains a disjunctive relation between D the decision of the conditional statement, and C_{Then}, C_{Else} which are associated to each part of the conditional. By using logical operators, the relation maintained by $ite(D, C_{Then}, C_{Else})$ can be formulated as $(D$ and $C_{Then})$ or $(\neg D$ and $C_{Else})$. Nevertheless, constraint-based reasoning can be used to reason on this conditional constraint by using case-based reasoning and constructive disjunction. *Case-based reasoning* tries to refute one part of disjunction by checking its inconsistency with the other constraints from the constraint system [4]. In the program foo of Fig. 2, if one knows that $u \leq 8$, case-based reasoning can deduce that the **else** part of the first conditional is inconsistent because it assigns u to 100 which is not possible. *Constructive disjunction* tries to extract as much information as possible from the analysis of the conditional without knowing which part of the conditional would be selected to satisfy the test objective. For example, constructive disjunction can determine that, whatever be the part of the conditional which is taken in the first conditional of program foo, there are only two possible outcomes for u after its execution: $u \in \{5, 100\}$.

4.1.3 Iteration

Iterative statements include many different constructions in programming languages such as **while-do**, **do-while**, **for**, etc. However, handling **while-do** is sufficient to understand how to handle all of them because there exist automatic transformations which allow compilers to switch from one construction to another. Dealing with iterations is challenging in automatic test data generation because the number of iterations for satisfying a test objective is unknown beforehand. Usual methods assign a maximum value to the number of possible iterations within a loop but this approach is debatable when the termination condition of the loop depends on input variables. In the program divide of Fig. 1, the number of iterations of loops cannot be predicted beforehand as it depends on input variable n, which is unknown, and also on computations realized within the loops. On the one hand, assigning a too low value to the maximum number of iterations can miss to spot faults which require a higher number of iterations. On the other hand, assigning a too high value can lead to unacceptable delays in the generation of test inputs, especially when programs contain several loops. Note also that imbricated loops in programs often introduce a dependency between the number of iterations in each loop. Without an approach which captures this dependency, the process is doomed to consider many spurious program behaviors which cannot be executed.

Instead of bounding a priori the number of iterations in each loop, it is possible to introduce a mechanism which unroll loops on-demand in the generated constraint system. Similarly to the treatment of conditional statements, one can introduce a special constraint noted $w(Dec, \mathcal{M}_1, \mathcal{M}_2, \mathcal{M}_3, C_{Body})$ where Dec stands for the decision of the loop, C_{Body} stands for the constraints of the body of the loop, and $\mathcal{M}_1, \mathcal{M}_2, \mathcal{M}_3$ stands for memory states[6]. These memory states allow the constraint solver to deal with the appropriate program variables. Further details are given below in Section 4.7. The implementation of w is also based on case-based reasoning and constructive disjunction. Case-based reasoning on iterations relies on the following simple remark: if a variable used after the loop has a value which is different from the value it had before, then this variable has necessarily been modified within the loop body. Then, the loop is necessarily unrolled at least once. So, by reasoning on the states before and after each loop iteration, it is possible to derive deduction rules for handling $w(Dec, \mathcal{M}_1, \mathcal{M}_2, \mathcal{M}_3, C_{Body})$ in a constraint solver [4, 49]. Additionally, when no strong deduction can be made on whether the process should unroll the loop or not, constructive disjunction can take place by extrapolating the computations realized in the loop, whatever be the number of iterations. This process has been formalized by using an Abstract Interpretation operator called widening [63]. Further details can be found in [64].

4.2 Constraint Solving and Optimization

Program verification can often be reduced to the problem of showing that a constraint system is satisfiable or unsatisfiable [65, 66]. For example, verifying the absence of null pointer dereference in an imperative program is equivalent to showing that any constraint system that characterizes a path

---

[6] Memory states can be understood as mappings from program variables to values.

through a state where a null pointer is dereferenced is unsatisfiable. Recently, much attention has been devoted to the usage of constraint-solving and constraint optimization tools in constraint-based testing. Techniques such as linear programming, SAT and SMT solving, constraint programming have been used for that purpose.

These techniques can be compared regarding to their ability to handle various types of constraints and variables. Table 1 shows a comparison between the solving technologies used in constraint-based testing with respect to the type of data which are natively handled by their solvers. Some answers in the table contains an additional parameter referring to the underlying technique used to solve the constraints. For example, Boolean-typed variables can be handled by the usage of integer linear programming (ILP). Bounded Integers variables are usually encoded with a fixed length sequence of bits (typically over 32 or 64 bits) while Integers variables are encoded with a nonfixed length sequence of bits, meaning that their representation can be extended as much as needed for a given computation. Floating-point variables represent various types of floating-point numbers, encoded with a fixed-length sequence of bits (s,m,e) where s is the sign bit, m is a fixed-length sequence for the mantissa and e is a fixed-length sequence for the exponent. Real variables represent rational or real numbers that can be encoded with pairs of integers or pairs of floating-point numbers in order to form an interval which contains the represented real. In addition, arrays represent indexed values that can be accessed and updated with possibly unknown indexes.

Based on Table 1, a couple of observations can be made. Linear programming and its extension to deal with Integers is really powerful to deal with bounded and unbounded Integers. These techniques, have been developed

Table 1 Comparison of Different Constraint-Solving Technologies Used in Constraint-Based Testing in Their Native Handling of Different Type of Data

Approaches	Booleans	Bounded Int.	Integers	Floats	Reals	Arrays
Linear prog.	Yes (ILP)	Yes (ILP)	Yes (ILP)	No	Yes	No
SAT solving	Yes	No	No	No	No	No
SMT solving	Yes (SAT)	Yes (ILP)	Yes (ILP)	No	Yes (LP)	Yes
Constraint prog.	Yes (FD)	Yes (FD,ILP)	No	Yes	Yes (CD,LP)	Yes

ILP stands for integer linear programming, FD stands for finite domains, CD stands for continuous domains.

up to a point where thousands of constraints and variables can be handled without any difficulty by mature tools. For Booleans and Bounded Integers, constraint programming has introduced Finite Domains (FD) constraint solving which takes advantage of the bounds of variable domains to prune the search space. Based on constraint propagation and filtering, constraint programming is a versatile technique to deal with bounded domains, but, unlike ILP, it cannot deal with unbounded Integers. Regarding floating-point computations, very few constraint solvers have been developed. Those which have reached a certain level of maturity are also based on constraint filtering over bounded domains in constraint programming. Linear programming is the core technique to deal with real and rational variables. There are also constraint propagation and filtering techniques which have been developed for continuous domains (CD) but they have been very seldomly used for test input generation. Finally, constraint solvers able to deal with arrays adopt either an axiomatic reasoning approach developed in SMT solving or a constraint filtering approach developed in constraint programming.

It is also worthwhile to compare these techniques (linear programming, SAT solving, SMT solving, and constraint programming) with respect to the type of constraints and constraint reasoning they can handle. Table 2 compares the ability of the techniques to deal with linear and nonlinear arithmetical constraints, symbolic constraints, constraint solving and optimization, and their usage of global reasoning. For a constraint solver, dealing with nonlinear arithmetical constraints is notoriously difficult. Almost all the simple program examples shown in this chapter contain instructions which have to be interpreted as nonlinear constraints. For example, an assignment instruction such as $z = x * y$ is nonlinear when both x,y are unknown input variables. Of course, there are many other operators in programming languages which lead to nonlinear constraints, such as division, mult-add, etc. Another source of nonlinearity comes from disjunctions when or-statements, conditionals or iterative statements have to be handled. In constraint-based testing, symbolic constraints are used to deal with indirect accesses to the memory. It is thus beneficial to have some native support for encoding these accesses through symbolic reasoning. Some constraint solvers, in addition to solving constraints, can also optimize a cost function in order to find test inputs which maximizes or minimizes a test objective. Finally, some constraint-solving approaches for constraint-based testing adopt a global reasoning over the constraints, as opposed to a simpler local reasoning approach. Table 2 shows that there

Table 2 Comparison of Different Constraint-Solving technologies Used in constraint-based testing in Their Handling of Constraints

Approaches	Linear Arithm.	Nonlinear Arithm.	Symbolic Ctr.	Ctr. Solving	Ctr. Optimization	Global
Linear prog.	Yes	No	No	Yes	Yes	Yes
SAT solving	No	No	No	Yes	No	Yes
SMT solving	Yes	No	Yes	Yes	No	Yes
Constraint prog.	Yes	Yes	Yes	Yes	Yes	No

is no silver bullet for constraint-solving in constraint-based testing. The distinct technologies are complementary, having their own strengths and weaknesses for test input generation. The rest of the section if dedicated to the description in more depth of these technologies.

4.3 Linear Programming for Test Data Generation

Historically, linear programming techniques in combination with ad hoc techniques were the first automatic constraint solving the be used in order to generate test inputs for path conditions [3, 33, 45, 67, 68]. By switching path conditions solving into a constrained optimization problem, Boyer *et al.* and Clarke [33, 67] have explored several distinct linear programming techniques, including the cut generation algorithm of Gomory for integer computations and the Benders decomposition technique. A linear constraint is of the form $a_1 * x_1 + \ldots a_n * x_n \leq b$ and it is well known that many constraints (symbolic or numeric) can be transformed or approximated by using one or several linear constraints. Solving a set of linear inequalities is possible by using a combination of various techniques including Fourier elimination and simplex algorithm. Note that, in the context of test input generation, Boyer *et al.* [67] also proposed to use the conjugate gradient algorithm to deal with quadratic and linear inequalities. Interestingly, Bicevskis *et al.* [45] proposed a tool called SMOTL, which contained an ad hoc procedure for solving inequalities over integer variables based on a domain pruning procedure. The constraint system is processed iteratively: the inequalities are used to prune the interval domain of each variable until no more pruning is possible. The lowest bounds of each interval are then suggested as potential input value for testing the program. DeMillo and Offut [3, 43] proposed a similar approach to kill mutated programs. Note, however, that in both cases, the proposed approaches were incomplete, that is, not capable of guaranteeing the generation of a test input satisfying the test objective, even if it existed. More recently, the DART [5] and CUTE [52] techniques were introduced to generate test inputs by combining program execution and symbolic execution. Both techniques used linear programming over mixed integer-real computations for solving the path conditions generated during program executions.

4.4 SAT and SMT Solving for Test Input Generation

Many developments in dynamic symbolic execution, a technique used to symbolically explore the execution paths of a program through a combination of symbolic reasoning and program executions, revealed the pressing needs for having at hand powerful constraint-solving methods. In this context, these methods have to decide efficiently of the satisfiability of first-order logic formulae and have to find models (i.e., solutions of these formulae) to automatically derive test inputs.

Despite the great success of dynamic symbolic execution tools, such as PEX [53], SAGE [54], or KLEE [58], cost-effective solving of intensive test inputs generation tasks requires efficient constraint solvers. In fact, dealing accurately and efficiently with all data and control structures of a programming language is difficult and requires dedicated *decision procedures*. The approach which consists in exploding basic types and data structures into bit vectors and using a SAT solver to reason on these vectors does not really scale up [62]. That is why special theories and associated decision procedures have been proposed to extend SAT solvers in a framework called SMT solving. SMT stands for *satisfiability modulo theory*. The most well-known theories of SMT are the *theory of uninterpreted functions (UF)* and the *theory of linear integer arithmetic (LIA)*. The theory UF considers function symbols in addition to equality and disequality over variables, where functions are of arbitrary arity and have no interpretation. The only assumption about a function f concerns its functional consistency: $\forall x,y(x = y \Rightarrow f(x) = f(y))$. The theory LIA considers linear inequalities over integer variables. These theories are decidable, meaning that there are decision procedures able to decide of the satisfiability of any formulae expressed in the language of these theories. In addition, several cooperation frameworks between decision procedures have been proposed to facilitate the resolution of formulae which combines the symbols from both theories; the most well known being the Nelson–Oppen cooperation framework [69]. It should be noted that most of these decision procedures handle only conjonctions of constraints and there is still a need to combine them with an external procedure based on SAT-solving when disjunctive formulae are considered. So, an SMT solver can be sought as a classical SAT solver extended with decision procedures for selected theories. The searching process is thus driven by the underlying SAT solver which delegates to the specialized decision procedure the handling of conjonction of constraints. Among the most successful SMT solvers developed in recent years and extensively used for test input generation, Z3 [70] and StP [57] can be mentioned.

Based on the analysis of an early attempt to combine SMT-based decision procedures and CP solvers [85], the following differences and complementarities have been noticed: SMT-based decision procedures bring *global reasoning* through the handling of specific theories and similar constraints (e.g., linear integer arithmetic, difference logic, nonlinear arithmetic, etc.,) while CP-based approaches, through the usage of consistency filtering algorithm, bring *local reasoning*. SMT solvers build upon a nice and neat separation of decision procedures through the *high-level* Nelson–Oppen combination framework while CP solvers implements complex reasoning at *low-level* within a single constraint propagation queue. Through their *rigidity* in terms of accepted inputs, SMT solvers come with strong correctness and completeness results, while CP solvers through their *flexibility* allows the users to define their own constraints and search procedures. These differences open the door for promising opportunities when handling complex constructions in constraint-based software testing approaches. Better optimized constraint solvers will be produced when a fruitful dialogue will be started on the marriage of these technologies.

4.5 Constraint Programming Approaches for Test Data Generation

Constraint-based test data generation involves solving constraint systems extracted from programs. In constraint programming, a constraint system is composed of variables, domains, built-in constraints and user–defined constraints. Variables represent unknown typed value and they are associated to a variation domain. When used to capture the possible values of a program variable, this domain is finite as it corresponds to a fixed-length bit sequence (i.e., integers, floating-point values or memory references). Built-in constraints include standard logical and arithmetic operations such as $=\leq$, $<$, $+$, $-$, $*$, ... They are usually supported by the constraint solver itself. User-defined constraints are additional constraints which implement special-purpose algorithms dedicated to the studied problem. In automatic test input generation and program analysis, these user-defined constraints are useful to deal with control and data structures.

Intuitively, a constraint program is solved with the interleaving of three processes, namely *local filtering*, *constraint propagation* and a *search procedure*.

- Given a constraint, *local filtering* prunes the domains of variables by eliminating values which cannot be part of any solution of the constraint. For example, the constraint $X \leq Y$ filters all values of X's domain which are greater than the upper bound of Y's domain and all values of Y's domain which are lower than the lower bound of X's domain. This filtering process is local because it considers only a single constraint at a time. When large domains are considered, local filtering usually considers only the bounds of domains and ignore internal values in order to preserve efficiency.

- *Constraint propagation* is the process which propagates domain pruning throughout the constraint system. Each constraint is treated in turn one by one in an iterative process. Local filtering is applied to the variable domain and thus, domain pruning is propagated throughout the constraint system until a fix-point is reached. Roughly speaking, this fix-point corresponds to a state where no more pruning can be performed. When all the domains are finite, termination is guaranteed by the fact that only a finite number of value can be removed from the domains.

- The *search procedure* instantiates each variable X_i to a value v_j from its domain in order to form a satisfying assignment for all the constraints. The process can be implemented by adding a new constraint $X_i = v_j$ to the constraint system and by triggering constraint propagation, so that further domain pruning of other variables is possible. When the domain of any variable becomes empty, then the constraint system is showed to be contradictory. It means that the current assignment $X_i = v_j$ is incoherent with the constraints. Then, the search procedure can backtrack to one assignment $X_i = v_j$ and revise it by either selecting another variable to assign or another value. This search procedure is parametrized by a value-selection and variable-selection strategy that is called *search heuristics*.

As an example, consider the following nonlinear constraint system over two unsigned 32-bits integer variables:

$$X, Y \in 0..2^{32} - 1, X * Y = 6, X + Y = 5.$$

Local filtering on constraint $X * Y = 6$ prunes the domain of X and Y to 1..6 as values 0,7,8,... violate the constraint. Ideally, local filtering could also detect that other assignments within 1..6 violate the constraint (e.g., $X = 5$ is impossible) but usually only the boundaries of the domains are checked for violations, to preserve efficiency. Then, the constraint $X + Y = 5$ is considered and local filtering prunes the domain of both X and Y to 1..4. In fact, the values 5 and 6 for X and Y are incoherent with the constraint. Finally, the constraint $X * Y = 6$ woke up through constraint propagation and local filtering prunes the domain of X and Y to 2..3. From there, local filtering cannot prune the domain anymore and thus, the Cartesian product of the domains is a fix-point. The search procedure can then be triggered and, depending on the search heuristics that is employed, the solutions $(X = 2, Y = 3)$ and $(X = 3, Y = 2)$ are found.

Constraint programming has be tuned to test input generation in many different ways. Tools such as InKa [49, 50], PathCrawler [6], Osmose [61], Euclide [10] have explored different search heuristics, local filtering algorithms and constraint propagation strategies. For instance, considering distinct priorities over constraints allows the system to prioritize the treatment of the most powerful constraints when it comes to their pruning capabilities [10]. Local filtering is also parametrized by the level of consistency to be achieved. In most cases, however, the most important feature of these tools is related to their treatment of control structures and how they explore the program under test.

4.6 User-Defined Constraints

As said above, in constraint programming environments, one can add user-defined constraints able to capture the essence of constraint reasoning for selected control structures. This feature requires to define:

1. A named interface on a set of variables, which establishes the relation to be added. For example, we previously introduced *ite* and *w* to represent **if-then-else** and **while-do**;
2. The wake-up conditions. A user-defined constraint is awaked when either the domain of one of its variables is pruned, or one of its variables

is instantiated, or a new constraint related to its variables is added to the constraint system;

3. An algorithm to call on wake-up. The purpose of this algorithm is to check whether the constraint is consistent or inconsistent with the new domains of variables, but also to prune the domains when no final answer can yet be given regarding to its consistency. This algorithm is typically defined with graph traversal techniques or specific domain filtering.

4.7 The *w* Constraint for Handling Loops

The user-defined $w(Dec, \mathcal{M}_1, \mathcal{M}_2, \mathcal{M}_3, Body)$ constraint captures the essence of iterative computation [4, 49, 63, 64] where Dec represents the decision of the loop and $Body$, its execution body. Recall that a memory state is actually a mapping from program variables to values.

The w constraint maintains a relation over three distinct memory states: $\mathcal{M}_1$ a state before the loop execution, $\mathcal{M}_2$ a state after one iteration of the loop, and $\mathcal{M}_3$ a state after the complete execution of the loop. Note that $w(Dec, \mathcal{M}_1, \mathcal{M}_2, \mathcal{M}_3, Body)$ is compositional, meaning that $Body$ may also contain other constraint operators such as *ite* and *w*. The semantics of w corresponds to the repetitive application of $Body$, while Dec is true.

As a user-defined constraint, w has an interface $w(Dec, \mathcal{M}_1, \mathcal{M}_2, \mathcal{M}_3, Body)$, a set of awakening conditions and a filtering algorithm. Awakening conditions for w are triggered by any modification within $\mathcal{M}_1$ or $\mathcal{M}_3$, meaning that some new information about the memory states before or after the loop execution is known. The filtering algorithm of w can be expressed as a set of conditional constraints of the form $C_1 \rightarrow C_2$ and implemented as such within a constraint solver having an appropriate interface. Such a conditional constraint is treated as follows: if C_1 is entailed by the current set of constraints then C_2 is added to the set and w is solved and removed from the constraints set. If C_1 is disentailed (meaning that its negation is entailed), then the conditional constraint is discarded and removed from the set of conditional constraints. At last, if no entailment or disentailment can be shown, then the conditional constraint suspends until possible further application when the w constraint is awaken. These conditional constraints are considered each time the constraint w awakes during the constraint solving process. By using variable substitution, some of them implements the iteration process by rewriting it into recursive calls. $Dec_{\mathcal{M}_3 \leftarrow \mathcal{M}_1}$ denotes constraint Dec where all the program variables from $\mathcal{M}_3$ have been substituted by the same variables from $\mathcal{M}_1$. With these notations, the filtering algorithm of w is expressed as follows:

$w(Dec, \mathcal{M}_1, \mathcal{M}_2, \mathcal{M}_3, Body)$ iff

- $Dec_{\mathcal{M}_3 \leftarrow \mathcal{M}_1} \rightarrow Body_{\mathcal{M}_3 \leftarrow \mathcal{M}_1} \wedge w(Dec, \mathcal{M}_2, \mathcal{M}_{new}, \mathcal{M}_3, Body_{\mathcal{M}_2 \leftarrow \mathcal{M}_{new}})$
- $\neg(Dec_{\mathcal{M}_3 \leftarrow \mathcal{M}_1}) \rightarrow \mathcal{M}_3 = \mathcal{M}_1$
- $\neg(Dec_{\mathcal{M}_3 \leftarrow \mathcal{M}_1} \wedge Body_{\mathcal{M}_3 \leftarrow \mathcal{M}_1}) \rightarrow \neg(Dec_{\mathcal{M}_3 \leftarrow \mathcal{M}_1}) \wedge \mathcal{M}_3 = \mathcal{M}_1$
- $\neg(\neg Dec_{\mathcal{M}_3 \leftarrow \mathcal{M}_1} \wedge \mathcal{M}_3 = \mathcal{M}_1) \rightarrow Dec_{\mathcal{M}_3 \leftarrow \mathcal{M}_1} \wedge Body_{\mathcal{M}_3 \leftarrow \mathcal{M}_1}$
$$\wedge w(Dec, \mathcal{M}_2, \mathcal{M}_{new}, \mathcal{M}_3, Body_{\mathcal{M}_2 \leftarrow \mathcal{M}_{new}})$$
- $join(Body_{\mathcal{M}_3 \leftarrow \mathcal{M}_1} \wedge w(Dec, \mathcal{M}_2, \mathcal{M}_{new}, \mathcal{M}_3, Body_{\mathcal{M}_2 \leftarrow \mathcal{M}_{new}}), \mathcal{M}_3 = \mathcal{M}_1)$

By evaluating the entailment of Dec, the first two conditional constraints implement the operational semantics of a while loop within an imperative programming language. If Dec is entailed, a recursive call which posts a new w is performed. The next two conditional constraints implement backward reasoning by examining the differences between the memory states before and after the execution of the loop. These conditional constraints are convenient to perform deductions about the loop itself. For example, knowing that a variable modified within the loop has a value after the execution of the loop which is different from its value before the execution, necessarily means that the loop must be unrolled. For the last deduction rule, an additional operator is introduced. The *join* operator implements the union of memory states when none of the previous conditional constraints can be triggered. This operator performs some deductions, even if the number of iterations performed in the loop is ignored.

4.8 Illustrative Example

The program of Fig. 3 illustrates the behavior of w. A typical constraint-based testing problem consists in finding a value of i such that statement 6. is executed. Existing approaches for solving this reachability problem propose to select a path passing through statement 6. For instance, the path 1-2-4-5-6 can be selected, and the approach will try to solve the *path condition* associated to this path. In this case, it means extracting the path conditions $j_1 = 100, i_1 \leq 0, j_1 > 500$ and solving it. Actually, this constraint system is contradictory and thus the path 1-2-4-5-6 is infeasible. Then, the process can backtrack and select another path. For instance, the path 1-2-3-2-4-5-6 can be selected with path conditions $j_1 = 100 \wedge i_1 > 0 \wedge j_2 = j_1 + 1 \wedge i_2 = i_1 - 1 \wedge i_2 \leq 0 \wedge j_2 > 500$. Repeating the process leads again to contradictory path conditions. Actually, this example is problematic for path-oriented approaches, as only the paths which iterate more than

```
int goo(int i,...)
1.    int j = 100 ;
2.    while (i > 0)
3.         {j = j + 1 ; i = i - 1} ;
4.    ... ;
5.    if (j > 500)
6.         ... ;
```

Figure 3 An example with constraint w (where unknown statement 4 is supposed to avoid modifying variable j).

400 times in the loop can reach statement 6. This deduction is unfortunately difficult to obtain without a strong and powerful program analysis. Hopefully, using the constraint operator $w(i > 0, \mathcal{M}_1, \mathcal{M}_2, \mathcal{M}_3, j = j + 1 \wedge i = i - 1)$, it is possible to deduce that the loop must be iterated at least 400 times to reach statement 6. Interestingly, this deduction is performed without backtracking. The relational analysis performed on w is highly beneficial here as it entails the expected deduction. By using powerful constraint reasoning, constraint-based testing can perform deductions which are sometimes outside the scope of other traditional testing techniques.

5. EXTENSIONS

This section presents two extensions of constraint-based testing towards programming paradigms which are traditionaly left apart from introductory books in software testing. The first extension is about the difficulty to test numerical programs, that is, programs which contain floating-point computations and how to perform constraint-based testing for them. The second extension introduces the problems of dealing with object-oriented constructions such as inheritance and polymorphism.

5.1 Constraint Solving for Floating-Point Computations

Programs with floating-point computations are notoriously difficult to test. The main problems with floating-point computations are the rounding errors which are difficult (sometimes almost impossible) to predict and eliminate from programs. One could argue that rounding errors leading to large deviations are not so frequent and can probably often be ignored in many cases. That would be dangerous as these errors are a major source of critical defects in embedded systems, sometimes yielding to catastrophic consequences.

A typical approach used when testing floating-point computations consists in selecting special execution paths of the program and trying to find test inputs to activate these paths. It requires the resolution of constraints over floating-point computations and unfortunately, existing constraint solvers over the real numbers or the rational numbers do not work properly for this purpose. In fact, operations over the floating-point numbers cannot easily be captured by constraints over the real numbers and conversely. Let us illustrate this statement on a simple example. The constraint system $(x > 0.0, x + 1.0e12 = 1.0e12)$ where x is a 32-bits floating-point number, accepts all the floating-point numbers within the closed interval $[1.4012984643248171e - 45, 32768.0]$ as possible solutions for x. In fact, due to the limited representation of x, any float from this interval will be "absorbed" by $1.0e12$. Yet, a simple reasoning over the constraints indicates that the system has no solution over the reals $(x > 0, x = 0)$, which is an incorrect deduction over the floats. Any solver working properly over the reals or the rationals will get immediately to this conclusion. Conversely, the constraint system $(x < 10000.0, x + 1.0e12 > 1.0e12)$ accepts all the reals within the open interval $(0, 10000.0)$ as solutions, as it simplifies to $(x > 0.0, x < 10000.0)$ over the reals. Yet, there is not a single floating-point number that can solve this constraint system as any float encoded over 32 bit from this interval will be absorbed by $1.0e12$.

Although automatic test input generation is not a recently addressed research problem, there are only few studies that have genuinely sought to reason correctly about floating-point computations. In 2001, Michel *et al.* proposed in [71] a first constraint solver based on constraint programming. The solver was able to deal correctly with floating-point computations, even if its algorithms could hardly scale up to more than a couple of variables and constraints. These algorithms were based on a dichotomy-based exploration of the interval associated to each variable in order to find correct floating-point values satisfying the floating-point constraints. In 2002, Michel [72] proposed a theoretical framework to achieve what was called *FP-2B-consistency*, a dedicated filtering property of constraints for floating-point computations. This theoretical work opened up the road to the realization of efficient solvers for floating-point constraints. In 2006, Botella *et al.* developed a first operational symbolic executor for floating-point computations [73] based on FP-2B-consistency. In this work, techniques were proposed to correctly handle path conditions involving floating point calculations, with the development of projection functions for floating-point constraints. Recently, new improvements on these projection functions for two basic arithmetical operations, namely addition and subtraction, were proposed in [74]. These improvements take advantage of the representation of floating-point numbers to increase the accuracy of deductions obtained with constraint propagation over floating-point constraints. These optimizations were implemented and generalized to nonlinear operators in [75]. Using the terminology *"filtering by ULP-Max,"* Carlier and Gotlieb defined optimized projection functions for the four basic operations, and obtained some advanced experimental results on an industrial C program related to in-flight anti-collision for drones [76].

Automatic test data generation for floating-point computations is a recent but very promising research topic, within the scope of constraint-based testing. Observing that floating-point computations are used everywhere in embedded systems design, it is believed that industrial needs for approaches able to analyze and process correctly floating-point computations are immense.

5.2 Test Input Generation for Object-Oriented Code

Constraint-based testing of object-oriented code requires to deal with inheritance, operator overloading, (dynamic) method calls and polymorphism. These features are difficult to handle correctly and only a few approaches have achieved to address them successfully in constraint-based testing. An early attempt to deal with inheritance is present in the work of Buy *et al.* in [77] and Souter *et al* in [78]. Testing polymorphic relations was early recognized as difficult, especially if one wants to formally extend the coverage criteria classically used in testing [79]. In the context of sequential code, the handling of dynamic data structures in constraint-based testing approaches has initially been proposed by Sen *et al.* in [52]. This approach was further refined and developed by the design of two SMT-based test input generators, namely PEX in [53] and SAGE [54]. By compromising on the completeness of constraint solving and search during test input generation, these approaches can deal with very large object oriented .NET programs. These tools opened the door to the large-scale industrial adoption of constraint-based testing. Based on the constraint model of [11] dedicated to complex dynamic data structures, Charreteur and Gotlieb [18] proposed to handle inheritance and virtual method calls for Java Bytecode in constraint-based testing. In this approach, each Bytecode is seen as a relation among two abstract memory states and constraint reasoning is used to perform deductions on variables of these abstract states. This technique revealed itself to be powerful enough to deal with complex decisions and data structures. For instance, a decision of the form `p == p.next` can be satisfied only by creating a cyclic data structure referenced by `p`. This deduction is difficult to implement in a constraint-based testing tool unless it is based on a relational model to reason over references and data structures [18]. However, the complexity of the abstract memory models requested for dealing with such data structures entails performance issues when handling large programs.

Similarly, dealing with virtual method calls is difficult as it is impossible to know at compile-time exactly which method in the inheritence tree will be called. An approach in constraint-based testing consists in exploring the various possibilities until one of them is found to be satisfactory. This approach can be implemented using a simple deep-first search exploration of the inheritence tree. Handling correctly virtual method calls as well as operator overloading in a constraint model associated to a program under test demands great efforts in the design of a constraint-based tool as this requires to understand the semantics of each construction and to model it as relations. There is room for improvement in this area where only very few approaches have been designed.

6. PERSPECTIVES

The increasing complexity of software systems requires the development of more effective techniques for their validation and verification. This increased complexity is not only due to the growth of the number of components of the system, but also to the growth of the number of features and configuration parameters. Nowadays, it is not uncommon to see software systems that can be configured in several million different ways depending on the diversity of their configuration settings. Testing these highly configurable software systems is an emerging challenge which is driven by strong industrial needs. Among the issues brought by these needs, the selection of error-prone test configurations, the optimization of test suites and the scheduling of test executions are typical highly combinatorial problems that can be addressed by constraint-based testing approaches. Although most of the underlying fundamental problems are NP-hard (e.g., selecting a minimum subset of test cases in a test suite that covers a set of existing test requirements), it is of paramount importance to find practical solutions that can compromise between the effort devoted to the test preparation and the quality of the test processes. Developing models and techniques that can effectively deal with the combinatorial explosion of the number of possible configurations of a software system is highly desirable, as well as selecting test configurations based on their relevance to their exposure to software errors.

To face these challenges, research perspectives in the domain of constraint-based testing have been identified. At the crossroads of software testing techniques based on constraint solving and variability management practices, fundamental and applied research work can develop new bridges between constraint programming and software testing. In fact, constraint programming can solve hard combinatorial problems such as staff allocation or task scheduling, opening up great perspectives for solving software testing problems with similar characteristics. Fruitful initial results have already been obtained in test suite optimization [80], but these efforts have to be further extended and generalized.

According to this vision, the development of more optimized and generalized constraint-solving techniques will be a key factor of the success of constraint-based testing. In particular, the remarkable development of global constraints [81] will open up great perspectives for the creation of new innovative tools and processes in this area.

The industrial adoption of constraint-based testing is in progress with several pioneering experiences. Di Alesio *et al.* introduced in [82] a constraint optimization model for generating robustness test scenarios for safety-critical real-time-embedded systems of the Maritime domain. Gotlieb and Marijan presented in [80] a constraint optimization model based on global constraints for test suite optimization. Its usage on real-world software product lines enables the automatic selection of minimal test suites for videoconferencing systems. Another industrial example is given by the development of a constraint programming model for generating test sequences for integrated painting systems embedded onto industrial robots [83, 84]. Interestingly, this constraint-based testing approach is now deployed in an industrial continuous integration environment. All these case studies are promising regarding the industrial adoption of constraint-based testing and they are part of a broad perspective to demonstrate the high potential of constraint-based testing in software testing.

REFERENCES

[1] B. Littlewood, L. Strigini, Validation of ultrahigh dependability for software-based systems, Commun. ACM 36 (1993) 69–80.
[2] E. Weyuker, Translatability and decidability questions for restricted classes of program schemas, SIAM J. Comput. 8 (4) (1979) 587–598.

[3] R. DeMillo, J. Offut, Constraint-based automatic test data generation, IEEE Trans. Softw. Eng. 17 (9) (1991) 900–910.

[4] A. Gotlieb, B. Botella, M. Rueher, Automatic test data generation using constraint solving techniques, in: Proc. of Int. Symp. on Soft. Testing and Analysis (ISSTA'98), 1998, pp. 53–62.

[5] P. Godefroid, N. Klarlund, K. Sen, DART: directed automated random testing, in: Proc. of PLDI'05, Chicago, IL, 2005, pp. 213–223.

[6] N. Williams, B. Marre, P. Mouy, M. Roger, PathCrawler: automatic generation of path tests by combining static and dynamic analysis, in: Proc. Dependable Computing–EDCC'05, 2005.

[7] C. Cadar, V. Ganesh, P. Pawlowski, D. Dill, D. Engler, EXE: automatically generating inputs of death, in: Proc. of Comp. and Communications Security (CCS'06), Alexandria, VA, 2006, pp. 322–335.

[8] P. Boonstoppel, C. Cadar, D. Engler, RWset: attacking path explosion in constraint-based test generation, in: Int. Conference on Tools and Algorithms for the Construction and Analysis of Systems (TACAS'08), 2008, pp. 351–366.

[9] J. Burnim, K. Sen, Heuristics for scalable dynamic test generation, in: ASE'08: 23rd IEEE/ACM International Conference on Automated Software Engineering, IEEE Computer Society, Washington, DC, ISBN: 978-1-4244-2187-9, 2008, pp. 443–446, ISSN 1527-1366.

[10] A. Gotlieb, EUCLIDE: a constraint-based testing platform for critical C programs, in: 2th IEEE International Conference on Software Testing, Validation and Verification (ICST'09), Denver, CO, 2009.

[11] F. Charreteur, B. Botella, A. Gotlieb, Modelling dynamic memory management in constraint-based testing, J. Syst. Softw. 82 (11) (2009) 1755–1766, special Issue: TAIC-PART 2007 and MUTATION 2007.

[12] F. Degrave, T. Schrijvers, W. Vanhoof, Towards a framework for constraint-based test case generation, in: Logic-Based Program Synthesis and Transformation, 19th International Symposium, LOPSTR 2009, Coimbra, Portugal, September 2009, Revised Selected Papers, 2009, pp. 128–142.

[13] D. Marinov, S. Khurshid, TestEra: a novel framework for automated testing of java programs, in: Proc. of the 16th IEEE Int. Conf. on Automated Soft. Eng. (ASE'01), 2001, p. 22.

[14] C. Boyapati, S. Khurshid, D. Marinov, Korat: automated testing based on Java predicates, in: Proc. of the Int. Symp. on Soft. Testing and Analysis (ISSTA'02), Roma, Italy, 2002, pp. 123–133.

[15] S. Khurshid, C. Pasareanu, W. Visser, Generalized symbolic execution for model checking and testing, in: Proc. of the 9th International Conference on Tools and Algorithms for the Construction and Analysis of Systems (TACAS'03), Warsaw, Poland, 2003.

[16] K. Sen, G. Agha, CUTE and jCUTE: concolic unit testing and explicit path model-checking tools, in: 18th Int. Conf. on Computer Aided Verification (CAV'06), Lecture Notes in Computer Science 4144, Seattle, WA, 2006, pp. 419–423.

[17] B. Elkarablieh, D. Marinov, S. Khurshid, Efficient solving of structural constraints, in: Proc. of the Int. Symp. on Software Testing and Analysis (ISSTA'08), Seattle, WA, 2008, pp. 39–50.

[18] F. Charreteur, A. Gotlieb, Constraint-based test input generation for java bytecode, in: Proc. of the 21st IEEE Int. Symp. on Softw. Reliability Engineering (ISSRE'10), San Jose, CA, 2010.

[19] D. Lewin, L. Fournier, M. Levinger, E. Roytman, G. Shurek, Constraint satisfaction for test program generation, in: IEEE International Phoenix Conference on Communication and Computers, 1995, 1995.

[20] E. Bin, R. Emek, G. Shurek, A. Ziv, Using a constraint satisfaction formulation and solution techniques for random test program generation, IBM Syst. J. 41 (3) (2002).

[21] S.K.S. Hari, V.V.R. Konda, V. Kamakoti, V.M. Vedula, K.S. Maneperambil, Automatic constraint based test generation for behavioral HDL models, IEEE Trans. Very Large Scale Integr. Syst. 16 (2008) 408–421, ISSN 1063-8210.

[22] R.H. Carver, Testing abstract distributed programs and their implementations: a constraint-based approach, J. Syst. Softw. 33 (3) (1996) 223–237.

[23] D. Jackson, M. Vaziri, Finding bugs with a constraint solver, in: Proc. of ISSTA'00, Portland, OR, 2000, pp. 14–25.

[24] B. Legeard, F. Peureux, Generation of functional test sequences from B formal specifications–presentation and industrial case-study, in: Proc. of the 16th IEEE Int. Conf. on Automated Software Engineering (ASE 2001), IEEE Computer Society Press, San Diego, CA, 2001, pp. 377–381.

[25] A. Pretschner, H. Ltzbeyer, Model based testing with constraint logic programming: first results and challenges, in: 2nd ICSE Int. Workshop on Automated Program Analysis, Testing, and Veri. (WAPATV'01), 2001.

[26] B. Marre, B. Blanc, Test selection strategies for lustre descriptions in GATeL, Electron. Notes Theor. Comput. Sci. 111 (2005) 93–111.

[27] F. Bouquet, F. Dadeau, B. Legeard, M. Utting, JML-testing-tools: a symbolic animator for JML specifications using CLP, in: Tools and Algorithms for the Construction and Analysis of Systems, 11th International Conference (TACAS'05), Edinburgh, UK, 2005, pp. 551–556.

[28] A. Gotlieb, B. Botella, Automated metamorphic testing, in: 27th IEEE Annual International Computer Software and Applications Conference (COMPSAC'03), Dallas, TX, 2003.

[29] T. Denmat, A. Gotlieb, M. Ducassé, Proving or disproving likely invariants with constraint reasoning, in: Proc. of the 15th Workshop on Logic-Based Methods in Programming Environments (WLPE'05), Sitges, Spain, 2005, satelite Event of International Conference on Logic Programming (ICLP'2005).

[30] H. Collavizza, M. Rueher, Exploring different constraint-based modelings for program verification, in: Proc. of CP2007, Lecture Notes in Computer Science 4741, 2007, pp. 49–63.

[31] H. Collavizza, M. Rueher, P. Van Hentenryck, CPBPV: a constraint-programming framework for bounded program verification, in: Proc. of CP2008, Lecture Notes in Computer Science 5202, 2008, pp. 327–341.

[32] J. King, Symbolic execution and program testing, Commun. ACM 19 (7) (1976) 385–394.

[33] L. Clarke, A system to generate test data and symbolically execute programs, IEEE Trans. Softw. Eng. 2 (3) (1976) 215–222.

[34] W. Howden, Reliability of the path analysis testing strategy, IEEE Trans. Softw. Eng. 2 (3) (1976) 208–214.

[35] D. Yates, N. Malevris, Reducing the effects of infeasible paths in branch testing, in: Proc. of Symposium on Software Testing, Analysis, and Verification (TAV3), in: Software Engineering Notes, vol. 14(8), 1989, pp. 48–54, Key West, FL.

[36] B. Blanchet, P. Cousot, R. Cousot, J. Feret, L. Mauborgne, A. Miné, D. Monniaux, X. Rival, Design and implementation of a special-purpose static program analyzer for safety-critical real-time embedded software, invited chapter, in: T. Mogensen, D. Schmidt, I. Sudborough (Eds.), in: The Essence of Computation: Complexity, Analysis, Transformation. Essays Dedicated to Neil D. Jones, Lecture Notes in Computer Science 2566, Springer-Verlag, 2002, pp. 85–108, ISBN 3-540-00326-6.

[37] T. Ball, V. Levin, S.K. Rajamani, A decade of software model checking with SLAM, Commun. ACM 54 (2011) 68–76.

[38] P. Godefroid, Software model checking improving security of a billion computers, in: C. Pasareanu (Ed.), in: Model Checking Software, Lecture Notes in Computer Science, vol. 5578, Springer, Berlin, 2009, pp. 146–162.

[39] R. Leino, Efficient weakest preconditions, Inf. Process. Lett. 93 (6) (2005) 281–288.

[40] B. Marre, Toward automatic test data set selection using algebraic specifications and logic programming, in: K. Furukawa (Ed.), Proc. of the Eight Int. Conf. on Logic Prog. (ICLP'91), MIT Press, Paris, 1991, pp. 202–219.

[41] J. Dick, A. Faivre, Automating the generation and sequencing of test cases from model-based specifications, in: Proc. of the FME'03: Industrial Strength Formal Methods, Lecture Notes in Computer Science 670, 1993.

[42] J. Jaffar, J.-L. Lassez, Constraint logic programming, in: POPL, ACM, Munich, 1987, pp. 111–119.

[43] R. DeMillo, J. Offut, Experimental results from an automatic test case generator, ACM Trans. Softw. Eng. Methodol. 2 (2) (1993) 109–127.

[44] W. Howden, Symbolic testing and the DISSECT symbolic evaluation system, IEEE Trans. Softw. Eng. 3 (4) (1977) 266–278.

[45] J. Bicevskis, J. Borzovs, U. Straujums, A. Zarins, E. Miller, SMOTL–a system to construct samples for data processing program debugging, IEEE Trans. Softw. Eng. 5 (1) (1979) 60–66.

[46] B. Korel, Automated software test data generation, IEEE Trans. Softw. Eng. 16 (8) (1990) 870–879.

[47] N. Gupta, A. Mathur, M. Soffa, Automated test data generation using an iterative relaxation method, in: Foundations on Software Engineering, ACM, Orlando, FL, 1998.

[48] N. Tracey, J. Clark, K. Mander, Automated program flaw finding using simulated annealing, 23 (2) (1998) 73–81.

[49] A. Gotlieb, B. Botella, M. Rueher, A CLP framework for computing structural test data, in: Proceedings of Computational Logic (CL'2000), LNAI 1891, London, UK, 2000, pp. 399–413.

[50] A. Gotlieb, B. Botella, M. Watel, Inka: ten years after the first ideas, in: 19th Int. Conf. on Soft. and Systems Eng. and their Applications (ICSSEA'06), Paris, France, 2006.

[51] R. Cytron, J. Ferrante, B. Rosen, M. Wegman, F. Zadeck, Efficently computing static single assignment form and the control dependence graph, ACM Trans. Program. Lang. Syst. 13 (4) (1991) 451–490.

[52] K. Sen, D. Marinov, G. Agha, CUTE: a concolic unit testing engine for C, in: Proc. of ESEC/FSE-13, ACM Press, Lisbon, Portugal, 2005, pp. 263–272.

[53] N. Tillmann, J de Halleux, Pex: white box test generation for .NET, in: Proc. of the 2nd Int. Conf. on Tests and Proofs, Lecture Notes in Computer Science 4966, 2008, pp. 134–153.

[54] P. Godefroid, M.Y. Levin, D.A. Molnar, Automated whitebox fuzz testing, in: NDSS'08: network and distributed system security symposium, The Internet Society, San Diego, CA, 2008.

[55] A. Gotlieb, T. Denmat, B. Botella, Constraint-based test data generation in the presence of stack-directed pointers, in: 20th IEEE/ACM International Conference on Automated Software Engineering (ASE'05), Long Beach, CA, 2005, 4 pages.

[56] A. Gotlieb, T. Denmat, B. Botella, Goal-oriented test data generation for pointer programs, Inf. Softw. Technol. 49 (9-10) (2007) 1030–1044.

[57] V. Ganesh, D.L. Dill, A decision procedure for bit-vectors and arrays, in: Proceedings of the 19th International Conference on Computer Aided Verification, CAV'07, Berlin, Germany, 2007, pp. 519–531.

[58] C. Cadar, D. Dunbar, D. Engler, KLEE: unassisted and automatic generation of high-coverage tests for complex systems programs, in: USENIX Symposium on Operating Systems Design and Implementation (OSDI 2008), San Diego, CA, 2008.

[59] P. Cousot, R. Cousot, Abstract interpretation : a unified lattice model for static analysis of programs by construction or approximation of fixpoints, in: POPL, ACM, 1977, pp. 238–252.

[60] A. Gotlieb, TCAS software verification using constraint programming, Knowl. Eng. Rev. 27 (3) (2012) 343–360.

[61] S. Bardin, P. Herrmann, Structural Testing of Executables, in: 1th Int. Conf. on Soft. Testing, Verif. and Valid. (ICST'08), 2008, pp. 22–31.

[62] S. Bardin, P. Herrmann, F. Perroud, An alternative to SAT-based approaches for bit-vectors, in: Tools and Algorithms for the Construction and Analysis (TACAS'10), Paphos, Cyprus, 2010, pp. 84–98.

[63] T. Denmat, A. Gotlieb, M. Ducasse, An abstract interpretation based combinator for modeling while loops in constraint programming, in: Proceedings of Principles and Practices of Constraint Programming (CP'07), Lecture Notes in Computer Science 4741, Springer-Verlag, Providence, RI, 2007, pp. 241–255.

[64] A. Gotlieb, T. Denmat, N. Lazaar, Constraint-based reachability, in: Electronic Publication in Theoretical Computer Science (EPTCS)–Invited presentation of Infinity workshop 2012, Paris, Aug. 2012, 2013, http://dx.doi.org/10.4204/EPTCS.107.4, source: arXiv.

[65] A. Podelski, Model checking as constraint solving, in: Proceedings of Static Analysis Symposium (SAS'00), in: Lecture Notes in Computer Science, vol. 1824, Springer-Verlag, Santa Barbara, CA, 2000, pp. 22–37.

[66] C. Flanagan, Automatic software model checking via constraint logic, Sci. Comput. Program. 50 (1-3) (2004) 253–270.

[67] R. Boyer, B. Elspas, K. Levitt, SELECT–a formal system for testing and debugging programs by symbolic execution, ACM SIGPLAN Not. 10 (6) (1975) 234–245.

[68] C. Ramamoorthy, S. Ho, W. Chen, On the automated generation of program test data, IEEE Trans. Softw. Eng. 2 (4) (1976) 293–300.

[69] G. Nelson, D.C. Oppen, Simplification by cooperating decision procedures, ACM Trans. Program. Lang. Syst. 1 (1979) 245–257.

[70] L. De Moura, N. Bjørner, Z3: an efficient SMT solver, in: TACAS'08/ETAPS'08: Proceedings of the Theory and Practice of Software, 14th International Conference on Tools and Algorithms for the Construction and Analysis of Systems, Springer-Verlag, Budapest, Hungary, 2008, pp. 337–340.

[71] C. Michel, M. Rueher, Y. Lebbah, Solving constraints over floating-point numbers, in: Proceedings of Principles and Practices of Constraint Programming (CP'01), Springer-Verlag, Paphos, Cyprus, 2001, pp. 524–538.

[72] C. Michel, Exact projection functions for floating point number constraints, in: Seventh Int. Symp. on Artificial Intelligence and MAthematics (7th AIMA), Fort Lauderdale, FL, 2002.

[73] B. Botella, A. Gotlieb, C. Michel, Symbolic execution of floating-point computations, Softw. Test Verif. Rel. 16 (2) (2006) 97–121.

[74] B. Marre, C. Michel, Improving the floating point addition and subtraction constraints, in: Principles and Practice of Constraint Programming–CP'2010, Lecture Notes in Computer Science, vol. 6308, 2010, pp. 360–367.

[75] M. Carlier, A. Gotlieb, Filtering by ULP maximum, in: Proc. of the IEEE Int. Conf. on Tools for Artificial Intelligence (ICTAI'11), Boca Raton, FL, 2011, short paper, 4 pages.

[76] R. Bagnara, M. Carlier, R. Gori, A. Gotlieb, Symbolic path-oriented test data generation for floating-point programs, in: Proc. of the 6th IEEE Int. Conf. on Software Testing, Verification and Validation (ICST'13), Luxembourg, 2013.

[77] U. Buy, A. Orso, M. Pezzè, Automated testing of classes, in: Proc. of the Int. Symp. on Software Testing and Analysis, Portland, Oregon, 2000.

[78] A.L. Souter, T.M. Wong, S.A. Shindo, L.L. Pollock, TATOO: testing and analysis tool for object-oriented software, in: Proc. of the 9th International Conference on Tools and Algorithms for the Construction and Analysis of Systems (TACAS), Genova, Italy, 2001.

[79] R.T. Alexander, A.J. Offut, Criteria for testing polymorphic relationships, in: 11th International Symposium on Software Reliability Engineering, San Jose, CA, 2000, pp. 15–23.

[80] A. Gotlieb, D. Marijan, FLOWER: optimal test suite reduction as a network maximum flow, in: Proc. of Int. Symp. on Soft. Testing and Analysis (ISSTA'14), San Jos, CA, 2014.

[81] J.-C. Regin, Global constraints: a survey, in: P. van Hentenryck, M. Milano (Eds.), in: Hybrid Optimization, Springer Optimization and Its Applications, vol. 45, Springer, New York, NY, 2011, pp. 63–134. URL, http://dx.doi.org/10.1007/978-1-4419-1644-0_3, ISBN 978-1-4419-1643-3.

[82] S. Di Alesio, A. Gotlieb, S. Nejati, L. Briand, Worst-case scheduling of software tasks: a constraint optimization model to support performance testing, Principles and Practice of Constraint Programming (CP'14)–Application track, 2014, Lyon, France.

[83] M. Mossige, A. Gotlieb, H. Meling, Using CP in automatic test generation for ABB robotics' paint control system, Principles and Practice of Constraint Programming (CP'14)–Application track–Awarded Best Application Track paper, 2014, Lyon, France.

[84] M. Mossige, A. Gotlieb, H. Meling, Testing robot controllers using constraint programming and continuous integration, Inf. Softw. Technol. 57 (2015) 169–185.

[85] S. Bardin, A. Gotlieb, FDCC: a combined approach for solving constraints over finite domains and arrays, in: Proc. of Constraint Programming, Artifical Intelligence, Operational Research (CPAIOR'12), May 2012, Nantes, France.

ABOUT THE AUTHORS

The author of this chapter, Dr. Arnaud Gotlieb, is the leader of Certus SFI, Simula's Centre for Research-based Innovation (SFI) on software verification & validation. Dr. Gotlieb's expertise is on the application of constraint solving to software testing. At the beginning of his career, he spent 7 years in industry working for Dassault Electronics, Thomson-CSF, and Thales. He joint INRIA, the French National Institute on Computer Science and Automatisms in 2002 where he worked as a research scientist in a group specialized in semantical analysis of software systems. He has contributed to several projects that aimed at improving static analysis and testing of critical embedded software system of the civil and military avionics industry. He was the scientific coordinator of the ANR CAVERN project (2008–2011) that explored the capabilities of constraint programming for program verification and participated to several other scientific projects. Since October 2011, he has joint SIMULA Research Laboratory in Norway, as a senior research scientist. He is the main author of more than 30 publications and coauthor of more than 60, and he is the main architect of several constraint-based testing tools for the testing of C and Java critical programs, including InKa, FPSE, and Euclide. He has served in the program committee, the IEEE International Conference on software testing, validation and verification (ICST) for many years; since 2008, he cochaired the SEIP track of IEEE ICSE 2014. He initiated the Constraints in software testing, verification and analysis (CSTVA) workshop series and was its main organizer during the first editions. Dr. Gotlieb completed his PhD on automatic test data generation using constraint logic programming techniques (2000) at the University of Nice-Sophia Antipolis and get habilitated in 2011 from University of Rennes, France.

CHAPTER THREE

Automated Fault Localization: Advances and Challenges

Wes Masri

Electrical and Computer Engineering Department, American University of Beirut, Beirut, Lebanon

Contents

Advances in Computers, Volume 99
ISSN 0065-2458
http://dx.doi.org/10.1016/bs.adcom.2015.05.001

Abstract

Following a program failure, the main concern of the developer is to identify what caused it in order to repair the code that induced it. The first activity is termed *fault localization*, whereas the second is referred to as *fault repair*. Even though both activities are very important, this chapter will only focus on automated fault localization research. First, it presents the background that provides the bases for the main existing fault localization techniques. Second, it describes early research and relevant shortcomings. Finally, it presents the latest major advances in this area of research.

1. INTRODUCTION

During the debugging process, the developer replicates the failure at hand in order to (1) identify what caused it and (2) prevent it from happening again by modifying, adding, or deleting code. The first activity is termed *fault localization*, whereas the second is referred to as *fault repair* or more commonly as *bug fixing*. Both of these activities are time consuming and difficult, but fault localization is considered to be more critical since it is a prerequisite for performing fault repair. In recent years, a number of automated fault repair techniques have been proposed, most of which were based on evolutionary algorithms [1] or formal methods [2,3]. Pertaining to the subject matter, for over three decades, researchers have proposed a plethora of automated fault localization techniques and tools of which we will try to select and present the state of the art. However, before embarking on our subject, we first need to define the goals of automated fault localization, which we do next.

If one complies with a literal interpretation of *automated fault localization*, the ideal goal of any proposed technique should basically be: *to automatically and accurately identify the cause of the failure in order to provide the developer with a report that pinpoints the parts of the code that need to be repaired*. Such goal is not achievable in most cases for many reasons that are actually inherent to real programs; for example: (1) the abundance of transitive dependences in programs [4,5] makes it almost impossible to locate the root cause of the failure within long dependence chains [6]; (2) it is not even possible to pinpoint the parts of the code that need to be repaired in case the fault involves omitted code or missing conditionals; and (3) most bug fixes could be achieved in numerous different ways and/or possibly at different locations in the program. For such reasons, researchers readjusted their expectations and revised their idealistic goal based on a looser interpretation of automated fault localization, to become: *to identify some program event(s) or state(s) that cause or correlate with the failure in order to provide the developer with a report that will aid fault repair.* This latter interpretation will sound more and more adequate as the chapter progresses.

We recognize two general categories of techniques for addressing automated fault localization. In the first category, the techniques require executing the subject program using one or more test cases, namely, *dynamic* or *test-driven* techniques. Those in the second do not require any test cases and are typically referred to as *static* or *formal* techniques. The focus of this chapter is mainly on test-driven techniques, but for completeness, several techniques that leverage formal methods will also be covered.

The presented techniques are based on various and possibly multiple established methods, namely: (1) program dependence analysis, (2) analysis of structural execution profiles, (3) causal inference, (4) information theory, and (5) formal methods. Section 2 provides background for some of the above base methods. Sections 3 and 4 present early work, shortcomings, and advances in spectrum-based fault localization research. Section 5 discusses program slicing in the context of fault localization. Section 6 introduces delta debugging and presents one of its applications. Section 7 presents two techniques that are based on formal methods, and Section 8 concludes.

2. BACKGROUND

2.1 Program Dependence Analysis

Program dependence analysis [4,5,7,8] aims at determining whether a given statement may influence another statement due to a chain of data and/or control dependences. A statement t is *directly data dependent* on a statement s if (1) s defines a variable v; (2) t uses v; and (3) there is at least a path between s and t along which v is not redefined. A statement t is *directly control dependent* on a statement s if (1) s is a conditional statement and (2) s's outcome determines whether t is executed or not. The definitions of indirect (or transitive) data and control dependence follow from the definitions of their direct counterparts. It should also be noted that data and control dependences can occur either intraprocedurally or interprocedurally, depending on whether t and s (and the paths along which the dependences occur) belong to the same procedure or to different procedures.

Program dependence analysis can be computed using either *static* or *dynamic* approaches. Static dependence analysis computes dependences without executing the program, by analyzing the program code. Dynamic dependence analysis, conversely, uses data collected during one or more specific program executions to detect dependences that occurred during such execution(s). Static dependence analysis can compute all potential dependences in a program, but it typically also includes spurious ones. Dynamic dependence analysis can compute more precise results, but is inherently incomplete because it identifies only observed dependences. In other words, static dependence analysis can overestimate the solution while not omitting any actual information; i.e., it is safe, conservative, and prone to false positives. Dynamic analysis can underestimate the solution while possibly omitting actual information, i.e., it is unsafe, precise, and prone to false negatives. Figures 1 and 2 illustrate the concept.

Referring to Fig. 1, static dependence analysis would determine that: (a) s_3 is dependent on s_0; (b) s_4 is dependent on s_0, s_1, and s_3; (c) s_5 is dependent on s_0, s_1, and s_2; and (d) s_6 is dependent on s_0, s_1, s_2, s_3, s_4, and s_5.

Referring to Fig. 2 and assuming the execution trace $\langle s_0, s_1, s_2, s_3, s_5, s_6 \rangle$, dynamic dependence analysis would determine that: (a) s_3 is dependent on s_0; (b) s_5 is dependent on s_0, s_2, and s_3; and (c) s_6 is dependent on s_0, s_2, s_3, and s_5. Note how dynamic analysis has determined that s_6 is influenced by only four statements, whereas static analysis would have determined that it is influenced by six statements.

Program dependence analysis provides the basis for addressing numerous problems in many software engineering areas. For example, in software testing and debugging, program dependences are important because they contribute both to triggering the effects of faults and to propagating those effects to a program's output. For the purpose of automated fault localization,

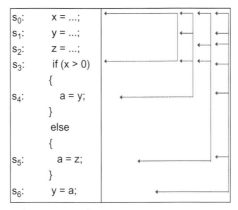

Figure 1 Static dependence example.

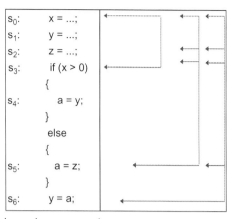

Figure 2 Dynamic dependence example.

researchers have used derivates of dependence analysis (mostly in the dynamic context), several of which are informally described below:

(1) *Def-use pair* is a triple $DUP(v, d, u)$, where d is a statement that defines v, u is a statement that uses v, and there is at least a def-clear path from d to u, i.e., u is *directly data dependent* on d. For example, $DUP(x, s_0, s_3)$ and $DUP(z, s_2, s_5)$ are two def-use pairs in Fig. 2.

(2) *Program slice* is a set of statements that influence a given statement via data or control dependences. The slice at s_5 is $\{s_0, s_2, s_3, s_5\}$, for example.

(3) *Information flow* is a set of variables that influence a given variable via data or control dependences. For example, the information flow into a at s_5 is $\{x, z\}$, meaning that at s_5, variable a is influenced by x and z.

(4) *Information flow pair* is a couple $IFP(v, u)$ where information flowed from v into u; e.g., $IFP(x, a)$ and $IFP(z, a)$ are two information flow pairs.

(5) *Chop* is the set of statements that relate a source to a sink via data or control dependences. For example, $\{s_0, s_3, s_5, s_6\}$ is the chop from s_0 to s_6.

(6) *Dependence chain* is a sequence of statements of a given length related via data or control dependences; e.g., $\langle s_0, s_3, s_5 \rangle$ is a dependence chain of length 2.

Finally, aiming at further improving the precision of dynamic dependence analysis, Masri and Podgurski [4,5] used statistical and information theoretic metrics to quantify the strength of the dependence between every pair of program variables that are connected via a dynamic dependence chain. This *strength-based dependence analysis* has potential applications in many areas of software analysis including compiler optimization [9], program slicing, and fault localization.

2.2 Structural Execution Profiles

Structural execution profiles form the basis of many dynamic program analysis techniques developed to solve problems in fields such as software testing, fault localization, and program comprehension. A typical profile comprises information that approximates the execution path of a program [10], specifically, the frequency of occurrence of program elements, such as statements or branches.

Previous empirical studies [11] have shown that the effectiveness of coverage-based software testing improves by increasing the granularity of the profiled program elements. This is due to the fact that simple profile elements, such as statements and branches, cannot characterize and ultimately reveal nontrivial faults. For this reason, more complex program elements were explored when profiling for testing or fault localization. Specifically, in addition to statements and branches, some researchers used def-use pairs, information flow pairs, and dependence chains of varying lengths. In the literature, the automated fault localization techniques that rely on analyzing structural execution profiles are referred to as *spectrum based* or *coverage based*.

Note that several early techniques have augmented branch profiles with simple predicates inserted at the sites of function calls and definition statements. For example, at each scalar-returning function call site, the techniques presented in Refs. [12–14] track six predicates: whether the returned value is ever <0, ≤ 0, >0, ≥ 0, $=0$, or $\neq 0$. And at each definition statement that assigns a value to x, they identify each same-typed in-scope variable y_i and each constant expression c_j. For each y_i and each c_j, they track six relationships to the new value of x: $<$, $\leq$, $>$, $\geq$, $=$, and $\neq$.

Finally, given that a typical profile comprises a large number of program elements, in the order of thousands or higher, and knowing that according to the *curse of dimensionality*, an increase in the size of the execution profiles might diminish the effectiveness of the techniques at hand. Farjo *et al.* [15] devised techniques to reduce the size of execution profiles by identifying and discarding redundant profiling elements. They also showed that such reduction benefits software testing.

2.3 Causal Inference

In statistics, an *association* is a bidirectional relationship between two random variables that are statistically dependent, and *correlation* coefficients measure the strength of a given association. It is common to use correlation and association interchangeably in the literature. In information theory, *mutual information* also measures the strength of an association by quantifying the amount of information flowing between the two associated variables. A common misconception is that if two variables are correlated, then one causes the other, i.e., a cause-and-effect relationship connects them. In fact, correlation and mutual information do not imply causation, but causation implies mutual information and nonlinear correlation. Causality, a unidirectional relation, is clearly more desirable than correlation for the purpose of fault localization, since the ultimate goal is to identify and repair the code that caused the failure and not just any code that correlated with it.

A representative spectrum-based fault localization technique computes a suspiciousness score for a program element by contrasting the percentage of failing runs to the percentage of passing runs that covered it; a higher ratio of these respective entities implies a higher score. Early spectrum-based work (erroneously) used correlation to compute the suspiciousness score in order to infer the causal effect of individual program elements on the occurrence of failure. The scores they used suffer from *confounding bias*, which occurs when an *apparent* causal effect of an event on a failure may actually be due to an unknown confounding variable, which causes both the event and the failure. Confounding bias might explain the high rate of *false positives* exhibited by such spectrum-based techniques [16,17].

Given a program and a test suite, assume, for example that, all failing test cases induce dependence chain $e_1 \rightarrow e_2 \rightarrow e_{bug} \rightarrow e_3 \rightarrow e_4 \rightarrow e_{fail}$ and all passing test cases induce $e_1 \rightarrow e_2$ only, where e_{bug} exercises the fault and e_{fail} indicates a failure. A correlation-based approach would determine that any of e_{bug}, e_3, or e_4 is equally suspected to be the cause of the failure, thus resulting in two false positives, whereas a causation-based approach that considers dependences to have causal effect would determine that e_4 is the least suspect and e_{bug} the most suspect. This is because: (1) confounding bias weakens the causal relationship; and (2) when computing the suspiciousness scores, the confounding bias to consider for e_4 would involve e_3 and e_{bug}, for e_3 it would involve e_{bug}, and no confounding is involved when computing the suspiciousness score of e_{bug}.

Confounding bias is a common phenomenon that needs to be identified, controlled, and reduced. Recent advances in causal inference [18–21] research allow for graphically identifying confounding bias and reducing it by employing causal-effect estimators. Next, we provide background needed to understand the fault localization techniques that we present later and are based on causal inference, specifically Pearl's *back-door criterion* [18,19].

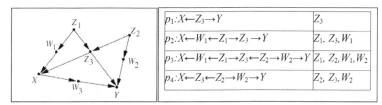

$p_1: X \leftarrow Z_3 \rightarrow Y$	Z_3
$p_2: X \leftarrow W_1 \leftarrow Z_1 \rightarrow Z_3 \rightarrow Y$	Z_1, Z_3, W_1
$p_3: X \leftarrow W_1 \leftarrow Z_1 \rightarrow Z_3 \leftarrow Z_2 \rightarrow W_2 \rightarrow Y$	Z_1, Z_2, W_1, W_2
$p_4: X \leftarrow Z_3 \leftarrow Z_2 \rightarrow W_2 \rightarrow Y$	Z_2, Z_3, W_2

Figure 3 Causal graph and back-door paths.

First, a *causal graph* or *causal Bayesian network* is a directed acyclic graph whose nodes represent random variables, corresponding to causes and effects, and whose edges represent causal relationships. Assume a scenario in which we need to find the effect of X (treatment) on program outcome Y (response). The causal graph in Fig. 3 captures the causal relationships involving X and Y, and other relevant variables, namely, W_1, W_2, W_3, Z_1, Z_2, and Z_3. Note how each of Z_1, Z_2, and Z_3 causes both X and Y, and thus these are confounding variables (covariates) that need to be controlled to reduce confounding bias.

Pearl's *back-door criterion* provides a graphical method of selecting possible sets of covariates to be controlled; it (briefly) states that for a set of variables S to be admissible:

1. No element of S is a descendant of X.
2. The elements of S *block* all *back-door* paths from X to Y. A *back-door* path is any path that on one end points with an arrow to X and on the other end points with an arrow to Y. A node is said to *block* a path p, if p contains the node and it is arrow emitting.

The table in Fig. 3 shows a subset of the back-door paths in the depicted causal graph, and the right column lists the corresponding blocking nodes for each given path. We opted not to consider the full list of back-door paths for space and clarity considerations, but the reader should assume that the discussion refers to all back-door paths.

Minimal sets are desirable in practice, Pearl's approach identifies the following minimal sets: $\{Z_1, Z_3\}$, $\{Z_2, Z_3\}$, $\{W_1, Z_3\}$, and $\{W_2, Z_3\}$, in addition to other nonminimal sets such as $\{Z_1, Z_2, Z_3\}$. To illustrate why these sets are admissible, take $\{W_1, Z_3\}$, for example, Z_3 blocks p_1, p_2, and p_4; and W_1 blocks the last remaining path, p_3. Note that since p_1 can only be blocked by Z_3, any admissible set must include Z_3. As expected, any of the above minimal sets is adequate for controlling the confounding bias of all three of Z_1, Z_2, and Z_3. For example, if $\{W_2, Z_3\}$ is picked, Z_3 is controlled directly when p_1, p_2, and p_4 are taken, and W_2 allows for controlling Z_1 and Z_2 when p_3 is taken, thus resulting in Z_1, Z_2, and Z_3 being controlled.

In summary, the intuition behind the back-door criterion is as follows. The back-door paths in the diagram carry spurious associations from X to Y, while the paths directed along the arrows from X to Y carry causative associations. Blocking the back-door paths, by leveraging the elements of a set S that satisfy the back-door criterion, ensures that the measured association between X and Y is purely causative, namely, it correctly represents the target quantity, i.e., the causal effect of X on Y [18].

Finally, a fault localization technique that leverages causal inference should perform the following steps for each program element pe: (1) build a causal graph around pe and the program outcome Y, possibly derived from prior analyses of the program; (2) use the *back-door criterion* method to identify which covariates to control; and (3) devise an estimator for the suspiciousness of pe using coverage information about pe and the controlled covariates and the program outcome.

2.4 Formal Methods

Many computer scientists believe that software testing is only effective in the early stages of development, i.e., when the program is infested with a large number of bugs, while it suffers from a sharp decrease in effectiveness as the program becomes more stable. In other words, they argue that testing is likely to reveal the easier bugs in a reasonable amount of time, but might require an unreasonable amount of time and resources to reveal the complex bugs. Given that testing explores only a subset of all possible program behaviors, they advocate *formal verification* which aims at *an exhaustive exploration of all possible behaviors*. Actually, such aim is not always feasible for the following reasons: (1) formal verification explores bounded partial paths as opposed to complete paths; (2) even exploring all complete paths does not guarantee that all behaviors are explored, e.g., program states should also be considered; (3) most formal techniques require the developer to augment the code with detailed properties when most developers are reluctant to do that, furthermore, the properties themselves could be faulty; and (4) scalability is a major issue, due to *state explosion*, which makes most formal techniques only applicable to smaller programs such as device drivers, or specific critical components within large systems.

The main formal methods that might assist automated fault localization include model checking, symbolic execution, SAT solving, and SMT solving. Model checkers take as input a program and a set of formal properties therein and check whether the properties hold for the program. In general, a model checker either returns with a proof that the properties hold for the program, returns a counterexample (a failing execution trace with the associated failing input) illustrating how the program violates the properties or returns an inconclusive result when they reach computational bounds such as memory or timeout limits. In order to construct the counterexample, a model checker relies on symbolic execution to determine the path condition (a predicate formula) leading to the violated property and then uses an SMT solver to solve that condition in order to generate a failing test case. Since SAT solvers are capable of solving propositional logic, and SMT solvers aim at solving predicate logic which subsumes propositional logic, typically, an SMT solver has an SAT solver at its backend.

The example in Fig. 4 illustrates how model checking works assisted with symbolic execution and an SMT solver. The code is augmented with a property at s_6 that, if violated, the model checker would return a counterexample in the form of a failing execution trace and values for x and y that induce the failure. We will walk through the case when the explored execution trace is $\langle s_0, s_1, s_3, s_4, s_6 \rangle$, and the property is violated, i.e., one of the possible failing traces. The symbolic execution associates a symbolic value with each variable in the program and builds a path condition (shown in the third column) that must be `true` for a given execution trace to be realized. The execution starts at s_0 with the variables x and y assuming the symbolic values of A and B, respectively, and then builds the path condition as the branches of the conditional statements are explored. For example, for s_4 to be reached via $\langle s_0, s_1, s_3, s_4 \rangle$, A should be >0 and B should be ≥ 0. And for the property to get violated at s_6, condition `(true && A>0 && B≥0 && !(−B<0))`, which is equivalent to `(A>0 && B==0)`, should evaluate to `true`. Finally, in order to generate a counterexample that will violate the property via trace

	Symbolic operations	Path condition
s0 input(x,y);	x = A, y = B	true
s1 if (x <= 0) {	if (A ≤ 0)?	true
s2 y = x;		
}		
s3 if (y >= 0) { // fault: should be (y > 0)	if (B ≥ 0)?	true && A > 0
s4 z = -y;	z = -B	true && A > 0 && B ≥ 0
} else {		
s5 z = y;		
}		
s6 assert(z <0); // property to be held	assert(-B < 0)	true && A > 0 && B ≥ 0 && !(-B < 0)

Figure 4 Model checking example.

$\langle s_0, s_1, s_3, s_4, s_6 \rangle$, the model checker uses an SMT solver to solve for A and B in
(A >0 && B ==0), yielding failing input $(x=1, y=0)$ as one possibility.

Fault localization researchers have leveraged the ability of model checkers to identify counterexamples. For example, Ball *et al.* [22] contrasted
the counterexamples (failing traces) to traces that conform to the property
(passing traces) and reported the differences as fault localization aids to the
developer. This formal approach and another are discussed in Section 7.

3. SPECTRUM-BASED TECHNIQUES: EARLY WORK AND SHORTCOMINGS

3.1 Early Techniques

Typically, *spectrum-based fault localization* (SBFL) approaches work by observing the behavior of a number of passing and failing executions, performing
statistical inference based on the observed behavior in order to rank program
elements in terms of their likelihood of being relevant to the failure. This
section mainly discusses one representative early SBFL technique, namely,
Tarantula. For a comprehensive survey, the reader can refer to Ref. [23].

Jones *et al.* [24] presented a technique that uses visualization to assist with
locating faults. They implemented their technique in a tool called *Tarantula*.
The technique uses color and brightness to visually map the participation of
each program statement in the outcome of the execution of the program
with a test suite, consisting of both passing and failing test cases. To provide
the visual mapping, the program statements are colored using a continuous
spectrum from red to yellow to green: the greater the percentage of failing
test cases that execute a statement, the brighter and more red the statement
should appear. A statement s_1 is considered more suspicious (more red) than
statement s_2 if $M(s_1) > M(s_2)$ where

$$M(s) = \frac{F(s)}{F(s) + P(s)}$$

and

$F(s) = (\text{\# of failing runs that executed } s)/(\text{total \# of failing runs}),$
$P(s) = (\text{\# of passing runs that executed } s)/(\text{total \# of passing runs}).$
The brightness of statement s is determined by the following equation:

$$M_b(s) = \text{MAX}(P(s), F(s))$$

Given two statements s_1 and s_2 such that $M(s_1) = M(s_2)$ and $F(s_1) > F(s_2)$, the intuition behind M_b is that s_1 is more likely than s_2 to be the faulty statement and thus should be presented more brightly to attract the user's attention. Subsequently, Jones *et al.* [25] presented an approach based on *Tarantula*, termed *parallel debugging*, that enables multiple developers to simultaneously debug multiple faults by associating each fault with a specialized test suite.

Denmat *et al.* [26] studied the limitations of *Tarantula*. They argued that for it to be effective, the following three requirements must hold: (1) a defect is due to a single faulty statement; (2) statements are independent of each other; and (3) executing a faulty statement leads most of the time to a failure. Clearly, the aforementioned requirements are not likely to be fulfilled when dealing with complex programs involving nontrivial defects. Baah *et al.* later showed in [27] that the *Tarantula* metric and the popular *Ochiai* metric [28] are both grounded in statistical methods, specifically, correlation.

Other select early works include the technique presented by Renieris and Reiss [29] which produces a report of the "suspicious" parts of a program by analyzing the spectra differences between a faulty run and the correct run that most resembles it. Liblit *et al.* [12,13] proposed a statistical fault localization method that is based on branch coverage and a set of predicates, as described in Section 2.2. Liu *et al.* [14] proposed SOBER which also ranks predicates based on their suspiciousness.

Finally, most fault localization techniques adopt one of the following two code examination strategies. The first strategy, used by Renieris and Reiss [29], Cleve and Zeller [30], and SOBER [14], assumes that only a subset of statements are identified as suspicious and expect the developer to examine them first and then move on to examining the statements that are statically data and/or control dependent on them. The second strategy, used in *Tarantula* [24], assumes that all statements are ranked (i.e., tagged with a level of suspiciousness) and expects the developer to examine statements from the top of the ranking scale and then down until a faulty statement is found.

3.2 Shortcomings in Early SBFL Techniques

Parnin and Orso [17] conducted a study trying to understand why spectrum-based techniques to date have yet to be widely adopted by practitioners. The first major reason they identified is that these techniques assume *perfect bug understanding*; that is, by having access to a ranked list of suspicious statements, the developer would understand and fix the bug at hand by simply examining one (or few) suspicious statement(s) in isolation. Thus, they ignore the fact that understanding the root cause of a failure typically involves complex activities, such as navigating program dependencies and reexecuting the program with different inputs. The second and more important reason is that the provided lists of suspicious statements are unmanageably large in most cases, as they require the developer to examine around 5–10% of the code, on average. Obviously, localizing a fault down to 10% or even 1% of the code size is hardly a success for large programs, e.g., those over 50,000 lines of code. Such localization inaccuracy is due to several reasons that we discuss next.

3.2.1 Correlation Versus Causation

As argued in Section 2.3, causality is more desirable than correlation for the purpose of fault localization, since the ultimate goal is to identify and repair the code that caused the failure and not just any code that correlated with it.

Early SBFL techniques exhibit high rates of false positives due to the fact that they rely on correlation, as opposed to causation, to compute their respective suspiciousness scores. That is, they do not attempt to control or reduce potential confounding bias.

3.2.2 Test Suite Quality

The test suite used has a great impact on the performance of spectrum-based fault localization. To start with, the size of the test suite matters. A small set of test cases having the right characteristics might be adequate to narrow down the search to 5–10% of the code [31]. But to pinpoint a bug down to a handful of statements, one may need thousands of test cases (with the right characteristics) that are unlikely to be available.

In addition, the empirical study we conducted in Ref. [16], using 148 seeded versions of 10 subject programs, showed that in 24% of the versions, *a considerable number of program elements were covered by all failing runs but by no passing runs*. Specifically, in 36 of 148 versions, the set of statements that executed in all failing runs and in no passing runs ranged from 2% to 16% of the total number of executed statements. All of these statements will be assigned a maximum suspiciousness score, thus yielding a high rate of *false positives*. Therefore, it is desirable to have a test suite in which the failing test cases are as similar as possible to the passing test cases, as suggested by Renieris and Reiss [29].

3.2.3 Granularity and Type of Profiling Elements

The initial goal of spectrum-based techniques is to identify program elements that are highly correlated with failure. This goal might not be met in case the profiling type used is unable to characterize the fault at hand. For example, statements and branches might be too simple to characterize some complex faults, such as those that induce failures exhibiting some unique execution patterns, e.g., particular sequences of statements, branches, and def-uses. The inability of identifying program elements that are highly correlated with failure leads to a high rate of *false negatives*, since the fault cannot be identified to start with.

One solution is to use more complex profiling types with higher granularity such as information flow pairs or dependence chains. Doing so will likely reduce the rate of false negatives because complex profiling types will enable for identifying both simple and complex faults. However, if the profiling type happened to be more complex than the fault at hand, more spurious statements will be tagged as highly suspicious, thus leading to a higher rate of *false positives*.

Finally, it is plausible that some fault might not be characterized by any failing path or any set of structural program elements. In such case, execution profiles that are based on structural elements would not be of much benefit. Therefore, it is also worth exploring profiles that approximate the *program states* as opposed to the program paths, as discussed in Ref. [32].

3.2.4 Coincidental Correctness

According to the *Propagation–Infection–Execution* model presented in Ref. [33], for failure to be observed, the following three conditions must be met: C_R = *the defect was executed or reached*; C_I = *the program has transitioned into an infectious state*; and C_P = *the infection has propagated to the output*. Coincidental correctness (CC) arises when the program produces the correct output while condition C_R is met but not C_P. We recognize two forms of CC, weak and strong. In *weak CC*, C_R is met, whereas C_I might or might not be met; while in *strong CC*, both C_R and C_I are met [34]. Hence, a test case that satisfies the strong form of CC also satisfies its weak form. SBFL is based on the premise that if a run fails, the defect must have executed, i.e., C_R was met; therefore, weak CC is more relevant to SBFL than strong CC is.

3.2.4.1 CC Is a Source of *False Negatives*

We now demonstrate how weak CC has a safety reducing effect on SBFL; i.e., it leads to higher rates of *false negatives*. Specifically, we show that the presence of CC tests leads to suspiciousness scores that underestimate the suspiciousness of faulty program elements. We carry this out in the context of two metrics, *Tarantula* and *Ochiai*. The main *Tarantula* suspiciousness metric is defined as follows:

$$M(e) = \frac{F(e)}{F(e) + P(e)}$$

where

    $e =$ faulty program element,
    $a_{11}(e) = \#$ of failing runs that executed e,
    $a_{01}(e) = \#$ of failing runs that did not execute e,
    $a_{10}(e) = \#$ of passing runs that executed e,
    $a_{00}(e) = \#$ of passing runs that did not execute e,
    $f_T =$ total $\#$ of failing runs $= a_{11}(e) + a_{01}(e)$,
    $p_T =$ total $\#$ of passing runs $= a_{10}(e) + a_{00}(e)$,
    $F(e) = a_{11}(e)/f_T$,
    $P(e) = a_{10}(e)/p_T$.

In case of n CC tests, the more accurate metric would then be $M'(e) = F(e)/(F(e) + P'(e))$, where $P'(e) = (a_{10}(e) - n)/(p_T - n)$. It could be easily shown that $M'(e) \geq M(e)$. To verify, $M'(e) \geq M(e) \Rightarrow 1/M'(e) \leq 1/M(e) \Rightarrow P'(e)/F(e) \leq P(e)/F(e) \Rightarrow P'(e)/P(e) \leq 1$, which holds since $a_{10}(e) \leq p_T$.

Similarly, the *Ochiai* metric is defined as follows:

$$M(e) = \frac{a_{11}(e)}{\sqrt{(a_{11}(e) + a_{01}(e)) \times (a_{11}(e) + a_{10}(e))}}$$

To arrive at a more faithful suspiciousness value, we should subtract n from $a_{10}(e)$ leading to $M'(e) = a_{11}(e)/\sqrt{(a_{11}(e) + a_{01}(e)) \times (a_{11}(e) + a_{10}(e) - n)}$, which is clearly larger than $M(e)$.

In the above, we have shown that cleansing test suites from CC would improve the task of identifying failure-correlated program elements by assigning the faulty code higher (or equal) suspiciousness values.

3.2.4.2 CC Is Prevalent

In Ref. [16], we conducted an empirical study involving 148 seeded versions of 10 subject programs to identify the distribution of strong and weak coincidentally correct tests.

Figure 5 summarizes our results regarding strong CC. The horizontal axis represents the percentages of strong coincidentally correct tests. Each bar corresponds to a range of size 10%. The vertical axis represents the percentage of seeded versions that exhibited a given range. The following observations could be made about the seeded versions exhibiting strong CC:

- 28% did not exhibit any;
- 40% exhibited a low level, in the range [0%, 10%];
- 19% exhibited a medium level, in the range [10%, 60%];
- 13% exhibited a high level, in the range [60%, 100%];
- The average over all 148 seeded versions is 15.7%.

Clearly, the exhibited levels of strong CC are significant.

More importantly, Fig. 6 summarizes our results for weak CC. The following observations could be made from the figure:

- 3.5% seeded versions did not exhibit any weak coincidentally correct tests;
- 8% exhibited a low level, in the range [0%, 10%];
- 30% exhibited a medium level, in the range [10%, 60%];
- 28.5% exhibited a high level, in the range [60%, 90%];
- 30% exhibited an ultrahigh level, in the range [90%, 100%];
- The average over all seeded versions is 56.4%.

The exhibited levels of weak CC are very significant. This factor is expected to have a considerable negative impact on the safety of SBFL.

Finally, *strength-based dependence analysis* quantifies the amount of information flowing from one program variable to another that are connected via a dynamic dependence chain. In Ref. [4], we conducted an empirical

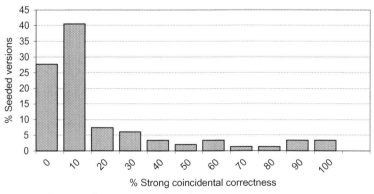

Figure 5 Distribution of strong coincidental correctness.

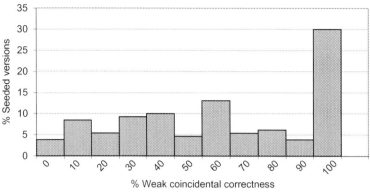

Figure 6 Frequency of weak coincidental correctness.

study showing that weak information flows are prevalent, and that actually most of them have zero *strength*. This means that it is likely that many infectious states might get canceled and not propagate to the output, thus leading to a potentially high rate of CC due to condition C_p not being met. These results support our other findings regarding the prevalence of CC.

3.2.4.3 Why Is CC Prevalent?

As illustrative examples, consider the three snippets of code below where x takes on the values [1,5], and specifically the value 4 when the program is in an infected state:

```
eg1: y = x * 3;
eg2: y = x % 3;
eg3: if (x >=3) {
        y =1;
     } else {
        y =0;
     }
```

In *eg1*, there is a clear one-to-one mapping between the x values and y values: $\{1 \rightarrow 3, 2 \rightarrow 6, 3 \rightarrow 9, 4^* \rightarrow \underline{12}^*, 5 \rightarrow 15\}$; therefore, when x is infected, the corresponding y value which is unique will successfully propagate the infection past *eg1*. In other words, the infection $x=4$ leads to the infection $y=12$.

In *eg2*, the mapping is as follows: $\{1 \rightarrow \underline{1}, 2 \rightarrow 2, 3 \rightarrow 0, 4^* \rightarrow \underline{1}, 5 \rightarrow 2\}$, which shows that there is no unique value of y that captures the infection; noting that $y=1$ is not an infection since it also results from $x=1$. In this case, the infection was nullified or canceled by the execution of *eg2*. Similarly, in *eg3* where the mapping is: $\{1 \rightarrow 1,\ 2 \rightarrow 1,\ 3 \rightarrow \underline{0},\ 4^* \rightarrow \underline{0},\ 5 \rightarrow \underline{0}\}$, no unique value of y captures the infection ($y = 0$ is not an infection), which means that the infection was also nullified.

These examples explain our empirical findings related to the prevalence of CC, since programming patterns similar to *eg3* are widely used in code.

4. ADVANCES IN SPECTRUM-BASED FAULT LOCALIZATION

We now cover recent selected work that attempt to address the above shortcomings; i.e., our coverage is by no means comprehensive.

4.1 Using Causal Inference

Baah *et al.* were the first to investigate the application of *causal inference* in SBFL [27]. Given a statement s in program P, the aim of their work is to obtain a causal-effect estimate of s on the outcome of P that is not subject to severe confounding bias, i.e., a causation-based suspiciousness score of s. They applied Pearl's back–door criterion (see Section 2.3) to program control dependence graphs in order to devise an estimator based on the following linear regression model:

$$Y_s = \alpha_s + \tau_s T_s + \beta_s C_s + \varepsilon_s$$

This model relates the event of program failure Y_s with not only the event of covering statement s (i.e., T_s), but also the confounding events, listed in C_s. The model is fit separately for each statement s, using statement execution profiles that are labeled as passing or failing.

Given that causal graphs are not known in practice, this work assumes that: (1) if s is faulty, covering it will cause a failure; and (2) if s is dynamically directly control dependent on statement s', s' causes the execution of s and possibly the failure; i.e., s' is the only source of confounding bias and C_s becomes a single indicator of whether s' was covered. In other words, this work assumes that the causal graph is made up of the following three edges only: $T_s \rightarrow Y_s$, $C_s \rightarrow T_s$, and $C_s \rightarrow Y_s$. Therefore, the only back–door path to be controlled is $T_s \leftarrow C_s \rightarrow Y_s$. More importantly, since τ_s is the average effect of T_s on Y_s, the work uses an estimate of τ_s to quantify the failure-causing effect of s, i.e., the suspiciousness of s.

Note that neither of the above assumptions is sure to hold. For example, due to CC, covering a faulty statement will not necessarily cause a failure;

and due to the transitivity of control/data dependences in programs, direct control dependences might not be the only source of confounding bias. Nevertheless, using the above model is likely to yield more accurate suspiciousness scores than simply relying on correlation. In fact, the empirical study conducted in Ref. [27], which involved 9 subject programs and 168 faulty versions, indicated that the proposed causal-effect estimator can significantly improve the effectiveness of fault localization over existing correlation-based metrics.

In Ref. [35], Baah *et al.* presented a new technique that also uses causal inference to compute the suspiciousness of a statement s. They assumed the following: (1) if s is faulty, covering it will cause a failure; and (2) if s is dynamically directly control and/or data dependent on statement s', s' causes the execution of s and possibly the failure; i.e., the set of covariates includes zero or one decision statement, and zero or more definition statements.

The proposed technique is based on the premise that to reduce any confounding biases due to dynamic dependences, the treatment group of executions (those covering s) and the control group of executions (those not covering s) should be *balanced*; i.e., they should exhibit the same pattern of dependences. Having access to such balanced groups is hard to satisfy (for each s) as the test cases used in SBFL are usually collected from the field or originated from an existing regression test suite. However, to achieve relative balance, for each statement s, the proposed technique identifies one treatment execution and one or more control executions, such as they are most similar in regard to the set of covariates of s. If the matching did not succeed, the suspiciousness score of s is estimated using a linear regression model similar to the one presented in Ref. [27]. However, following a successful match, the score is estimated based on the outcomes of the matched executions. Specifically, it is the difference between the outcome of the treatment execution (1 for failing and 0 for passing) and the average outcome of the control executions. For example, the highest score of 1.0 is achieved if the treatment execution failed and all control executions passed; and the lowest score of -1.0 is achieved if the treatment execution passed and all control executions failed.

Finally, the observed empirical results indicate that this technique is more effective overall than early correlation-based techniques, and the causation-based techniques presented in Ref. [27]. Podgurski *et al.* later proposed the use of other causal inference techniques in method-level fault localization [36] and in fault localization focused on numeral software [37].

4.2 Using Complex Profiling Elements

Generally, simple profiling elements can only characterize simple faults, as discussed in Section 3.2.3. Below we present two approaches that address this limitation.

4.2.1 Covering Information Flow Pairs

Information flow analysis, which originated in the field of computer security, is used to determine if information stored in a sensitive variable or object can flow or actually has flowed to a variable or object that is accessible to an untrusted party. There are both static and dynamic variants of information flow analysis, which is closely related to program slicing. *Dynamic information flow analysis (DIFA)* [7], which seeks to identify (direct and indirect) information flows between variables at runtime, is capable of modeling complex interactions between program elements. In the context of this work [38], *complex interactions* refer to a set of execution events involving different types of simple program elements that are possibly located far apart in the program, e.g., a combination of def-use pairs and branches executed in some specific order. Also in this work, a defect involving complex interactions will be termed a *hard to debug defect* since it clearly requires the developer to exert considerable manual effort to locate. This work proposes using information flows, identified using DIFA, to locate hard to debug defects. Information flows are relatively more complex and potentially more effective since they capture the transitive interactions (data and control dependences) of both statements and program variables. The fault localization technique proposed here adopts a *Tarantula* style suspiciousness metric and code examination strategy [24] tailored for *information flow profiles*. For example, the suspiciousness score of a given information flow is computed first; then that score is assigned to all the statements belonging to the dependence chain (dynamic chop) leading from its source to its target.

An *information flow profile* indicates the execution frequency of the flows that occurred during a program run. The elements that constitute the profiles used in the proposed technique are *information flow pairs (IFPs)*. An *IFP* is defined as follows: for each combination of (s, x) and (t, y) such that (a) statement s last defined object x and statement t last defined object y and (b) information flowed dynamically from x into y in at least one run, an *IFP* profile contains a count of how many times such a flow occurred in the current run. If the count is zero, it means that the *IFP* never occurred in the current run but it did occur in at least one other run. Note that the flow $x \rightarrow y$ is uniquely identified by the quadruple (s, x, t, y).

We now provide a motivating example based on the Java program shown in Table 1a. Given a string representing an eight-digit binary number, `decimal()` returns its decimal conversion. Due to an overflow problem in statement 2, `powers[0]` takes on the value −128 as opposed to `128`, thus causing a failure whenever the input string has its leftmost bit set. Table 1 shows four passing and two failing test cases, in addition to statement coverage, branch coverage, and def-use coverage. None of these three types of coverage provides any assistance in locating the defect since all tests exhibit the same respective profiles.

Table 2 provides the corresponding information flow coverage. It shows that flows `(2, powers[0], 8, decimal)` and `(2, powers[0], 10, decimal)` are two IFPs that are uniquely induced by both of the failing test cases and, thus, would be ranked highest, but with a tie. The proposed approach breaks the tie by assigning the shorter flow a higher rank. The reason behind this is that when a defect is exercised, its resulting infectious state propagates transitively to many objects down the dependence chain, thus inducing many additional suspicious flows, but the prime interest of the developer is to examine the earliest flow where things went wrong. Therefore, `(2, powers[0], 8, decimal)` having a length of 1 is ranked higher than `(2, powers[0], 10, decimal)` which has a length of 2. Finally, note how several other flows also have statement 2 as a source and statement 8 or 10 as a target, e.g., `(2, powers[1], 8, decimal)`, `(2, powers[4], 8, decimal)`, `(2, powers[1], 10, decimal)`, and `(2, powers[4], 10, decimal)`. These would be ranked lower since they are not as highly correlated with the two failing test cases. This demonstrates that SBFL using information flow coverage not only is capable of localizing the faulty statement but can also identify the specific object/variable, in this case array element `powers[0]`, which was involved in the failure.

To show its potential, the technique was applied to several open source Java programs and was compared, with respect to its fault localization effectiveness, to three other coverage techniques that use similar style metrics that are defined for statements, branches, and def-use pairs, respectively. The results revealed that information flow, branch, and def-use coverage performed consistently better than statement coverage. Also, in a considerable number of cases, information flow coverage performed better than branch and def-use coverage. Specifically, it was always safer but not always more precise. In other words, using a complex profiling element such as IFPs yields a very low rate of false negatives, but possibly at the expense of an increased rate of false positives.

Table 1 (a) Java Code and Statement Coverage, (b) Branch Coverage, and (c) Def-Use Coverage

(a)

/* Given a string representing an 8 digit binary number, decimal() returns its decimal conversion. Due to overflow, failure occurs whenever the input string has its leftmost position set. */ public class BinarytoDecimal { static byte powers[] = new byte[8];	Passing Test Cases				Failing Test Cases	
	"00001100"	"01011001"	"00110100"	"01111101"	"10101110"	"10000100"
public static void main(String args[]) {						
1 for (int i1 = 0; i1 < powers.length; i1++) {	✓	✓	✓	✓	✓	✓
2 powers[i1]=(byte)Math.pow(2.0,(double)(7-i1)); }	✓	✓	✓	✓	✓	✓
3 decimal(args[0]); }	✓	✓	✓	✓	✓	✓
public static int decimal(String binary) {						
4 int decimal = 0;	✓	✓	✓	✓	✓	✓
5 for (int i2 = 0; i2 < binary.length(); i2++) {	✓	✓	✓	✓	✓	✓
6 char ch = binary.charAt(i2);	✓	✓	✓	✓	✓	✓
7 if (ch == '1') {	✓	✓	✓	✓	✓	✓
8 decimal += powers[i2]; }	✓	✓	✓	✓	✓	✓
9 }						
10 return decimal; } }	✓	✓	✓	✓	✓	✓

(b)

	Passing Test Cases				Failing Test Cases	
Branch (Source Statement, Target Statement)	"00001100"	"01011001"	"00110100"	"01111101"	"10101110"	"10000100"
(1,2)	✓	✓	✓	✓	✓	✓
(1,3)	✓	✓	✓	✓	✓	✓
(5,6)	✓	✓	✓	✓	✓	✓
(5,10)	✓	✓	✓	✓	✓	✓
(7,8)	✓	✓	✓	✓	✓	✓
(7,9)	✓	✓	✓	✓	✓	✓

Table 1 (a) Java Code and Statement Coverage, (b) Branch Coverage, and (c) Def-Use Coverage—cont'd
(c)

Def-Use (Def Statement, Use Statement)	Passing Test Cases				Failing Test Cases	
	"00001100"	"01011001"	"00110100"	"01111101"	"10101110"	"10000100"
(i1,1,2)	✓	✓	✓	✓	✓	✓
(i2,5,6)	✓	✓	✓	✓	✓	✓
(binary,3,6)	✓	✓	✓	✓	✓	✓
(binary,3,5)	✓	✓	✓	✓	✓	✓
(ch,6,7)	✓	✓	✓	✓	✓	✓
(decimal,4,8)	✓	✓	✓	✓	✓	✓
(decimal,8,10)	✓	✓	✓	✓	✓	✓
(powers[],2,8)	✓	✓	✓	✓	✓	✓

4.2.2 Covering Profiling Elements with Increasing Structural Complexity

As observed in the study conducted in Ref. [38], using a complex profiling element will improve the safety of spectrum-based fault localization but might reduce its precision. Ideally, the used profiling element should closely characterize the fault at hand; i.e., it should be no less complex than the fault (to evade false negatives) and no more complex than the fault (to evade false positives). In Ref. [6], we presented an SBFL approach that builds on that in order to identify program elements that are highly correlated with failure. With E denoting the profiling type, e an instance of E, and the suspiciousness metric:

$$M_E(e) = F - P$$

where

$F = \%$ of failing runs that executed e,

$P = \%$ of passing runs that executed e.

The steps of the approach are as follows:

1. Specify E to represent statements (the simplest profiling type considered);
2. Compute $M_E(e)$ for all executing statements;
3. Exit if the highest score was 1.0 (a failure-correlated statement was found);

Table 2 Information Flow Coverage Information

Flow (Source Statement, Source Object, Target Statement, Target Object)	Passing Test Cases "00001100"	"01011001"	"00110100"	"01111101"	Failing Test Cases "10101110"	"10000100"
(2,powers[0],8,decimal)					✓	✓
(2,powers[0],10,decimal)					✓	✓
(2,powers[6],8,decimal)					✓	
(2,powers[6],10,decimal)					✓	
(2,powers[5],8,decimal)	✓		✓	✓	✓	✓
(2,powers[5],10,decimal)	✓		✓	✓	✓	✓
(6,ch,7,-)	✓	✓	✓	✓	✓	✓
(8,decimal,10,-)	✓	✓	✓	✓	✓	✓
(5,-,6,ch)	✓	✓	✓	✓	✓	✓
(4,decimal,8,decimal)	✓	✓	✓	✓	✓	✓
(7,-,8,decimal)	✓	✓	✓	✓	✓	✓
. . .	.	.	.			
(2,powers[2],8,decimal)			✓	✓	✓	
(2,powers[2],10,decimal)			✓	✓	✓	
(2,powers[4],8,decimal)	✓	✓			✓	✓
(2,powers[4],10,decimal)	✓	✓			✓	✓
(2,powers[1],8,decimal)		✓		✓		
. . .	.	.	.	.		

In case the source or target is conditional or return statements, a " - " is used in place of the object name.

4. Specify E to represent dependence chains of length 1 (a more complex type);
5. Compute $M_E(e)$ for all executing chains;
6. Exit if the highest score was 1.0 (a failure-correlated chain was found);
7. Increase the complexity of E, i.e., alternate between (a) augmenting the covered chain with a set of predicates and (b) increasing the length of the chain by 1;
8. Exit if the complexity of E renders profile collection infeasible;
9. Go to Step 5.

The sequence of covered elements would then be (1) statements, (2) dependence chains of length one, (3) dependence chains of length one augmented with predicates, (4) chains of length two, (5) chains of length two augmented with predicates, and so on. Basically, the algorithm searches for a highly correlated program element starting with the simplest profiling type (statement). If no element is found, it increases the complexity and searches again. This is repeated until a highly correlated element is found, or the resources are exhausted.

The predicates used are to some extent similar to what is used in Ref. [13]; they are computed for a given dependence chain, as follows:

- *Source predicates*
    - source = *True*, source = *False*; applicable when the source is a *boolean*;
    - source > 0, source = 0, source < 0; applicable when the source is a *scalar*;
    - source = *null*, source ≠ *null*; applicable when the source is an *object reference*;
- *Target predicates* (similar to source predicates)
- *Relationship predicates*
    - source > target, source = target, source < target; applicable when the source and target are *scalars*;
    - source = target, source ≠ target; applicable when the source and target are *booleans* or *references*.

To evaluate the approach, we conducted experiments involving 18 seeded versions from the Siemens benchmark. First, we describe some additional metrics that we computed:

Max_s = max M_E score attained by a statement,

$Fault_s$ = M_E score of the faulty code,

Max_c = max M_E score attained by a dependence chain,

$Fault_c$ = max M_E score attained by a chain that traverses the fault.

The following observations could be made based on our experiments:

1. *In 17 versions, Max_c was > Max_s, and the chains were ≤ 3 in most cases.* That is, in most cases, the technique succeeded at finding program elements that have a higher suspiciousness score than when using statement coverage. And this was achieved by using moderately complex profiling elements.

2. *In nine versions, Max_c was 1.0.* That is, in 50% of the cases, the technique found elements that are highly correlated with failure. Note that not attaining a score of 1.0 means that: (a) we ran out of resources, (b) the fault cannot be characterized by a dependence chain, or (c) the test suite contained coincidentally correct tests.

3. *In seven versions, predicates improved Max$_c$.*

4. *In 15 versions, the most suspicious chain had a length greater than one and/or was augmented with predicates.* This basically suggests that simple profiling types are not adequate enough.

5. *Fault$_c$ was always greater than (or equal to) Fault$_s$.* Suggesting a lower rate of false negatives.

4.3 Cleansing CC Test Cases

As noted in Section 3.2, CC is a source of false negatives and is prevalent. In Refs. [34,39], we presented techniques to cleanse test suites from CC test cases. Figure 7 depicts a test suite T with its various relevant components. It comprises a set of passing tests T_P and a set of failing tests T_F, where T_P might be composed of a subset of coincidentally correct tests T_{CC} and another subset of true passing tests T_{trueP}; T_{CC} refers to either weak or strong coincidentally correct tests. Our aim is to identify T_{CC} given T_F and T_P so that the tests in T_{CC} would be discarded from T in order to enhance the safety of SBFL. A passing test identified by our techniques as a potential CC test is called a cc_t; and the set of identified cc_t's, our estimate of T_{CC}, is called T'_{CC}. In Refs. [34,39], we presented two techniques to achieve our goal, both of which are based on analyzing structural execution profiles; here, we describe the simpler of the two, namely, *Tech-I*.

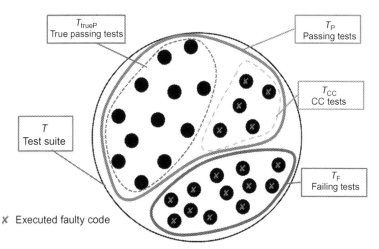

Figure 7 A test suite with its various components.

Given a program element e, we denote by $F(e)$ the ratio of failing test cases executing e and by $P(e)$ the ratio of passing test cases executing e. Each test case t_i is associated with a characteristic function f_i defined as follows:

$$f_i(e) = \begin{cases} 1 & \text{if } e \text{ is exercised by } t_i \\ 0 & \text{otherwise} \end{cases}$$

Given a test suite T that exercises elements $e_1, e_2, \ldots, e_n$, a test case t_i in T is represented by the feature vector $V_i = [f_i(e_1)f_i(e_2)\ldots f_i(e_n)]$. Our technique assumes that (1) there exists a set of elements, which we call cc_e's, that correlate with CC and (2) a good candidate for a cc_e is any program element that occurs in all failing runs and in a nonzero but not excessively large percentage of passing runs.

Tech-I conjectures that coincidentally correct tests are similar to failing tests in terms of their execution profiles and hence are expected to automatically cluster together. Our approach is to use cluster analysis, and specifically *k-means* clustering, to partition the whole test suite into two clusters, pick the cluster containing the majority of failing tests and label all passing tests within it as cc_t's. We use the Euclidean metric as a distance measure and discard elements that are not cc_e's. In fact, since *Tech-I* considers an element e to be a cc_e iff $F(e) = 1$ and $0 < P(e) < 1$, it follows that all failing runs would collapse to the same point in the clustering process. The distance between two tests t_i and t_j is defined as follows:

$$d(t_i, t_j) = \sqrt{\sum_{\substack{k=1 \\ e_k \text{ is a } cc_e}}^{n} \left(f_i(e_k) - f_j(e_k)\right)^2}$$

where the two initial means consist of the common failing point and the most distant passing test.

We conducted an empirical study involving 105 versions of 15 subject Java and C programs. *Tech-I* resulted in a low rate of false negatives of 3% and a high rate of false positives of 39%, on average; noting that 18 of the versions exhibited no false negatives and no false positives. Even though the average rate of false positives is high, it is the low rate of false negatives that is most beneficial for SBFL, as the end goal is to identify and discard most of the CC tests in order to arrive at a more faithful value of the suspiciousness score.

4.4 Isolating Failure Causes Through Test Case Generation

Starting with a single failing test case and a simple oracle, *BugEx* [40] is an approach that leverages automated test case generation to isolate the facts that highly correlate with failure. In its current implementation, a *fact* is an execution of a branch or a state of the visible variables at a method entry.

BugEx combines lessons learned from SBFL and experimental approaches. The first and most representative experimental technique, delta debugging (see Section 6), starts with only one failing and one passing run and isolates minimal failure-inducing differences in inputs or program states [30]. One shortcoming of experimental techniques is that they might identify suspicious entities that correspond to executions that are not feasible (i.e., no test case could induce them), which will mislead the developer. The executions considered by *BugEx* are all feasible since they are induced by real test cases that were automatically generated, whereas executions in experimental techniques are arrived at through internally manipulating other executions. More importantly, *BugEx* evades the SBFL shortcomings related to test suite quality (see Section 3.2.2) by generating failing and passing test cases that are similar to each other and to the originally provided failing test case, which ensures low rates of false positives. Furthermore, depending on where the oracle (check that distinguishes failing from passing runs) is placed in the code, *BugEx* might inadvertently evade the negative effect of CC; i.e., if the check happened to be very close to the faulty code, a CC test case might serendipitously get categorized as failing.

Given a failing test case t_{fail} and assuming that the executions of branches are the only facts considered, we now discuss the steps of *BugEx*:

Step 1 $F_{\text{correlating}}$ is a set comprising the facts to be considered. This step initializes $F_{\text{correlating}}$ with the branches covered in t_{fail}.

Step 2   A branch f is randomly picked from $F_{\text{correlating}}$.

Step 3   One passing and another failing test case are generated that satisfy the following requirements: (1) Both must reach the last branch before the failure occurs; to ensure a good level of similarity. (2) Both must evaluate f differently than t_{fail}; this ensures that it would be possible to assess the correlation of f with the program outcome. (3) If several test cases fulfill the first two requirements, the one most similar to t_{fail} is selected. In summary, optimally, *BugEx* seeks tests (passing and failing) that are as similar to t_{fail} as possible but differ from t_{fail} with respect to f, which is rarely achievable in practice, however.

Step 4   Include the two additional test cases in recomputing the suspiciousness scores of all branches that have been covered so far and store them in $F_{correlating}$. Proceed to Step 5 if no new branches emerged as a result of the two additional test cases; otherwise go to Step 2.

Step 5   Rank the branches in $F_{correlating}$. *BugEx* only returns the top-ranked facts and cuts the result off where the difference in ranking between two successive facts exceeds an order of magnitude.

BuxEx uses *EvoSuite* [41] as a test case generation tool, which implements an evolutionary search approach enhanced with dynamic symbolic execution; alternatively, other tools based on this or other approaches could also be integrated within. Regarding the evaluation of *BugEx*, the authors conducted experiments using seven defects/failures which showed that: (1) In six of them, the facts reported by *BubEx* explained the failure effectively. (2) In all seven, *BugEx* focused on a far smaller number of branches than traditional spectrum-based techniques. (3) In all seven, *BugEx* reported a small number of branches; in particular, it reported a single branch in four of them. These impressive results can somewhat justify the title of the paper which refers to the failure-correlated facts as *failure causes*. As a final note, the current implementation of *BugEx* uses simple facts; more complex facts might have to be considered in order to address complex bugs. Apparently, this was not necessary in the small experimental study conducted by the authors.

4.5 Purifying JUnit Test Cases to Improve SBFL

The use of unit testing frameworks, such as the xUnit family of products, has become a near de facto practice in most development environments. It is the case because these frameworks tremendously facilitate regression testing and test-driven development. Therefore, when applying SBFL to Java programs, the available test suites are likely to be sets of JUnit test cases.

Given a method m to be tested, a set of inputs and an expected output, a JUnit test is a method consisting of code that typically invokes m with the set of inputs and checks whether its returned output matches what is expected. The checks are done using a family of *assertions* provided by the framework, which also provides support for bundling tests into test suites. As its name suggests, each unit test should test only one behavior of a method, or a single limited functionality of the application, but unfortunately, tests writers do not follow this guideline. For example, *Apache Commons Lang v2.6* is a project consisting of 1874 JUnit test cases comprising 10,869 assertions; i.e., each test case includes 5.80 assertions on average, whereas an average closer to 1.0 would be desirable. This fact is problematic for maintaining the unit tests and for SBFL as argued by Xuan and Monperrus [42] who went on to develop a tool that transforms JUnit test cases containing k assertions into k

```
public class T1 {   // Test suite
    void t1() { // fails
        assertEquals(1.2f, utils.min(1.2f, 2.5f, Float.NaN));                          // passes
        assertEquals(2.5f, utils.max(1.2f, 2.5f, Float.NaN));                          // fails
        float [] aF = new float[] {1.2f, Float.NaN, 3.7f, 27.0f, 42.0f, Float.NaN}; // never reached
        assertEquals(42.0f, utils.max(aF));                                            // never reached
    }
    void t2() { // fails
        assertEquals(1.2f, utils.min(1.2f, 2.5f, Float.NaN));                          // passes
        float [] aF = new float[] {1.2f, Float.NaN, 3.7f, 27.0f, 42.0f, Float.NaN};
        assertEquals(42.0f, utils.max(aF));                                            // fails
    }
}
public class T2 {   // Test suite
    void t1() { // passes
        assertEquals(1.2f, utils.min(1.2f, 2.5f, Float.NaN));                          // passes
    }
    void t2() { // fails
        assertEquals(2.5f, utils.max(1.2f, 2.5f, Float.NaN));                          // fails
    }
    void t3() { // fails
        float [] aF = new float[] {1.2f, Float.NaN, 3.7f, 27.0f, 42.0f, Float.NaN};
        assertEquals(42.0f, utils.max(aF));                                            // fails
    }
}
```

Figure 8 Unit test suites: T_1 and T_2.

tests each containing a single assertion. They termed this transformation, *test case purification*. To motivate their work they used a variant of the example presented below.

The table below shows several methods for calculating the maximum and the minimum of floating numbers. Line 9 contains an injected fault that negates the conditional expression *Float.isNaN(a)*. The table also shows statement coverage information for two separate JUnit test suites, T_1 comprising test cases with multiple assertions and T_2 containing *purified* tests with a single assertion only. Figure 8 shows the actual JUnit tests in T_1 and T_2. However, not shown in the figure or table is the information about other passing tests that make T_1 and T_2 achieve full statement coverage.

Considering T_1, SBFL would suggest that statements $\{1, 2, 4, 5, 7, 9, 10\}$ are all suspicious whereas, if T_2 is considered, only $\{9, 10\}$ would be deemed suspicious. This demonstrates a serious negative side effect of not writing focused and compact JUnit tests, i.e., tests containing single assertions.

The authors in Ref. [42] recognized the prevalence of this problem in existing unit test suites, and developed an automated tool to address it. They also conducted an empirical study showing the major improvement achieved in SBFL when the test suites are "purified" using their tool.

	T_1		T_2		
`public class utils {` `public static float min(float a, float b, float c) {`	t_1	t_2	t_1	t_2	t_3
1 `return min(min(a, b), c);`	✓	✓	✓		
`}` `public static float min(float a, float b) {`					
2 `if(Float.isNaN(a))`	✓	✓	✓		
3 `return b;`					
4 `else if(Float.isNaN(b))`	✓	✓	✓		
5 `return a;`	✓	✓	✓		
6 `else`					
7 `return Math.min(a, b);`	✓	✓	✓		
`}` `public static float max(float a, float b, float c) {`					
8 `return max(max(a, b), c);`	✓			✓	
`}` `public static float max(float a, float b) {`					
9 `if(!Float.isNaN(a)) // Fault: added negation`	✓	✓		✓	✓
10 `return b;`	✓	✓		✓	✓
11 `else if(Float.isNaN(b))`		✓			✓
12 `return a;`		✓			✓
`else`					
13 `return Math.max(a, b);`					
`}` `public static float max(float[] array) {`					
14 `float max = array[0];`		✓			✓
15 `for (int j = 1; j < array.length; j++)`		✓			✓
16 `max = max(array[j], max);`		✓			✓
17 `return max;`		✓			✓
`}` `}`	Fail	Fail	Pass	Fail	Fail

4.6 Reproducing and Debugging Field Failures

4.6.1 BugRedux: *Reproducing Field Failures*

In Ref. [43], Jin and Orso presented *BugRedux*, an approach for synthesizing executions that mimic an observed field failure. Given a program P, a field execution e of P that results in a failure f, and a set of crash data D for e, *BugRedux* can synthesize an in-house execution e' with two main characteristics: (1) e' results in a failure f' that has the same observable behavior of f (e.g., it violates the same assertion that f violates at the same program location) and (2) e' is an actual execution of P, i.e., *BugRedux* generates an actual input that, when provided to P, results in e'. The set of crash data D is an ordered list of program points, which can be seen as breadcrumbs to be followed to get to the failure. The last point in the list is the actual failure point. Given D, *BugRedux* performs an optimized, guided forward symbolic analysis to synthesize an execution e' that reaches the goals in the right order. It then checks whether e' fails in the same way as the observed field execution e and, if so, provides e' and its corresponding input to the developer.

4.6.2 F^3: *Fault Localization for Field Failures*

Although reproducing field failures is very helpful, *BugRedux* does not provide any explicit support for fault localization. To address this limitation, Jin and Orso presented a new technique called F^3 (Fault localization for Field Failures) [44], which extends *BugRedux* to support SBFL. F^3 comprises two main components: the *execution generator* and the *fault localizer*, described next.

4.6.2.1 Execution Generator

The *execution generator* generates a set of executions (and associated tests) that mimic a field execution e. The generated set contains both failing and passing executions, such that the failing executions (*FAIL* set) fail for the same reasons as e, and the passing executions (*PASS* set) are "similar" to e. The use of similar tests (passing or failing) is expected to improve the effectiveness of SBFL.

The *execution generator* takes as input an ordered list of program locations l that guides the generator in synthesizing an execution that mimics e and reproduces field failure f. The original *BugRedux* implementation [43] used l to generate a single failing execution. Within F^3, *BugRedux* was extended so that it continues to synthesize executions that mimic e until it reaches a given time limit.

By construction, all the synthesized executions reach the point of failure and share with e a set of intermediate execution points, but they are likely to follow different paths than e. It is worth noting that they do not necessarily all result in failure f, but in practice they do in most cases. However, in case no passing executions were generated, F^3 starts by eliminating a single entry from l in order to induce a slight diversion from e and hopefully arrive at a passing execution. This elimination process is repeated until one or more passing execution is synthesized or a time limit is reached. Obviously, reducing l would yield executions that are dissimilar from e, which is harmful to SBFL. Fortunately, in practice, it was observed that the execution generator did not have to eliminate many entries in l to generate passing executions, and the degree of similarity between the synthesized executions and e was not considerably affected.

4.6.2.2 Fault Localizer

Using the synthesized *FAIL* and *PASS* sets and an SBFL technique, the *fault localizer* aims at producing a list of program elements ordered in terms of their likelihood of being faulty. The current implementation of F^3 uses the Ochiai [28] and observation-based model [45] techniques enhanced by the three means described next. First, F^3 filters the executions in order to discard the program elements (branches) that are deemed irrelevant for the failure according to some heuristics. For example, it considers only branches that are exercised in all failing executions and exclude all other branches from the statistical analysis. Furthermore, it also excludes those branches that are exercised in all passing executions. Second, F^3 uses profiling as opposed to coverage, i.e., it takes into consideration how many times a branch got executed, and not just whether it got executed or not. To support profiling, the SBFL metrics had to be modified. Third, F^3 recognizes the fact that developers operate at the source code level and not at the instruction level at which the analysis was conducted. Therefore, it presents the developer with a ranked list of suspicious source code statements, which requires suitable grouping of low-level program elements. To achieve that, F^3 adopts the following heuristic: program elements having the same suspiciousness value and belonging to either the same line of code or consecutive lines are grouped together and reported as a single entry.

Finally, the empirical study conducted in Ref. [44] showed that the *execution generator* was always able to synthesize multiple passing and failing executions, and that the simple modifications made to the *fault localizer* had a positive effect in most cases.

4.7 Prioritizing Test Cases for Fault Localization

Test case prioritization is a regression testing approach which aims at ordering test cases for early fault detection. The assumption behind test case prioritization is that there may not always be enough time to execute the entire test suite; therefore, test cases that are more likely to reveal the faults should be executed first. Since fault detection information is not known until after testing is finished, surrogates such as code coverage information are usually used when prioritization test suites.

Regression testing and fault localization are complementary [46]. The program is tested to see if change has introduced a fault and, in case it has, the focus is switched from regression testing to debugging and fault fixing. Following a successful fix, the focus is switched back to regression testing and so the cycle continues. This "test-find-debug-fix" cycle is a common scenario in practice. In order to automate the debugging phase within this cycle, automated fault localization could be used, which poses the following new challenge.

Typically, a test suite is required to be executed in its entirety before applying automated fault localization on a program. Following a failure, it may not be realistic to expect the developers to wait for all test cases to be executed before they can start applying automated fault localization (i.e., to initiate debugging and fixing). One approach would be to use the set of test cases executed up to the point at which the failure was observed. In some situations, this may be all that is required. However, there may be too few test cases for effective automated fault localization, particularly if the first failure is observed early in the testing process. In this situation, testing will need to continue for a while to provide a sufficiently large pool of test cases for effective localization. This raises the question that Yoo *et al.* try to address in Ref. [46]:

> *Having observed a failure, what is the best order in which to rank the remaining test cases to maximize early localization of the fault?*

As an illustration, Table 3 shows coverage information for statements s_1 to s_9 resulting from executing test cases t_1 to t_4 that are prioritized based on the statement coverage. That is, t_1 covers the most statements; t_2 covers the second most not covered before, etc. The prioritized test suite detects the first fault with t_2, which covers the faulty element s_7. Suppose that there is only time to execute one additional test, either t_3 or t_4. If t_3 is chosen, the *Tarantula* suspiciousness scores for s_7 would be 0.67, and 1.0 for s_6 and s_8, which is misleading, whereas, if t_4 was chosen, the scores for s_7, s_6, and s_8 would all be

Table 3 Illustrating Example

Statements	t_1	t_2	t_3	Score	t_4	Score
s_1	✓	✓	✓	0.5		0.33
s_2	✓		✓	0.0		0.0
s_3	✓		✓	0.0		0.0
s_4	✓			0.0		0.0
s_5	✓		✓	0.0		0.0
s_6		✓		1.0	✓	1.0
s_7 (fault)		✓	✓	0.67	✓	1.0
s_8		✓		1.0	✓	1.0
s_9	✓	✓		0.67	✓	0.5
Outcome	P	F	P		F	

1.0, which is a more accurate result. This shows that the choice of the next test case to execute can affect the accuracy of the suspiciousness metric when test suite execution is terminated at an arbitrary point.

Yoo *et al.* leverage information theory to determine which test to execute next following an initial failure. Below is their formulation of fault localization as an entropy reduction process.

4.7.1 Fault Localization as an Entropy Reduction Problem

Let $S = \{s_1, \ldots, s_m\}$ be the set of statements in the subject program such as a single element in S is faulty. Let $T = \{t_1, \ldots, t_n\}$ be the test suite, $F(t)$ a boolean statement indicating that t has failed, and $B(s)$ a boolean statement indicating that s is faulty.

Assume the situation in which the ith test fails during testing. Let T_{i-1} be the set of the first $i-1$ tests, $\{t_1, \ldots, t_{i-1}\}$, that have passed, and t_i be the first failing test. Shannon's entropy, or the measure of uncertainty, regarding the locality of the fault can be defined as follows:

$$H_{T_i}(S) = -\sum_{j=1}^{m} P_{T_i}\big(B(s_j)\big) \cdot \log P_{T_i}\big(B(s_j)\big) \qquad (1)$$

where $T_i = T_{i-1} \cup \{t_i\}$, $\tau(s_j | T_i)$ denotes the *Tarantula* suspiciousness score of s_j calculated using T_i. And the approximated probability that statement s_j is faulty, based on T_i, is the normalized suspiciousness metric for s_j:

$$\tau_{\text{norm}}\left(s_j | T_i\right) = P_{T_i}\left(B\left(s_j\right)\right) = \frac{\tau\left(s_j | T_i\right)}{\sum_{j=1}^{m} \tau\left(s_j | T_i\right)} \tag{2}$$

$P_{T_i}\left(B\left(s_j\right)\right)$ is more sensible than $\tau(s_j | T_i)$ at assessing the suspiciousness of s_j, since it accounts for false positives. For example, if s' is the only statement correlated with failure, then both $\tau(s' | T_i)$ and $P_{T_i}\left(B(s')\right)$ are 1.0; but if all statements are correlate with failure, then $\tau(s' | T_i)$ is 1.0 but $P_{T_i}\left(B(s')\right)$ would be smaller than 1.0.

Ideally, fault localization yields the best possible result when enough adequate tests are used to arrive at $H_{T_n}(s) = 0$. According to Eq. (1), this happens only in case when there is a single (faulty) statement s' with $P_{T_n}\left(B(s')\right) = 1$, and all remaining statements having $P_{T_n}\left(B(s)\right) = 0$. Therefore, the aim is to order the executed tests in a manner to arrive at the lowest possible value of $H_{T_n}(s)$ as fast as possible. Noting that the lowest value is not necessarily 0 since the pool of tests is provided and thus might not exhibit the quality characteristics to ever yield a $H_{T_n}(s) = 0$. It follows that the next test to execute, t_{i+1}, should be the one that yields the smallest $H_{T_{i+1}}(S)$. Therefore, the *lookahead entropy* $H_{T_{i+1}}(S)$ must be computed for all unexecuted tests.

4.7.2 Estimating the Lookahead Entropy

To estimate $H_{T_{i+1}}(S)$ on the basis of what is known so far, $P_{T_{i+1}}\left(B\left(s_j\right)\right)$ needs to be approximated. Since it is not possible to predict whether t_{i+1} will pass or fail, the authors use conditional probability to express both cases using the law of total probability:

$$P_{T_{i+1}}\left(B\left(s_j\right)\right) = P_{T_{i+1}}\left(B\left(s_j | F(t_{i+1})\right)\right) \times \alpha + P_{T_{i+1}}\left(B\left(s_j | \neg F(t_{i+1})\right)\right) \\ \times (1 - \alpha) \tag{3}$$

The authors base the approximation of α, the probability that t_{i+1} fails, on what was observed in T_i so far, it is computed as: $\alpha = TF_i / (TF_i + TP_i)$ where TP_i and TF_i are the total number of passing/failing tests, respectively, after executing the tests in T_i. For example, if a relatively high rate of failures was observed so far, the value of α would be high. The conditional probabilities in the above equation can be calculated using the *Tarantula* metric and Eq. (2) where $P_{T_{i+1}}\left(B\left(s_j | F(t_{i+1})\right)\right)$ assumes that t_{i+1} fails, and $P_{T_{i+1}}\left(B\left(s_j | \neg F(t_{i+1})\right)\right)$ assumes that t_{i+1} passes.

Now that $P_{T_{i+1}}(B(s_j))$ could be approximated, an estimate of the lookahead entropy $H_{T_{i+1}}(S)$ could be computed for every remaining test, which will enable to tester to choose the most appropriate one to execute next, i.e., the one yielding the lowest $H_{T_{i+1}}(S)$.

4.7.3 Example Walkthrough

Using the same example shown in Table 3, Table 4 shows the detailed steps of computing $H_{T_{i+1}}(S)$. Columns 5 and 6 show the *Tarantula* scores and normalized scores (calculated using Eq. 2) assuming that t_3 passes and fails, respectively. Similarly, columns 9 and 10 show the *Tarantula* scores and normalized scores assuming that t_4 passes and fails, respectively. After executing t_1 and t_2, the probability of the next test failing $\alpha = TF_i/(TF_i + TP_i) = 1/(1+1) = 0.5$.

Columns 7 and 11 show the lookahead probabilities of a statement being faulty, as computed using Eq. (3). For example, if t_3 is chosen, $P_{T_{i+1}}(B(s_9))$ is computed as follows:

$$P_{T_{i+1}}(B(s_9)) = P_{T_{i+1}}(B(s_9|F(t_{i+1}))) \times \alpha + P_{T_{i+1}}(B(s_9|\neg F(t_{i+1})))(1-\alpha)$$
$$= \tau_{\text{norm}}(s_9|F(t_3)) \times 0.5 + \tau_{\text{norm}}(s_9|\neg F(t_3)) \times (1-0.5)$$
$$= 0.07 \times 0.5 + 0.17 \times 0.5 = 0.12$$

Table 4 Detailed Steps of Computing $H_{T_{i+1}}(S)$

	t_1	t_2	t_3	τ/τ_{norm}		P(B(s))	t_4	τ/τ_{norm}		P(B(s))
				$\neg F(t_3)$	$F(t_3)$			$\neg F(t_4)$	$F(t_4)$	
s_1	✓	✓	✓	0.5/0.13	0.5/0.1	0.115		0.67/0.21	0.33/0.08	0.145
s_2	✓		✓	0/0	0.33/0.07	0.035		0/0	0/0	0
s_3	✓		✓	0/0	0.33/0.07	0.035		0/0	0/0	0
s_4	✓			0/0	0/0	0		0/0	0/0	0
s_5	✓		✓	0/0	0.33/0.07	0.035		0/0	0/0	0
s_6		✓		1.0/0.26	1.0/0.2	0.23	✓	0.67/0.21	1.0/0.26	0.235
s_7		✓	✓	0.67/0.17	1.0/0.2	0.185	✓	0.67/0.21	1.0/0.26	0.235
s_8		✓		1.0/0.26	1.0/0.2	0.23	✓	0.67/0.21	1.0/0.26	0.235
s_9	✓	✓		0.67/0.17	0.33/0.07	0.12	✓	0.5/0.16	0.5/0.13	0.145
	P	F	P		F	H=0.8	P		F	H=0.68

Finally, the lookahead entropy values for t_3 and t_4 are found to be 0.8 and 0.68, respectively. They are computed using Eq. (1) and the probabilities shown in columns 7 and 11. Since t_4 produces a lower value of $H_{T_{i+1}}(S)$, the tester is advised to execute t_4 before t_3.

5. PROGRAM SLICING

5.1 Program Slicing: Early Work

The first attempt to automate fault localization is *static slicing* [47,48], which is a technique that uses static dependence analysis to identify the set of program statements (*slice*), that could be responsible for an erroneous program state that occurred at a particular location in a program, termed *slicing criterion*. *Dynamic slicing* [7,8,49,50], a test-driven technique that extracts a slice from an execution trace, is potentially much more precise and, therefore, more beneficial for fault localization than static slicing, as it could be seen when contrasting Figs. 1 and 2 in Section 2.1. Despite this fact, dynamic slicing is still considered too imprecise, as dynamic slices are typically unmanageably large, which requires the developer to exert considerable effort to locate the faulty statements.

Depending on the problem at hand, two main types of slices could be computed, *backward* and *forward*. *Backward slices* include the statements that influence a given slicing criterion, whereas *forward slices* include the statements that get influenced by a given slicing criterion. Note that if the type of a slice is not specified, a backward slice is usually meant.

There are practically hundreds of early articles written on program slicing and dozens of proposed slicing techniques, but we opt not to further our discussion of earlier work since slicing, just by itself, has shown limited success in fault localization. One example of an early work that attempted to improve the fault localization capabilities of slicing is the technique presented by Agrawal *et al.* [51]. That technique is based on dicing, a dice being the set difference of two slices. It conjectures that the fault resides in the *execution slice* (trace) of a failing run but does not reside in the execution slice of a passing run, an assumption that does not generally hold.

5.2 Program Slicing: Shortcomings

Binkley *et al.* [52] have empirically shown that static slices range in size from 6% to 60% with an average of 30% of the size of the original program. The

Wisconsin Program-Slicing Tool 1.1 Reference Manual [53] also reported that, in six C programs, the average size of a static slice ranged from 19% to 97% of the program size. In addition, based on the experience with our own dynamic slicer [7,50], the sizes of dynamic slices average around 50% of the number of the executed statements. Therefore, in today's standards, program slicing alone, whether static or dynamic, might not be very effective for debugging; but it still attracts considerable interest as it benefits other software engineering areas, such as program comprehension and software maintenance.

5.3 Callstack-Sensitive Static Slicing

Horwitz *et al.* [54] proposed two complementary methods to assist the developer during the debugging process. First, since it is hard to pinpoint the statements that produce bad output in case of noncrashing failures, they developed a set of tools that help identify the points of failure of a given program. Second, in order to reduce the sizes of static slices, they recommended the use of *callstack-sensitive slicing* with the points of failure as slicing criteria.

In order to allow a programmer to pinpoint code that wrote each byte of (failing) output produced by a program, they implemented the following set of tools:

(1) The *Trace Tool* records output information in a trace file at runtime.

(2) The *Interactive Mapping Tool* allows a programmer to browse the program's output and, for each selected output character, to obtain the corresponding source code information from the trace file.

(3) The *What-Wrote Tool* finds and displays the associated source code information for an output stream of interest.

(4) The *Compare-Traces Tool* takes two programmer-specified traces as input (e.g., a trace representing correct output and a buggy trace containing bad output), finds the first byte of output at which the traces differ, and prints the source code information associated with that byte in the buggy trace.

When debugging, the developer could examine the backward slice built starting from the point of failure discovered using the provided tools above. The authors argue that dynamic slicing is too costly to be of practical use and thus recommend a variation of static slicing called *callstack-sensitive slicing*, an existing technique proposed by Binkley [55]. Given a point a failure s_f, both static slicing and *callstack-sensitive* slicing involve a backward traversal of the edges of the *System Dependence Graph* [56] of the program. The important difference arises when s_f is in a procedure P other than main. In that case, the full static slice follows edges back to all call sites that call P, while the callstack-sensitive slice only follows edges back to the call sites in the runtime callstack.

Consider the C program shown in the table below, which is supposed to compute and print either the product or the sum of the numbers from 1 to 10, depending on the command line argument. Function getChoice() is implemented incorrectly, which causes the product to be printed when the sum is expected, and vice versa. For a run with command line argument "sum," the program erroneously prints val: 3,628,800. Column 3 shows the full static slice computed with the slicing criterion at the point of failure (line 2), and column 4 shows the corresponding dynamic slice. The full slice is not helpful since it includes all 20 statements of the program, whereas, by excluding lines {6, 13, 14, 15, 16}, the dynamic slice reveals that the *product* is being computed and not the *sum*. However, as mentioned earlier, the support for dynamic slicing can introduce major slowdowns, which may be unacceptable for large programs. As an alternative, column 5 shows the callstack-sensitive slice, which by excluding lines {13, 14, 15, 16} provides enough information to reveal that the *product* is being erroneously computed. Note that the runtime callstack at line 2 ⟨main() line 20 → print() line 2⟩ indicates that print() was invoked at line 20, this explains why only statements that statically influence line 20 are included in the slice of column 5.

Callstack-sensitive slicing can be even more helpful when a single bug causes different test inputs to trigger failures with different sequences of active function calls. For example, if the program is tested with the command line argument "sum" and then "prod," the wrong output will be produced at line 2 in both runs. Since the suspicious code must be in both slices computed at line 2, their intersection is expected to be more helpful than each slice individually, as demonstrated by the slice shown in column 6.

Finally, the authors empirically demonstrated that, on average, a callstack-sensitive slice is about 0.31 time the size of the corresponding static slice, down to just 0.06 time in the best case. On the other hand, intersecting slices was found to be not as beneficial in practice.

		Static	Dynamic	Callstack	Intersection
		Sum	Sum	Sum	Sum/Prod
1	`void print(char *msg, int val) {`	✓	✓	✓	✓
2	`printf("%s %d\n", msg, val);`	✓	✓	✓	✓
	`}`				
3	`int getChoice(char *ch) {`	✓	✓	✓	✓
4	`if (strcmp(ch, "sum") == 0)`	✓	✓	✓	✓
5	`return 1;`	✓	✓	✓	✓
6	`else return 0;`	✓		✓	✓
	`}`				
7	`void main(int argc, char* argv[]) {`	✓	✓	✓	✓
8	`int sum = 0;`	✓	✓	✓	✓
9	`int prod = 1;`	✓	✓	✓	✓
10	`int k = 1;`	✓	✓	✓	✓
11	`int ch = getChoice(argv[1]);`	✓	✓	✓	✓
12	`if (ch == 0) {`	✓	✓	✓	✓
13	`while (k < 11) {`	✓			
14	`sum += k;`	✓			
15	`k++;`	✓			
	`}`				
16	`print("val: ", sum);`	✓			
	`} else {`				
17	`while (k < 11) {`	✓	✓	✓	
18	`prod *= k;`	✓	✓	✓	
19	`k++;`	✓	✓	✓	
	`}`				
20	`print("val: ", prod);`	✓	✓	✓	
	`}`				
	`}`				

5.4 Quantitative or Strength-Based Dynamic Slicing

Santelices *et al.* [57] proposed *quantitative slicing*, which assigns quantitative scores to statements in a slice that capture the level of relevance of such statements. The approach of computing these quantities is in essence identical to *strength-based dependence analysis* [4,5], an earlier work of Masri and Podgurski that was previously mentioned in this chapter. For this reason, we will refer to *quantitative slicing* as *strength-based slicing*, hereafter.

Even though *strength-based slicing* is applicable to fault localization, the work in Ref. [57] presents it in the context of *impact analysis* in which users assess the potential impact of changing some code on other parts of the program before proceeding with the change. Fault localization is concerned with what influenced a given point of failure, i.e., the backward slice computed starting from that point, whereas, given a change to be made to statement s, impact analysis is concerned with what s influences, i.e., the *forward* slice starting from s. This section discusses strength-based slicing in the context of fault localization.

In the code example below, consider the following scenarios:

(1) The value printed at s_{10} is observed to be erroneous, and the backward dynamic slice computed with s_{10} as the slicing criterion consists of $\{s_1, s_2, s_3, s_4\}$. Clearly, s_2 and s_4 are not responsible for the failure since their respective outcomes do not influence the output, whereas s_1 and s_3 are equally likely to be the culprits since they are both directly used in computing the output.

(2) The scenario involving s_9 is similar in that the slice is $\{s_1, s_2, s_3, s_4\}$, and s_2 and s_4 are not responsible for the failure at s_9. However, s_1 is less likely to be the culprit than s_3 is. This is because if h was infected at s_3, the infection will propagate to the output unobstructed, whereas, if c was infected at s_1, the infection might get masked (canceled) by the downcast from float to int, as discussed in Section 3.2.4.3.

(3) The scenario for s_8 is similar to that for s_9; i.e., s_1 is less likely to be the culprit than s_3 is. Here, if c was infected at s_1, the infection might get masked by the modulo operation.

(4) Now assume that the value printed at s_7 is erroneous. The backward dynamic slice computed at s_7 is $\{s_1, s_2, s_3, s_4, s_5, s_6\}$. Here also, s_2 and s_4 are not responsible for the failure; but $\{s_1, s_3, s_5, s_6\}$ are all equally likely to be responsible since the values for c, h, and x1 propagate unobstructed to s_7.

In the above scenarios, strength-based slicing would assign each statement within a dynamic slice a score indicating the strength of the dependence relating the statement to the failure point. In Refs. [4,5], the strength score between a source and a target statement was computed using statistical and information theoretic metrics, which requires: (a) the test suite to repeatedly execute (30 + times) the dependence chains relating the source to the target and (b) collecting the values computed at the source and target.

```
s1: float c = ...; // compute c
s2: if (c*c <= 100.0) {
s3:    float h = ...; // compute h
s4:    for (int i = 0; i < 10; i++) {
s5:       float x1 = c;
s6:       x1 = x1*h;
s7:       print x1;
s8:       print ((int)c % 10) + h;
s9:       print (int)c + h;
s10:      print c + h;
    }
}
```

Similarly, in Ref. [57] the strength score is computed using a statistical metric, specifically, the frequency of when a change in the source induces a change in the target. However, the main contribution of the work described in Ref. [57] is the development and use of a sensitivity-analysis tool (*SENSA*) to circumvent deficiencies in the provided test suites. *SENSA* takes as input a program P, a test suite T, and a statement c. For each test case t in T, *SENSA* executes t repeatedly; each time it replaces the value computed by c with a different value and checks which other statements were affected by these modifications. With this information, *SENSA* computes the sensitivity of each statement s (target) in P to the behavior of c (source) by measuring the frequency with which s is affected by c. These frequencies are the degree of dependence on statement c of all statements s in P, given T. For a backward slice from s, *SENSA* can be used to quantify the dependence of s on a selected statement c in that slice.

Finally, strength-based slicing alleviates the problem of having backward dynamic slices that are too large by ranking the statements within a slice with respect to their relevance to the observed value at the slicing criterion (or output).

6. DELTA DEBUGGING: AN EXPERIMENTATION-BASED APPROACH

Delta debugging [58] is an approach that originally aimed at simplifying a failing program input in order to facilitate the debugging task. Through experimentation, it iteratively reduces the size of a given failing input until it finds the smallest possible part of it that also causes failure. Delta debugging assumes that: (a) smaller inputs cover less code and thus require less debugging effort; and (b) inputs can be simplified and remain valid by omitting parts from within. Although neither of these assumptions generally holds, delta debugging has exhibited success not only in simplifying input but also in several other debugging contexts that aim at narrowing down failure causes.

For example, the work in Ref. [59] reduces the cause of failure to a small set of variables. It leverages *memory graphs* [60] to find the common variables between a passing run and a failing run. It then contrasts the program states, induced by the common variables, of the two runs. The suspiciousness of a given variable is assessed by replacing its value in the passing run with its corresponding value in the failing run and reexecuting the program. The variable is deemed suspicious if the identical failure is observed; otherwise, it is excluded from the set of failure-inducing variables.

One shortcoming of the technique in Ref. [59], and in delta debugging in general, is that it can alter the program state (or input) in a way that is impossible to achieve in the original setting, thus producing states (or inputs) that are infeasible, which will hinder the debugging task.

Given the relatively large body of work that is based on delta debugging, this section will only describe one representative recent work.

Failure reproduction is a prerequisite for fault localization and is necessary for subsequently demonstrating that the bug has been fixed. In Ref. [61], Burger and Zeller presented a technique for reproducing an observed failure in a minimal fashion. Given a single failing run, the interaction between program objects is recorded and reduced to arrive at a minimal unit test comprising a set of method calls that faithfully reproduces the failure. The proposed technique is enabled by JINSI, a tool developed by the authors that is based on the record/replay mechanism, delta debugging, and program slicing.

To illustrate the technique, Fig. 9 shows a snippet of code that interacts with the JODA TIME library (www.joda.org/joda-time/), a replacement for the JAVA date and time classes. This code works well when run in the UTC time standard, but crashes JODA TIME 1.6 when run west of

```
DateTimeZone America_Los_Angeles =
        new DateTimeZoneBuilder()
                .addCutover(-2147483648, 'w', 1, 1, 0, false, 0)
                .setStandardOffset(-28378000)
                .setFixedSavings("LMT", 0)
                .addCutover(1883, 'w', 11, 18, 0, false, 43200000)
                .setStandardOffset(-28800000)
                .addRecurringSavings("PDT", 3600000, 1918, ...)
                .addRecurringSavings("PST", 0, 1918, ...)
                .addRecurringSavings("PWT", 3600000, 1942, ...)
                .addRecurringSavings("PPT", 3600000, 1945, ...)
                .addRecurringSavings("PST", 0, 1945, ...)
                .addRecurringSavings("PDT", 3600000, 1948, ...)
                .addRecurringSavings("PST", 0, 1949, ...)
                .addRecurringSavings("PDT", 3600000, 1950, ...)
                .addRecurringSavings("PST", 0, 1950, ...)
                .addRecurringSavings("PST", 0, 1962, ...)
                .addRecurringSavings("PST", 0, 1967, ...)
                .addRecurringSavings("PDT", 3600000, 1967, ...)
                .addRecurringSavings("PDT", 3600000, 1974, ...)
                .addRecurringSavings("PDT", 3600000, 1975, ...)
                .addRecurringSavings("PDT", 3600000, 1976, ...)
                .addRecurringSavings("PDT", 3600000, 1987, ...)
                .toDateTimeZone("America/Los_Angeles");
```

Figure 9 Code that crashes JODA TIME when run in the western hemisphere.

Greenwich. This failure is hard to reproduce, as it depends on the current time zone. It is also hard to debug since the shown 23 method calls result in a trace containing close to 484,745 statement executions, covering 1528 of 26,534 lines of code.

JINSI uses capture/replay to reproduce the original failure. This complex mechanism is briefly summarized as follows: (a) it wraps around a component (e.g., the component building time zones) and records the instances of methods calls between the component and its environment and external services, like the operating system's time zone settings; (b) it then replays these captured methods' calls and thus reproduces the original failure. Obviously, in order to enable faithful replay of the method calls, ancillary data also needs to be captured, such as values of parameters, timing, and threading information.

The captured sequence of method calls might not all be relevant to the failure. To address this issue, JINSI applies delta debugging to systematically

```
DateTimeZone America_Los_Angeles =
    new DateTimeZoneBuilder()
        .addRecurringSavings("PDT", 3600000, 1987, ...)
        .toDateTimeZone("America/Los_Angeles");
```
Figure 10 Minimized code that reproduces the failure.

narrow down the sequence of failure-inducing calls. When treating the 23 calls in Fig. 9, delta debugging repeatedly omits one method call after another and reexecutes the program to check whether the failure persists. At the end, a minimal subset remains in which every method call would be relevant to reproduce the failure. Figure 10 shows the resulting minimal subset or minimized failing test, which consists of only three method calls.

As the subsequent step, JINSI computes the backward dynamic slice starting from the point of failure within the minimized failing test. In this manner, JINSI might reduce the number of lines to be inspected by the developer. For instance, in the example above, the minimized failing run covers 193 lines as opposed to 1528, and the slice computed at the point of failure consists of only 54 lines. Therefore, JINSI has narrowed down the search space to 54 lines, i.e., 3.5% of the originally executed lines and 0.2% of the JODA TIME code base. These are clearly better numbers than what is observed with SBFL techniques.

7. FAULT LOCALIZATION BASED ON FORMAL METHODS

Here, we present two representative fault localization techniques that are based on formal methods.

7.1 Using Model Checking to Contrast Failing and Passing Traces

As discussed in Section 2.4, following a property violation, model checking is an approach that returns a counterexample (an error trace) illustrating how the program violated the property. Ball et al. [22] argued that the produced error trace can be too long to be useful for pinpointing the causes of the failure; in addition, more than a single error trace might be needed. To address these two issues, they proposed an approach comprising the following steps:

Step 1 Extracting correct traces from the model checker's internal data structures at the point of the property violation, which are readily available.

Step 2 Identifying the parts of the error trace that are not in any of the correct traces. The identified parts and corresponding program statements are considered suspicious, as suggested by Agrawal *et al.* [51]. (This step addresses the first issue.)

Step 3 Inserting *halt* statements at the suspicious program locations resulting from Step 2 and rerunning the model checker. If a new error trace is found, go to Step 1, otherwise, exit. Note that a halt statement at a given location instructs the model checker to stop exploring paths through that location. (This step addresses the second issue.)

In the code example below, a correct behavior is one in which AcquireLock() and ReleaseLock() are invoked in strict alternation along all paths. When applying model checking, an error trace is produced, namely, $t_1 = \langle 1, 2, 4, 5 \rangle$. Step 1 extracts a single correct trace $t_2 = \langle 1, 2, 3, 5, 6, 7, 9 \rangle$. Step 2 identifies line 4 as suspicious since it is the only part of t_1 that does not appear in t_2, which is a correct judgment since the program is missing a call to ReleaseLock() on line 4. Step 3 inserts a *halt* statement at line 4 and invokes the model checker again, which reports a new error trace $t_3 = \langle 1, 2, 3, 5, 6, 8, 9 \rangle$. Step 2 contrasts t_3 with the correct trace t_2 deeming line 8 as suspicious. Step 3 inserts a *halt* statement at line 8, and the model checker is invoked for the third time yielding no additional error traces and causing the process to stop. To recap, the approach proposed in Ref. [22] identified line 4 and line 8 as suspicious and provided the two corresponding error traces. This information is more helpful than what a model checker alone would provide the developer, which is simply a single error trace.

```
  main() {
1   AcquireLock();
2   if (...)
3     ReleaseLock();
    else
4     ...;
5   AcquireLock();
6   if (...)
7     ReleaseLock();
    else
8     ...;
9   return;
  }
```

7.2 Fault Localization as a Maximum Satisfiability Problem

Given a Boolean formula in conjunctive normal form (CNF), the *Boolean satisfiability problem* asks whether there exists a truth assignment that makes all clauses true, whereas the *maximum satisfiability* (MAX–SAT) *problem* asks what is the maximum number of clauses in the formula that can be simultaneously satisfied by a truth assignment. For example, considering the CNF formula below:

$$(x_0 \vee x_1) \wedge (x_0 \vee \neg x_1) \wedge (x_0 \vee \neg x_1) \wedge (\neg x_0 \vee \neg x_1) \wedge (\text{false} \vee x_2)$$

No truth values assigned to (x_0, x_1, x_2) could satisfy the formula. However, if x_2 is *true*, four of five clauses would be *true* regardless of what is assigned to x_0 and x_1. Therefore, a MAX–SAT solver would determine that the answer is the number four and would provide the possible corresponding maximal set of clauses having a cardinality of 4.

Partial MAX–SAT solvers are a type of solvers that allow users to categorize the clauses within the formula as either *soft* or *hard*. Hard clauses denote the clauses that must be satisfied whereas soft clauses can be left unsatisfied. A partial MAX–SAT instance finds the maximum number of soft clauses that can be satisfied by a truth assignment while satisfying every hard clause.

Jose and Majumdar [62] reduced fault localization to the MAX–SAT problem, given a program, a property p within, and a failing input/trace that violates the property (a counterexample produced by a model checker). Their tool, *BugAssist*, performs the following steps in order to identify a minimal set of suspicious program statements:

Step 1 It constructs TF, a symbolic *trace formula* (in CNF) for the program path executed by the failing input.

Step 2 TF is extended to arrive at the formula $\text{ETF} \equiv I \wedge \text{TF} \wedge p$, where I is a formula that asserts that the input is actually the failing input, and p is the property that got violated by this same failing input. The extended formula ETF is clearly *unsatisfiable* since if I is *true*, p must be *false*.

Step 3 ETF is fed to a partial MAX–SAT solver with I and p categorized as hard, and the clauses in TF as soft. Obviously, the set of soft clauses returned by the solver could not contain all the clauses in TF since TF and ETF are both unsatisfiable. Actually, what interests us is what the solver does *not* return: the *complement* of the maximal set of soft clauses that can be simultaneously satisfied in TF. This complement set contains clauses that are candidates for change to make TF and ETF satisfiable, i.e., to make the failing input satisfy the property p (after a change is made in TF).

Step 4 The clauses in the complement set are mapped to their corresponding program statements, which will make up the minimal set of suspicious program statements.

Consider the C function below which returns a value of an element in `Array` [3]. The input is an index into the array which gets modified at lines 1–4 before being used at line 5 and ultimately at line 6. Line 5 also includes an assertion that guards the bounds of the array. However, there is a bug in this code: if the input `index` is 1, then line 4 assigns it a value of 3 leading to the assertion being violated. Model checking can produce the failing trace and the corresponding failing input, whereas *BugAssist* can pinpoint the bug as described next.

Given the failing trace $\langle 1, 4, 5 \rangle$ and corresponding failing input ($index = 1$), Step 1 constructs the following symbolic trace formula:

$$\begin{aligned} \text{TF} &\equiv \text{guard}_1 = (\text{index}_1 \neq 1) \wedge \\ &\quad \text{index}_2 = 2 \wedge \\ &\quad \text{index}_3 = \text{index}_1 + 2 \wedge \\ &\quad i = \text{guard}_1 ? \text{index}_2 : \text{index}_3 \end{aligned}$$

Step 2 extends TF to arrive at the unsatisfiable formula:

$$\text{ETF} \equiv I \wedge \text{TF} \wedge p \equiv (\text{index}_1 = 1) \wedge \text{TF} \wedge (i < 3)$$

Step 3 converts ETF to CNF and feeds it to a partial MAX-SAT with clauses ($\text{index}_1 = 1$) and ($i < 3$) tagged as hard, and all clauses in TF tagged as soft. The solver returns a set of clauses in TF of maximum cardinality that can be simultaneously satisfied by an assignment satisfying both hard clauses. *BugAssist* identifies the complement of the returned set of soft clauses.

Step 4 maps the complement clauses to their corresponding program statements and as a result considers the statement at line 4 as suspicious. Indeed, a bug fix could be carried out at line 4 by replacing constant 2 by any constant c such that $-2 < c < 2$.

```
    int Array[3];
    int testme(int index)
    {
      ...
1   if (index != 1)   // Potential Bug 2
2     index = 2;
3   else
4     index = index + 2;   // Potential Bug 1
      ...
5   i = index;       assert(i >= 0 && i < 3)
6   return Array[i];
    }
```

In case the developer did not see any potential bug fix on line 4, *BugAssist* can find additional suspicious statements as follows. It can invoke the partial MAX-SAT solver while also tagging the clauses that map to line 4 as hard. In this manner, line 4 will not be part of the solution. Doing so reveals another potential bug location at line 1. Actually, the program could be fixed by either changing the constant value at line 4 or the conditional statement at line 1. In addition, if line 1 was also discarded by the developer and the solver was invoked for a third time, *BugAssist* would determine that no clauses can be removed to make ETF satisfiable, and thus, no further suspicious statements could be found.

Finally, *BugAssist* is clearly more effective than (plain) model checking or the approach proposed by Ball *et al.* [22]. However, as it is the case for most fault localization techniques that are based on formal methods, scalability is a major issue for *BugAssist*.

8. CONCLUSION

The advanced techniques that were presented tried to address known shortcomings in earlier work. Confounding bias was reduced using causal inference methods. Complex profiling elements were used to identify non-trivial faults. The safety reducing effect of CC was mitigated by cleansing test suites. Program states were analyzed as an alternate to structural program constructs. Formal methods and tools were leveraged to achieve higher fault localization accuracy.

One additional advantage of the presented approaches is that they could be employed in tandem since each serves a different purpose. For example, when devising a new spectrum-based fault localization technique: (1) test suites could first be cleansed from coincidentally correct test cases, (2) complex structural profiles could be used and complemented with state profiles, and (3) confounding bias could be reduced.

Finally, it is somewhat surprising that even though fault localization and fault repair complement each other, researchers have tried to address these two tasks independently as if they are unrelated. We hope that this will be no longer the case in the future.

REFERENCES

[1] C. Le Goues, T.V. Nguyen, S. Forrest, W. Weimer, GenProg: a generic method for automated software repair, IEEE Trans. Softw. Eng. 38 (1) (2012) 54–72.

[2] D. Gopinath, M.Z. Malik, S. Khurshid, Specification-based program repair using SAT, in: 17th International Conference on Tools and Algorithms for the Construction and Analysis of Systems (TACAS), Saarbrucken, Germany, 2011, pp. 173–188.

[3] Y. Wei, Y. Pei, C.A. Furia, L.S. Silva, S. Buchholz, B. Meyer, A. Zeller, Automated fixing of programs with contracts, in: Proceedings of the 19th International Symposium on Software Testing and Analysis (ISSTA '10), ACM, New York, NY, 2010, pp. 61–72.

[4] W. Masri, A. Podgurski, Measuring the strength of information flows in programs, ACM Trans. Softw. Eng. Methodol. 19 (2) (2009), Article 5.

[5] W. Masri, A. Podgurski, An empirical study of the relationship between information flow and program dependence, in: 4th International Workshop on Dynamic Analysis (WODA 2006), Shanghai, China, 2006, pp. 73–80.

[6] R. Abou-Assi, W. Masri, Identifying failure-correlated dependence chains, in: 1st International Workshop on Testing and Debugging (TeBug 2011), Berlin, 2011.

[7] W. Masri, A. Podgurski, Algorithms and tool support for dynamic information flow analysis, Inf. Softw. Technol. 51 (2009) 395–404.

[8] W. Masri, N. Nahas, A. Podgurski, Memorized forward computational program slices, in: 17th IEEE International Symposium on Software Reliability Engineering (ISSRE 2006), Raleigh, NC, USA, 2006, pp. 23–32.

[9] W.J. Ghandour, H. Akkary, W. Masri, Leveraging strength-based dynamic information flow analysis to enhance data value prediction, ACM Trans. Archit. Code Optim. 9 (1) (2012), 33 pp (Article 1).

[10] T. Ball, J.R. Larus, Efficient path profiling, in: Proceedings of the 29th International Symposium on Microarchitecture, 1996, pp. 46–57.

[11] W. Masri, A. Podgurski, D. Leon, An empirical study of test case filtering techniques based on exercising information flows, IEEE Trans. Softw. Eng. 33 (7) (2007) 454.

[12] B. Liblit, A. Aiken, A. Zheng, M. Jordan, Bug isolation via remote program sampling, in: Proceedings of the ACM SIGPLAN 2003 International Conference on Programming Language Design and Implementation (PLDI '03), 2003, pp. 141–154.

[13] B. Liblit, M. Naik, A. Zheng, A. Aiken, M. Jordan, Scalable statistical bug isolation, in: Proceedings of the ACM SIGPLAN 2005 International Conference on Programming Language Design and Implementation (PLDI '05), 2005, pp. 15–26.

[14] C. Liu, L. Fei, X. Yan, J. Han, S. Midkiff, Statistical debugging: a hypothesis testing-based approach, IEEE Trans. Softw. Eng. 32 (10) (2006) 831–848.

[15] J. Farjo, R.A. Assi, W. Masri, Reducing execution profiles: techniques and benefits, J. Softw. Test. Verif. Rel. 25 (2) (2014) 115–137.

[16] W. Masri, R. Abou-Assi, M. El-Ghali, N. Fatairi, An empirical study of the factors that reduce the effectiveness of coverage-based fault localization, in: International Workshop on Defects in Large Software Systems, DEFECTS, Chicago, IL, 2009.

[17] C. Parnin, A. Orso, Are automated debugging techniques actually helping programmers? in: Proceedings of the 2011 International Symposium on Software Testing and Analysis, 2011, pp. 199–209.

[18] J. Pearl, Causal inference in statistics: an overview, Stat. Surv. 3 (2009) 96–146.

[19] J. Pearl, Causality: Models, Reasoning, and Inference, Cambridge University Press, San Francisco, CA, 2000.

[20] J.S. Neyman, On the application of probability theory to agricultural experiments. Essay on principles, Stat. Sci. 5 (1923) 465–480.

[21] D. Rubin, Estimating causal effects of treatments in randomized and nonrandomized studies, J. Educ. Psychol. 66 (1974) 688–701.

[22] T. Ball, M. Naik, S.K. Rajamani, From symptom to cause: localizing errors in counterexample traces, in: Proceedings of the 30th ACM SIGPLAN-SIGACT Symposium on Principles of Programming Languages (POPL '03), New York, NY, USA, 2003, pp. 97–105.

[23] W.E. Wong, V. Debroy, A Survey of Software Fault Localization, Technical Report UTDCS-45-09, Department of Computer Science, The University of Texas at Dallas, 2009.

[24] J. Jones, M.J. Harrold, J. Stasko, Visualization of test information to assist fault localization, in: Proceedings of the 24th International Conference on Software Engineering, 2001, pp. 467–477.

[25] J. Jones, J. Bowring, M.J. Harrold, Debugging in parallel, in: International Symposium on Software Testing and Analysis (ISSTA), London, UK, 2007, pp. 16–26.

[26] T. Denmat, M. Ducassé, O. Ridoux, Data mining and crosschecking of execution traces, in: International Conference on Automated Software Engineering, ASE, Long Beach, CA, 2005, pp. 396–399.

[27] G.K. Baah, A. Podgurski, M.J. Harrold, Causal inference for statistical fault localization, in: Proceedings of the 19th International Symposium on Software Testing and Analysis, 2010, pp. 73–84.

[28] R. Abreu, P. Zoeteweij, A.J.C. van Gemund, An evaluation of similarity coefficients for software fault localization, in: Proceedings of the 12th Pacific Rim International Symposium on Dependable Computing, 2006, pp. 39–46.

[29] M. Renieris, S. Reiss, Fault localization with nearest-neighbor queries, in: Proceedings of the 18th IEEE Conference on Automated Software Engineering, 2003, pp. 30–39.

[30] H. Cleve, A. Zeller, Locating causes of program failures, in: Proceedings of the International Conference on Software Engineering, St. Louis, Missouri, 2005, pp. 342–351.

[31] W.E. Wong, V. Debroy, B. Choi, A family of code coverage-based heuristics for effective fault localization, J. Syst. Softw. 83 (2010) 188–208.

[32] W. Masri, J. Daou, R. Abou-Assi, State profiling of internal variables, in: Regression/ICST 2014, Cleveland, 2014.

[33] J. Voas, PIE: a dynamic failure-based technique, IEEE Trans. Softw. Eng. 18 (8) (1992) 717–727.

[34] W. Masri, R. Abou Assi, Prevalence of coincidental correctness and mitigation of its impact on fault-localization, ACM Trans. Softw. Eng. Methodol. 23 (1) (2014) 8.

[35] G.K. Baah, A. Podgurski, M.J. Harrold, Mitigating the confounding effects of program dependences for effective fault localization, in: Proceedings of the 19th ACM SIGSOFT FSE Symposium and the 13th European Conference on Foundations of Software Engineering, 2011, pp. 146–156.

[36] G. Shu, B. Sun, A. Podgurski, F. Cao, MFL: method-level fault localization with causal inference, in: Proceedings of the 2013 IEEE 6th International Conference on Software Testing, Verification and Validation, 2013, pp. 124–133.

[37] Z. Bai, G. Shu, A. Podgurski, NUMFL: localizing faults in numerical software using a value-based causal model, in: 8th IEEE International Conference on Software Testing, Verification and Validation, 2015.

[38] W. Masri, Fault localization based on information flow coverage, J. Softw. Test. Verif. Rel. 20 (2) (2010) 121–147.

[39] W. Masri, R. Abou-Assi, Cleansing test suites from coincidental correctness to enhance fault-localization, in: 3rd International Conference on Software Testing, Verification and Validation (ICST 2010), Paris, France, 2010.

[40] J. Rößler, G. Fraser, A. Zeller, A. Orso, Isolating failure causes through test case generation, in: Proceedings of the 2012 International Symposium on Software Testing and Analysis, 2012.

[41] G. Fraser, A. Arcuri, Evolutionary generation of whole test suites, in: Proceedings of the 11th International Conference on Quality Software, 2011, pp. 31–40.

[42] J. Xuan, M. Monperrus, Test case purification for improving fault localization, in: Proceedings of the 22nd ACM SIGSOFT International Symposium on Foundations of Software Engineering, 2014, pp. 52–63.

[43] W. Jin, A. Orso, BugRedux: reproducing field failures for in-house debugging, in: Proceedings of the 34th International Conference on Software Engineering, 2012, pp. 474–484.

[44] W. Jin, A. Orso, F^3: fault localization for field failures, in: Proceedings of the 2013 International Symposium on Software Testing and Analysis, 2013, pp. 213–223.

[45] R. Abreu, P. Zoeteweij, A.J.C. van Gemund, An observation-based model for fault localization, in: Proceedings of the 2008 International Workshop on Dynamic Analysis, 2008, pp. 64–70.

[46] S. Yoo, M. Harman, D. Clark, Fault localization prioritization: comparing information-theoretic and coverage-based approaches, ACM Trans. Softw. Eng. Methodol. 22 (3) (2013) 19.

[47] M. Weiser, Program slicing, in: Proceedings of the 5th International Conference on Software Engineering (ICSE '81), IEEE Press, Piscataway, NJ, 1981, pp. 439–449.

[48] F. Tip, A survey of program slicing techniques, J. Program. Lang. 3 (3) (1995) 121–189.

[49] H. Agrawal, J. Horgan, Dynamic program slicing, ACM SIGPLAN Not. 25 (6) (1990) 246–256.

[50] W. Masri, Exploiting the empirical characteristics of program dependences for improved forward computation of dynamic slice, Empir. Softw. Eng. 13 (2008) 369–399.

[51] H. Agrawal, J. Horgan, S. London, W. Wong, Fault localization using execution slices and dataflow sets, in: IEEE International Symposium on Software Reliability Engineering, ISSRE, 1995, pp. 143–151.

[52] D. Binkley, N. Gold, M. Harman, An empirical study of static program slice size, ACM Trans. Softw. Eng. Methodol. 16 (2) (2007), Article 8.

[53] Wisconsin Program-Slicing Tool 1.1 Reference Manual, Wisconsin Alumni Research Foundation. http://www.cs.wisc.edu/wpis/slicing_tool/slicing-manual.ps, November 2000.

[54] S. Horwitz, B. Liblit, M. Polishchuk, Better debugging via output tracing and callstack-sensitive slicing, IEEE Trans. Softw. Eng. 36 (1) (2010) 7–19.

[55] D. Binkley, Semantics guided regression test cost reduction, IEEE Trans. Softw. Eng. 23 (8) (1997) 498–516.

[56] S. Horwitz, T.W. Reps, David Binkley: interprocedural slicing using dependence graphs, ACM Trans. Program. Lang. Syst. 12 (1) (1990) 26–60.

[57] R. Santelices, Y. Zhang, S. Jiang, H. Cai, Y.-J. Zhang, Quantitative program slicing: separating statements by relevance, in: Proceedings of the 2013 International Conference on Software Engineering, 2013.

[58] A. Zeller, R. Hildebrandt, Simplifying and isolating failure-inducing input, IEEE Trans. Softw. Eng. 28 (2) (2002) 183–200.

[59] A. Zeller, Isolating cause-effect chains from computer programs, in: Symposium on Foundations of Software Engineering (FSE), 2002, pp. 1–10.
[60] T. Zimmermann, A. Zeller, Visualizing memory graphs, in: Proceedings of the International Seminar on Software Visualization, Dagstuhl Castle, Germany, 2001, pp. 191–204.
[61] M. Burger, A. Zeller, Minimizing reproduction of software failures, in: Proceedings of the 2011 International Symposium on Software Testing and Analysis, 2011.
[62] M. Jose, R. Majumdar, Cause clue clauses: error localization using maximum satisfiability, in: Proceedings of the 32nd ACM SIGPLAN Conference on Programming Language Design and Implementation (PLDI '11), ACM, New York, NY, 2011, pp. 437–446.

ABOUT THE AUTHORS

Wes Masri is an Associate Professor in the ECE Department at the American University of Beirut. His research interest is in software engineering, primarily in software testing and analysis. He received his PhD in Computer Engineering from Case Western Reserve University in 2005, M.S. from Penn State in 1988, and B.S. also from Case Western Reserve University in 1986. He also spent over 15 years in the U.S. software industry mainly as a software architect and developer. Some of the industries he was involved in include medical imaging, middleware, telecom, genomics, semiconductor, document imaging, and financial.

CHAPTER FOUR

Recent Advances in Automatic Black-Box Testing

Leonardo Mariani*, Mauro Pezzè*,†, Daniele Zuddas†

*University of Milano–Bicocca, Department of Informatics, Systems and Communication, Italy
†Università della Svizzera italiana (USI), Faculty of Informatics, Lugano, Switzerland

Contents

Abstract

Research in black-box testing has produced impressive results in the past 40 years, addressing many aspects of the problem that span from integration with the development process, to test case generation and execution. In the past few years, the research in this area has focused mostly on the automation of black-box approaches to improve applicability and scalability. This chapter surveys the recent advances in *automatic black-box testing*, covering contributions from 2010 to 2014, presenting the main research results and discussing the research trends.

Advances in Computers, Volume 99
ISSN 0065-2458
http://dx.doi.org/10.1016/bs.adcom.2015.04.002

1. INTRODUCTION

Software testing and in particular black-box testing has attracted the attention of practitioners and researchers since the late sixties as witnessed by the seminal Myer's book on testing [1]. Despite the enormous progresses, there are still several open problems that are the targets of recent research activities.

In the first 40 years, research and development have produced impressive results in test case generation [2] and execution [3], black-box [4], white box [5] and fault-based testing approaches [6] and regression testing [7], and have investigated complementarities and synergies between program testing and analysis [8], as summarized in a recent book by Pezzè and Young [9].

The recent research in software testing, and in particular in black-box testing, has specifically focused on automation that has become a prominent problem due to the complexity of software systems and the effort required by testing and validation activities. While test automation has traditionally focused on test process management [10], test execution [11], structural testing [12] and regression testing [13], in the past years, research has increasingly focused on automatic black-box testing.

In this chapter, we survey the recent progresses in automatic black-box testing, covering contributions from 2010 to 2014. This survey discusses techniques that (1) are fully or mostly automatic (for instance, limiting the manual intervention to the definition of few configuration parameters), (2) do not require accessing the internals of the software under test (for instance, do not require access to the source code or to coverage data), and (3) are designed to reveal functional problems.

We have logically organized the most relevant recent advances in automatic software testing in four classes of approaches: random testing, model-based testing (MBT), testing with complex inputs, and combinatorial interaction testing. Each class has obtained a different level of attention by the community and approaches belonging to each class have reached different levels of maturity: some classes of approaches have been investigated only recently and their progresses are in a preliminary stage, for instance testing with complex inputs, while other classes of approaches have improved over the years and well consolidated research areas, and have reached industrial maturity, for instance MBT.

Among the many interesting recent research directions, there are a few novel approaches that can promisingly lead to influential solutions in automatic black-box testing:

- Heuristics for random testing: Random testing is a testing technique known for its simplicity and degree of automation, but also for its limited effectiveness. Recent results have greatly improved the effectiveness of random testing by introducing proper heuristics for efficiently exploring the input space.

- MBT from inferred models: MBT is a popular and effective approach, with an effectiveness limited by the cost of producing high quality models that can be used for test case generation. Recent relevant research in MBT has investigated the use of dynamic models, that is, models automatically derived from program execution. Using such models for generating test cases directly from the artifact under test is expected to mitigate the cost of producing high quality models. In a few years, approaches exploiting automatically generated models rather than manually specified models may succeed in providing an interesting tradeoff between costs and effectiveness.

- Testing with semantically complex inputs: The problem of generating syntactically complex inputs has been already investigated in many approaches. However, modern software systems require test cases that use not only syntactically complex inputs but also semantically legal values. For example, a map application requires proper location addresses to provide meaningful outputs. A few recent approaches have explored the problem of automatically generating semantically complex values. This kind of technology might influence future research in automatic generation of test inputs.

The rest of the chapter presents our survey of recent advances in automatic black-box testing, and gives insights about approaches, results and trends. Section 2 overviews the recent advances in automatic black-box testing. Sections 3–6 illustrate recent advances in random testing, MBT, generation of complex inputs, and combinatorial interaction testing, respectively. Section 7 summarizes the main contributions and indicates the current open research directions.

2. OVERVIEW

Recent advances in automatic black-box testing have produced relevant results in four main areas: random testing (RT), MBT, testing with complex inputs, and combinatorial interaction testing (CIT). Figure 1 illustrates the main advances that we discuss in this chapter, and presents the taxonomy that we use.

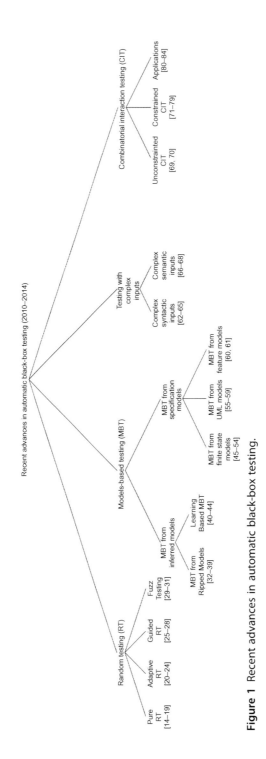

Figure 1 Recent advances in automatic black-box testing.

Random testing is a research area that is gaining increasing attention, after being nearly completely ignored for almost two decades. Random testing has attracted a lot of research interest from 1980s to 1990s, but without producing conclusive results [85, 86]. In the recent years, empirical and theoretical studies have contributed to clarify the role and the (nontrivial) effectiveness of random testing [14–16, 18]. More importantly, the research community has recently defined several approaches that extend random test case generation with informed and heuristic decisions that dramatically improved the capability to explore and sample the execution space [20, 21, 27, 30, 87, 88]. These algorithms, often referred to as randomized test case generation algorithms, since they include a significant number of random decisions but are not purely random, demonstrated their effectiveness and will likely influence research in black-box test case generation for the next few years.

MBT is a well-established and active research area, as suggested by the many papers published since the early seventies and from 2010 to 2014. We identified two main trends in MBT research and development: MBT from inferred modes, which is based on the novel idea of automatically deriving the models that can support test case generation from the application under test [32, 35, 40, 44]; and MBT from specification models, which consists in further developing and improving the well-established approaches about deriving test cases from specification models [45–47, 52, 55, 57, 61].

Techniques for deriving models from software artifacts have been studied and applied for a long time, but models dynamically derived from program executions have been only recently generated with the specific purpose of being used as software specifications. Modern approaches to generate specification models are often referred to as *specification mining techniques*. Examples of well-known specification mining techniques are Daikon [89], GK-tail [90], and Adabu [91]. Models obtained with specification mining techniques have been exploited for test case generation in multiple contexts, such as unit testing [92], integration testing [93], and system testing [94]. Recent approaches in black-box MBT have exploited models inferred from software mostly in the context of system testing [32, 33, 44]. The definition of testing approaches working with inferred models is a promising research direction that can perspectively overcome issues related to the costs of defining models that typically affect MBT.

Recent advances in testing based on specification models deal with three classes of popular models: finite state models [45, 48], UML models [56, 57], and feature models [60, 61]. Differently from testing based on inferred models, research in testing based on specification models has mostly focused on consolidating technical and scientific results, and on investigating specific aspects related to test case generation, for instance on generating optimal test suites from finite state models [52, 95].

Testing with complex inputs is a novel research area which aims is to generate inputs for functionalities that require complex data to be executed. Inputs might be complex for both syntactic reasons, for instance a method that requires a complex graph of objects as parameter, and semantic reasons, for instance a form that requires an address in a real city of a real country. The generation of syntactically complex inputs has been investigated only recently. After the early work on KORAT that addressed the construction of nontrivial data structures [96], recently many researchers have proposed new interesting approaches, due to the increasing popularity of applications that process real-world data, for instance gps systems and map services. This is a novel and promising research direction that will likely gain increasing attention, to a large extent due to the continuously increasing diffusion of software services that interact with physical and social systems.

Combinatorial interaction testing (CIT) has been introduced in the early nineties as a way to find a compromise between effort and effectiveness when testing interactions between multiple parameters [97–99]. Despite the long history of CIT, the research community is still actively working on the problem of generating test cases covering interactions between parameters. While little activity has been recorded for unconstrained CIT, a number of approaches have been recently defined to address the case of constrained CIT, in particular CIT problems proposed with a set of logical constraints to be satisfied [71, 74].

3. RANDOM TESTING

Random testing (RT) is a black-box software testing technique, where the core idea is to test a program by executing a set of randomly generated inputs. The recent research has improved random testing in four different ways that we summarize as: Pure RT, Adaptive RT, Guided RT, and Fuzz testing, as illustrated in Fig. 2.

Pure RT is the simplest approach to test case generation. It works by randomly generating independent test inputs, and only requires to know the interface of the SUT to be applied [85]. The main strengths of Pure RT are the low implementation cost and the limited time for generating test

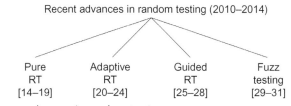

Figure 2 Recent advances in random testing.

cases. Another advantage of Pure RT is to be unbiased, since every test input has the same probability to be generated. Although the design of Pure RT approaches is a relatively active area, researchers are still studying the effectiveness of RT, compared to other testing approaches.

Differently from Pure RT, where each input has the same probability to be selected, faults are not evenly distributed in the input space. It is that failing inputs, i.e., inputs that cause the SUT to fail, tend to be clustered together creating contiguous failure regions [100, 101]. This implies that also nonfailure regions are contiguous. These intuitions led to the definition of *adaptive random testing* (ART), first introduced by Chen *et al.* in 2001 [88]. The key idea of ART is to sample the execution space by executing only those randomly generated test inputs that are far enough from the already generated inputs. This strategy increases the capability of the technique to evenly sample the execution space, compared to pure random testing, and increases the chance to hit failure regions. The research community is still actively studying different means of generating diverse test cases.

A novel and extremely prolific approach to RT is *guided RT*. The idea of Guided RT is to combine random decisions with heuristics and information about the software under test to make the testing process more effective. For instance, Randoop is a well-known and successful test case generation technique that dynamically adapts the test case generation process according to the results produced by the previously executed test cases [87]. Recent advances in this area mainly consisted of new techniques and heuristics to extend the applicability and effectiveness of Guided RT.

Finally, *fuzz testing* is a testing approach that aims at stimulating a SUT with semi-valid inputs, usually obtained by randomly mutating valid inputs [102]. For instance, a PDF reader can be fuzz tested by executing the application with a PDF file where some bits have been randomly flipped. Fuzz testing has already demonstrated its effectiveness in several domains, in particular the security domain, and is still widely studied and experimented.

In the following we discuss recent advances in these four areas.

3.1 Pure Random Testing

Although Random Testing techniques have a long history, they are still subjects of studies and experiments. In particular, their effectiveness has been recently studied both theoretically and empirically, and they have been compared to systematic approaches.

It is well known that RT has a little cost, but its fault-revealing ability is still controversial. Recently Oriol proposed to use the Michaelis–Menten equation to estimate the number of unique failures that can be detected with a given number of random tests [14]. The equation, which uses the number of randomly generated test cases and parameters that depend on the test code, has been evaluated with more than 6000 Java classes and against previous empirical studies with a correlation over to 80%.

The effectiveness of RT has been studied from a slightly different perspective by Arcuri *et al.* [15, 16], who studied the capability of RT to cover test targets, rather than looking at failures. Through a formal analysis, Arcuri *et al.* identified a nontrivial lower bound for the expected number of random test cases needed to cover a set of test targets, and showed that the best performance is achieved when all the test targets have the same probability of being covered, which is not usually the case in software systems. Moreover, they discovered that RT can scale up better than certain systematic techniques that are fast with small units, but do not efficiently scale to large systems.

Boheme and Paul compared RT and systematic techniques in a formal way [18], reporting results consistent with the study of Arcuri *et al.* In particular, Boheme and Paul discovered that there exist a size after which systematic approaches, although feasible, are less cost-effective than RT.

Finally, researchers are still investigating the effectiveness of RT compared to systematic approaches, consistently obtaining results that confirm the effectiveness of RT. A study with 13 container classes showed that RT and Shape Abstraction [103] achieve similar predicate coverage and mutation score, but RT is significantly less expensive than Shape Abstraction [17]. Another recent study compared RT to CIT techniques (see Section 6) demonstrating that RT can be preferable to CIT in many circumstances [19].

3.2 Adaptive Random Testing

ART is designed to improve RT following the intuition that diverse test cases are more likely to reveal failures than similar ones. A standard instantiation of ART consists of generating test cases using a normal distribution and then discarding the ones that do not have the required distance from the ones already generated. This strategy generates diverse test cases but introduces a significant computational overhead compared to RT [104].

Recent results focused on the definition of more effective implementations of ART and on empirically studying the effectiveness of ART. Liu et al. introduced the notion of test profile [20]. The idea is to use the already executed test cases to define a probability distribution, namely the test profile, which is then used to guide the random selection of the next test case that will be executed. Intuitively, the probability distribution assigns each test case with a probability to be selected that depends on the distance from the already executed tests (close points have smaller probability to be executed than distant points). Results show that this strategy has lower computational cost and higher effectiveness than standard ART. Shahbazi et al. suggested the use of Centroidal Voronoi Tessellations to generate test cases evenly spread in the input space with a cost similar to RT [21], and Liu et al. implemented ART for sequences of events using the Levenshtein distance to compute distance between test cases [22].

The empirical results on the effectiveness of ART are still controversial. In a recent survey, Chen et al. [23] discussed the advantages of ART compared to RT using F-measure, which measures the number of test cases needed in average to reveal the first fault. In another paper, Chen et al. demonstrated that the improvement of the F-measure obtained with ART is close to the best improvement that can be obtained without specific information about the failure regions [105], while studies of Arcuri et al. provided opposite evidences [24]. Although ART performs better than RT according to the F-measure, which depends on the number of executed test cases, it performs definitely worse when considering time, which is advocated as a more relevant measure of the cost of the technique. However, the studies of Arcuri et al. did not consider the technique by Shahbazi et al. [21], which has a cost comparable to RT. It would be interesting to extend these studies to this technique.

3.3 Guided Random Testing

Guided random testing (GRT) is an extremely promising and novel research direction, which aims is to augment random testing with heuristics and information about the software under test to improve the testing process.

There are several heterogeneous GRT techniques that depend on the specific target of testing. For instance, Ballerina is a technique for unit testing of multithreaded code [25], which creates the object under test, executes a random sequence of method calls using a modified version of Randoop [87], and then uses two threads to execute the same methods and cover interleavings that may detect concurrency bugs.

Wei *et al.* used GRT to address the problem of selecting the objects to be tested with RT in object oriented programs with contracts [26]. The approach exploits method pre- and postconditions to select objects covering different configurations, which are then tested with RT. This strategy dramatically increases the effectiveness of RT.

An interesting recent implementation of GRT is swarm testing [27], which is based on the innovative idea to generate random test cases using only a subset of the features, for instance the methods, available for test case generation. The intuition is that when using pure random testing, it might be extremely difficult to generate particular fault revealing test cases, such as a test case that calls 64 times method "open" without any call to method "close" in-between. To generate such test cases, swarm testing divides the time budget in slots where random testing is applied to a selection of features, for instance a subset of methods, thus increasing the likelihood to exercise interesting combinations of small sets of features.

Random test cases, such as the test cases generated with GRT, might be hard to debug due to the lack of meaningful identifiers and the lack of an explicitly purpose for the tests, compared to manual test cases. However, a recent study by Ceccato *et al.* revealed that random test cases are not harder to debug than manual test cases, on the contrary, due to their intrinsic simplicity, are often easier to debug [28].

3.4 Fuzz Testing

Fuzz testing is a testing approach, derived from RT, that aims to stimulate a SUT with semi-valid inputs [102]. Recently fuzz testing has been applied to client–server security protocols and virtual machines, as well as to the definition of a novel coverage criterion.

The application of Fuzz testing to security protocols and virtual machines is based on a same, commonly adopted, high level approach: collect valid inputs and mutate them to obtain novel inputs. Contributions are limited to the specific strategy used to mutate the inputs. In the case of client–server security protocols, fuzz testing has been implemented by capturing and mutating the messages exchanged between the client and the server [29]. In the case of virtual machines, fuzz testing has been implemented by capturing and mutating CPU states [31].

To measure the effectiveness of fuzz testing, Tsankov *et al.* recently defined semi-valid coverage, a novel criterion that measures how many semi-valid inputs (i.e., inputs that satisfy all correctness constraints but one) have been covered during a testing session [30]. This coverage criterion demonstrated to be more effective for fuzz testing than classic coverage criteria.

4. MODEL-BASED TESTING

MBT is a testing approach that uses models of software systems to guide test case generation [106, 107]. The key idea of MBT is to use a model that represents the intended behavior of a Software Under Test (SUT) to produce test cases that verify the conformance between the SUT and the specification.

A key benefit of MBT is the possibility to (formally) define criteria for effectively sampling the behavior of the SUT, in many cases even supporting the quantification of the thoroughness of the test suite. Unfortunately, defining useful models may be difficult and expensive, and the experience and ability of the software engineers who define the models play a critical role on the success of MBT.

We can distinguish two main approaches to MBT, as illustrated in Fig. 3: the recently investigated *MBT from inferred models*, which is the case of models derived from the SUT implementation, and the classic and still studied *MBT from specification models*, which is the case of models defined from the SUT specification.

Model inferred *from the program execution* are both generated automatically from the execution, and thus do not need human effort, and provide a description of the systems at the same abstraction level of the implementation, and thus deriving test cases does not require a mapping between the specification and the implementation. On the other hand, models derived from the program execution are partial, and thus the generated test cases cannot verify functionalities that have not been implemented. Moreover, failure detection is usually limited by the effectiveness of implicit oracles, which are oracles that can only capture failures like crashes and uncaught exceptions [108]. In fact, since the model reflects the behavior of the implementation, it is not possible to use the model to distinguish if a response of the SUT is correct or wrong.

MBT from inferred models is extremely useful in the many cases where MBT is difficult to apply due to lack of complete, consistent and updated

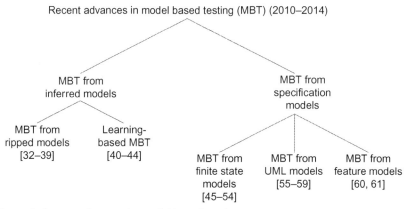

Figure 3 Recent advances in model-based testing.

models. Making MBT more practical and easier to apply is one of the main open challenges, and the recent trend of automatically extracting models from the application under test is an interesting first step in this direction. So far, MBT from inferred models has focused on system testing with an effectiveness limited to detecting faults that cause easy-to-detect failures, such as program crashes [33, 34, 109]. Another major open challenge is extending MBT from inferred models to a broader set of testing levels and faults.

When the model is obtained *from the specification*, test cases generated from the model can be used to check both correctness (i.e., to check if the SUT responds to stimuli as specified in the model) and completeness (i.e., to check if the SUT implements every behavior in the model). However, since the model is usually specified at a different abstraction level than the implementation, some effort might be necessary to turn the test case generated from the model into executable test cases.

MBT from specification models is a mature area that has demonstrated to be extremely effective when proper specification models are provided. This is also witnessed by the growing popularity of MBT in industry [110–113] and the increasing number of commercial tools available, such as Conformiq Designer [114], Smartesing CertifyIt [115, 116] and Microsoft Spec-Explorer [117].

Recent experimental results have confirmed the effectiveness of classic MBT from specification models. For instance, Schulze *et al.* compared MBT and manual testing, and discovered that MBT can reveal more faults than manual testing, although some specific tasks are still easier with manual testing [118]. Recent studies also demonstrated a comparable effort when debugging test cases generated with MBT and manual testing [119].

In the past 5 years research in MBT from specification models has been mostly incremental focusing on the definition of MBT approaches that target variants of models commonly supported in MBT, for instance timed automata [45], and specific aspects of test case generation, for instance generation of optimal test suites [52, 95].

In the rest of this section we discuss more in details the recent solutions to MBT, distinguishing approaches that work with inferred models and specification models.

4.1 MBT from Inferred Models

MBT can be applied only when a model of the application under test is available. In practice, specification models are often unavailable, and when they are available they are often outdated and incomplete. This significantly hinders the applicability of MBT.

To overcome these limitations, researchers have studied MBT techniques working with inferred models. Inferred models are not real specification models because they describe the actual behavior of the application rather than describing its intended behavior. Even if this difference might be significant in some cases, for instance inferred models cannot contain information about features that developers have not implemented, these models could still be used effectively in MBT.

Results produced in the past 5 years focused on system level testing of applications with a Graphical User Interface (GUI). This is mainly due to the availability of algorithms and technologies for analyzing GUIs that ease the extraction of GUI models that can serve the purpose of MBT testing.

In the following, we present recent achievements organized in two logical groups: *MBT from Ripped Models* and *Learning-based MBT*.

MBT from Ripped Models includes approaches that first automatically extract a model from a SUT and then use the model for testing. Learning-Based MBT includes approaches that infer a model of the SUT, generate test cases from the model, and keep iterating between these two phases, without always distinguishing between learning and testing.

4.1.1 MBT from Ripped Models

MBT from ripped models works by first extracting a model of the SUT, and then generating test cases from the extracted model. The most popular models used to this end are GUI models, that is models that represent the behavior of the SUT using GUI states and events. In the following, we illustrate the steps that typically compose the test case generation process.

1. *Extract a model*: The first step is extracting a model of the behavior of the SUT. This could be done by analyzing the code, or by running the system and analyzing the execution traces.

2. *Choose a test selection criterion*: In general, a model specifies an infinite number of behaviors, and thus an infinite number of test cases would be necessary to fully cover a model. To select a finite number of good test cases, testers can use a *test selection criterion*, which identifies a finite sets of test cases that can provide a certain confidence over the correctness of the system, once they are executed. Depending on the level of confidence that must be achieved, the selection criteria generate a variable number of test cases (usually higher confidence requires longer test execution time).

3. *Generate test cases*: In this step, automatic test case generation techniques are used to generate test cases from a given model according to the chosen test selection criterion.

4. *Run tests*: The test suite is executed and the program failures reported to the user.

Recent work has focused on steps 1 and 2, proposing novel models to represent the behavior of the SUT and novel criteria for generating test cases. While little attention has been paid to the generation and execution of test cases, which are usually considered mechanical and unchallenging steps. However, when the environment of the SUT is not trivial, for instance consider embedded, distributed, and database-intensive systems, specific techniques that can cope with the environment need to be defined. We expect that greater attention will be devoted to test execution in the future.

GUI Ripping extracts models interacting with the GUI of the SUT by executing events, for instance, clicking buttons and menu in a depth-first style [32]. In practice GUI Ripping traverses an application recursively and extracts two models: a *GUI Tree* and an *Event-Flow Graph (EFG)*. The GUI tree represents the hierarchical nature of the GUI. Each node in the tree represents windows as the list of the widgets available in such windows and their properties. The EFG model represents ordering between events. A node in the EFG is an executable GUI event and an edge from node *e1* to node *e2* indicates that *e2* can be executed immediately after *e1*. The EFG model is a valid source of test cases because new sequences of interaction can be conveniently generated by producing test cases that cover elements in the graph, such as nodes, and edges [32].

The idea of generating test cases from an EFG has recently evolved into test case generation from an *Event Semantic Interaction Graph* (ESIG), a graph similar to an EFG, but where dependencies between events have a different semantics. An edge from node *e1* to node *e2* indicates that *e1* influences the behavior of *e2*. The ESIG is generated with a ripping process similar to the one used for EFG [109]. The notion of semantics dependency between events demonstrated to be more useful for testing than the notion of dependency used in EFGs.

The idea of ripping, initially introduced for desktop applications, has been also explored in other domains. Amalfitano *et al.* defined a GUI ripping solution for Android applications [33]. Mesbah *et al.* defined an approach, called CRAWLAJAX, for building a state machine model of a Web application under test by exploring its GUI [120]. Interestingly, Schur *et al.* have investigated the problem of generating models of Web applications when multiple users might be present [34]. Their approach is implemented in the ProCrawl tool, which has the capability to interact with an application using multiple types of users, obtaining a deeper exploration of the business logic.

In the past years, several testing approaches have studied MBT from inferred models in contexts different than desktop applications, such as natural and Web interfaces. In particular, Hunt *et al.* addressed the problem of testing programs based on natural user interfaces, for instance a Kinect interface, by training a Markov Chain Model with real common gestures and skeletal positions, and using the model to synthesize new gestures, i.e., test cases [39]. Mesbah *et al.* have defined a test case generation strategy and an oracle strategy, based on the manual design of generic and application-specific invariants, that can reveal important classes of faults in Web applications [35]. Thummalapenta *et al.* have investigated the same problem considering business rules instead of invariants [36]. Black-box coverage criteria have been also recently defined to assess black-box techniques. For instance, DOM coverage has been defined to evaluate the thoroughness of black-box testing techniques for Web applications [121].

Other papers have investigated MBT from inferred models as means of detecting cross browser incompatibilities, that is an application that has different behaviors on different browsers [37, 38].

4.1.2 Learning-Based MBT

The effectiveness of the techniques relying on ripped models significantly depends on the completeness of the models. However, the ripping process is intrinsically a time-bounded, limited, and simple exploration of the execution space that may miss many relevant cases. Learning-based MBT addresses this issue by combining model inference and test case generation in an iterative way.

The idea is that the test cases generated to test the software can be used to augment the model, which in turn can be used to generate additional test cases, and so forth, for a given amount of time or until the process converges. In particular, the general process works as follows:

1. *Run the initial set of test cases*: A set of initial test cases are executed on the SUT.
2. *Augment the model*: The behavior shown by the SUT during test case execution is used to augment the current model using a learning algorithm (the first time the model is generated from scratch).
3. *Generate test cases*: The model is used to generate additional test cases. If no test cases can be generated, the testing process terminates.
4. *Execute the test cases*: The test cases are executed. If the SUT fails, the failure is reported to the user. If more time is available for testing, the process continues with step 2.

This general process indicated above has been recently instantiated in specific domains, such as reactive systems [40, 41] and numerical software [42], and reconsidered in a form that merges in an indistinguishable way testing and model inference [43, 44].

In the case of both reactive systems and numerical software, model checking technology has been used to generate test cases. The user is supposed to specify a set of requirements using a formal language. At every iteration, the requirements are checked on the model and the counter-examples are used as test cases that either reveal a fault, if the system fails when executing the test, or cover a behavior that can augment the model, if the system does not fail. In the specific case of reactive systems, researchers have investigated the use of Kripke structures, as a model, and formal requirements specified using temporal logic [40, 41]. In the case of numerical software, researchers have investigated the use of Piecewise polynomial models and formal requirements expressed as Hoare triples [42].

AutoBlackTest (ABT) implements a different approach to learning-based MBT [43, 44]. ABT is a system testing approach that merges test case generation and learning in a loop so close that the two phases become indistinguishable. In particular, ABT interacts with an application and after every interaction, for instance after clicking a button, updates the model, which is used to decide the next action to execute. The sequences of actions that are executed encode the test activity. Thus, the same sequences of actions are used to learn the model and test the application. ABT uses Q-Learning [122] to both represent the behavior of the application under test and select the actions that must be executed to test the SUT. Q-learning allows ABT to learn the complex sequences of actions that lead to useful computations and insist with these sequences to adequately test the relevant features of the SUT.

4.2 MBT from Specification Models

When the model is provided by the user, the test case generation process is defined as follows:

1. *Define model*: The first step is defining a model from the specification. Since a model is an abstraction, it may neglect certain aspects, for instance a model may represent the functional behavior of a system while neglecting timing and security aspects. Test case generation will clearly concern only the aspect represented in the model.

2. *Choose test selection criterion*: In general, a model specifies an infinite number of behaviors, and thus an infinite number of test cases would be necessary to fully cover a model. To select a finite number of good test cases, testers can use a *test selection criterion*, which identifies the sets of test cases that can provide a certain confidence over the correctness of the system, once they are executed. Depending on the level of confidence that must be achieved, the selection criteria generate a variable number of test cases (usually higher confidence requires longer test execution time).

3. *Generate test cases*: In this step, automatic test case generation techniques are used to generate test cases from a given model according to a test selection criterion. For instance, if the criterion requires covering all the transitions in a finite state machines, the generated test cases will cover every transition in the model at least once.

4. *Make test cases executable*: MBT produces test cases at the same abstraction level of the models; therefore the test cases may not be directly executable on the SUT, but need to be adapted and completed with additional implementation details to make them executable. The adaptation usually requires manual intervention.

5. *Run tests*: The test suite is executed. The output produced by each test case is compared to the expected output according to the model. Failures are reported to the user.

Note that this process differs from MBT from Ripped Model on two aspects: here the model is defined by the user, while in MBT from Ripped Model the model is extracted from the software; and here the test cases need to be turned into executable test cases, while the test cases generated from Ripped Models are usually directly executable.

Recent research in this area mostly focused on the definition of testing techniques for finite state models, UML models, and feature models, while little attention has been paid to the generation of executable test cases. In the following sections, we discuss major contributions in the area.

4.2.1 MBT from Finite State Models

Finite state models, finite state machines in particular, are frequently used to specify the behaviors of software systems. For instance, they have been used to describe the behavior of embedded systems [45], communication protocols [123] and reactive systems [124].

In the recent years, researchers have advanced MBT from FSM models in several ways: (1) they have extended test case generation algorithms to the *timing aspect*, (2) they have proposed *fault-based testing* as an alternative to structural-based testing, (3) they have addressed the *feasibility* of turning an abstract test case into a concrete test case, (4) they have exploited FSM models as *oracles* and (5) they have considered the problem of generating *optimal test suites*.

To address the *timing* aspect, which is particularly relevant for real-time embedded systems, Hansel *et al.* have recently defined a test case generation technique for UPPAAL timed automa [45], which are FSMs extended with clock variables and guards. The major challenge of testing such systems is that test cases have to be very long to cover interesting timing behaviors. This paper shows how to generate effective test cases using evolutionary algorithms.

An interesting alternative to generating test cases using classic structural criteria [125] is generating test cases according to a *fault model*. The core idea is to generate test cases that can reveal specific classes of problems, rather than covering behaviors in the model. Recent advances in the area consisted in new algorithms for fault-based testing with FSMs [46, 47], which work by first injecting a fault in the model (i.e., the model is transformed according to a pattern that matches a known type of fault) and then generating test cases that would fail if the implementation satisfies the mutated model rather than the original model. This process is repeated for all known classes of faults.

In general, test cases generated from FSM models are *abstract test cases that must be turned into concrete test cases* to be executed. Because of the gap between the abstract model and the actual implementation, sequences of operations generated from the model may turn out to be infeasible in practice. Tonella *et al.* addressed this issue by using N-grams [48], which are probabilistic models, often used in Natural Language Processing, that can predict the next item in a sequence. In this work, N-gram models are generated from usage data, for instance obtained by monitoring user activity, and used to increase the chance of selecting feasible sequences of operations when applying a test case selection criteria to the model.

In the context of MBT, finite state models have not been used only as artifact supporting test case generation, but also as *oracles* [108]. The idea is to represent the responses that the system is supposed to generate as reaction to external stimuli, and match the actual behavior of the system with the expected behavior. Recent advances investigated how to strengthen the fault detection capability of MBT using annotations [49] and developers-written assertions [50], and how to introduce a flexible matching between the actual traces and the model to reduce spurious failures for systems with highly nondeterministic behaviors [51].

In several cases, executing a test suite might be particularly expensive. This is true for instance for many industrial embedded systems, where the testing procedure requires setting a complex environment. In these cases, it is important to generate *optimal test suites* that can be executed cheaply and reveal faults early. Recent advances provided techniques for the computation of optimal test suites with integer linear programming algorithms [52, 95] and test suites with diverse test cases [53, 54]. In case the reduction must be achieved without affecting coverage of the requirements, FLOWER is a technique that may help achieving this goal [126].

4.2.2 MBT from UML models
The Unified Modeling Language (UML) is a language used in software engineering to visually specify the structure, the behavior and the architecture of a system [127]. UML tackles different aspects with different diagrams, for instance UML uses different diagrams to illustrate how a software component is decomposed into subcomponents, for instance using a UML Class Diagram, and how a component behaves, for instance using a UML Sequence Diagram.

Because of its popularity, many test case generation approaches have been designed to work with UML diagrams. Recent approaches have considered test case generation from sequence diagrams, use cases, and MARTE models.

In the case of *sequence diagrams*, Haitao *et al.* defined a formal testing framework that can be used to generate conformance test suites [55]; while Naslavsky *et al.* defined a technique that can select the interesting test cases that need to be reexecuted when domain and sequence diagrams are modified [56].

In the case of *use cases*, Sinnig *et al.* investigated how to generate test cases from use cases when task models are available [57]. Task models are models that specify how tasks can be executed with the user interface of a system [128]. Combining use cases with task models it is possible to determine how the functionalities of an application can be concretely used as part of complex and long scenarios.

In the case of the *MARTE* UML profile, which is a profile for modeling and analysis of real-time embedded systems, Arcuri *et al.* investigated several test case generation approaches, including random, adaptive random, and search-based test case generation strategies [58, 59], obtaining relevant results with random and search-based strategies.

4.2.3 MBT from Feature Models

Feature models are models that compactly represent combinations of features and their dependencies [129]. They are often used to describe software product lines, that is sets of related software products that share a core of features, but also include variations [130]. So far, several papers addressed the problem of generating test cases for instances of software product lines.

In contrast with these approaches, Lackner *et al.* [60] recently investigated the problem of testing the software product line per se. The idea is to model the software product line with a feature model, a 150% model—which is a UML state machine that accepts every behavior of every possible instance of the product line—and a mapping between them; and use these models to generate test cases. Lackner *et al.* define two approaches: product centered testing, which consists of generating test cases for a representative set of products, and product line centered testing, which consists of merging the model of every product in a single FSM model that can be used to generate test cases for the product line using standard techniques.

In a recent paper, Sanchez *et al.* have investigated the problem of prioritizing test cases for software product lines specified with feature models [61], proposing five prioritization criteria based on various heuristics.

5. TESTING WITH COMPLEX INPUTS

Modern software systems often require complex inputs with well-defined syntax and semantics to be tested effectively. For instance, testing a browser requires proper HTML pages, while testing a GPS system requires meaningful routes.

Non-trivial syntactically correct and semantically meaningful inputs can be hardly generated randomly. Consider for instance the chance of randomly generating a well-formed HTML page or the chance of generating two strings corresponding to two real addresses that can be accepted by a GPS system. Generating useful test cases for systems with complex inputs requires information about the nature of the inputs. In the past, this problem has been addressed only marginally with specification-based techniques. For instance, approaches based on constraint solving techniques have been proposed to generate test cases when the input structure is encoded with logical constraints [131, 132], and grammar-based approaches when the input structure is defined by means of grammars [133, 134].

The past years have seen interesting progresses in the generation of complex test inputs both for syntactically and semantically complex data, as summarized in Fig. 4. While the progresses in generating *syntactically complex inputs* are mostly extensions in line with classic work, the automatic generation of *semantically complex inputs* by exploiting resources available in the Web represents the main novelty of the recent research work. Indeed, Web services, Web pages, and Knowledge bases are huge sources of semantically relevant data available for many purposes. Several approaches investigated how to use these sources to obtain complex test inputs. This is a novel research direction that will likely influence testing of systems that process realistic data. In the following, we briefly describe advances in these two areas.

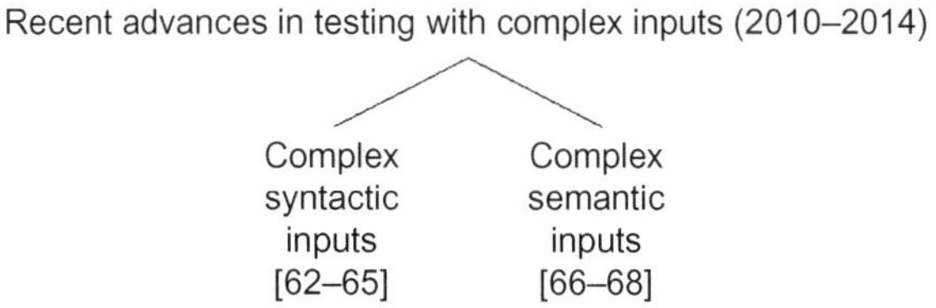

Recent advances in testing with complex inputs (2010–2014)

| Complex syntactic inputs [62–65] | Complex semantic inputs [66–68] |

Figure 4 Recent advances in testing systems with complex inputs.

5.1 Complex Syntactic Inputs

The approaches to generate syntactically complex inputs are all based on a specification of the input structure, and differ in the specifications and in the algorithms that constructively generates the inputs that cover the specification. Recent results covered different cases. Heam *et al.* presented SEED [62], which can generate tree-like recursive structures implementing the recursive method [135]. Zaeem *et al.* used dynamic programing [136] to generate complex recursive inputs. [63]. Mariani *et al.* defined strategies to samples multidimensional numeric input spaces [64]. Finally, Torlak *et al.* defined TestBlox [65], a technique for generating multidimensional data, where each dimension can be associated with statistical constraints.

5.2 Complex Semantic Inputs

Modern software applications require realistic and coherent data to be tested thoroughly. *Realistic* data are inputs semantically related to each other and to the reference environment, for example two addresses given as input to a GPS system shall correspond to addresses on the map (the reference environment). *Coherent* data are inputs composed by multiple semantically related fields, for instance the two addressed for to GPS system should correspond to locations connected by roads, and not separated by the ocean.

Albeit very useful for testing, the problem of automatically generating realistic and coherent values has been tackled only recently. The approaches studied so far work by composing Web Services, searching the Web and exploiting the Web of data.

Web Services

The inputs and the outputs of Web services can be described using ontologies, which are machine-processable artifacts that represent the knowledge of a certain domain in form of classes and relationships between classes [137]. Bozkurt *et al.* defined a testing technique that exploits the knowledge available in ontologies to automatically generate inputs for Web services [67]. The technique is particularly useful when the Web Service under test requires semantically meaningful values to be tested, such as a Web service that processes ISBN numbers. The idea is to generate semantically relevant test data, for example ISBN numbers, by looking for Web Services that can produce the data required in input to the Web Service under test. This search is recursively applied until discovering a composition of Web Services that can be used to generate semantic data. In principle, the technique can be extremely effective with Web Services, but its practical effectiveness is limited by the possibility to effectively build a composition using only the Web services readily available on the Web.

Web Searches

Shahbaz *et al.* proposed a technique that generates semantically relevant test inputs by looking for realistic inputs on the Web [68]. The idea is to extract the identifiers that describe the inputs that must be generated by analyzing the artifact under test, then searching both Web pages that contain occurrences of these identifiers and regular expressions that define how the data described by the identifiers should look like, and finally using the regular expressions to filter the content of the retrieved pages. The content selected with the regular expressions is used as test inputs. This technique can be potentially applied to many domains, but its effectiveness depends on the quality of the data in the Web pages and the quality of the regular expressions that are retrieved automatically from the Web.

Web of Data

The Web of Data is a huge aggregation of semantically interconnected and well-structured data available on the Internet [138]. Many data sources organized according to the Web of Data—called *knowledge bases*—can be readily queried using different protocols and techniques. For instance, *DBpedia*, which is one of the biggest knowledge bases, is obtained by extracting information from Wikipedia and encoding the extracted information in RDF [139], which can be easily processed by a machine. Link is a technique that uses the Web of Data to automatically generate complex inputs composed of multiple semantically coherent and meaningful fields [66]. In a nutshell, Link works at the user interface level by extracting the labels that describe the input fields, mapping them to corresponding concepts in a knowledge base, querying the knowledge base to extract sets of semantically coherent values and using the extracted values to test the system. Link is the only technique that can generate at the same time semantic and coherent inputs composed of multiple fields. Although it could be applied to many different domains, its practical effectiveness depends on the availability of properly populated knowledge bases.

6. COMBINATORIAL INTERACTION TESTING

When testing a software system, many mutually interacting factors may affect the behavior of the software under test and thus need to be taken into consideration. The obvious approach to testing is designing a test suite that covers all these factors and interactions, but this is often infeasible. For instance, if we consider a simple SUT with n binary configuration parameters, testing all possible interactions requires 2^n test cases.

Combinatorial Interaction Testing (CIT) aims to find a tradeoff between the cost of testing and the number of interactions covered by a test suite [140]. The basic idea of CIT is to cover all the interactions of size k (called combinatorial strength), rather than covering all combinations in general. This is motivated by the fact that most of the faults are triggered by the interaction of few parameters only [141–143].

More formally, given a combinatorial strength t and a SUT with n parameters $P = \{p_1, p_2, \ldots, p_n\}$ with $V_i = \{v_1, v_2, \ldots, v_{n_i}\}$ denoting the set of valid values for each parameter p_i, a CIT technique produces a t-way Covering Array (CA) defined as follows [144]: A CA is a two-dimensional array of size $m \times n$, where the i-th column denotes the parameter p_i and all the elements of this column are from the set V_i, such that every subarray of size $m \times t$ contains each possible combinations of the corresponding t parameters values at least once. A t-way combinatorial test suite, covering all the parameters interaction of size t, can be easily obtained from a t-way CA by mapping each row of the covering array to a test case of the combinatorial test suite.

Computing a t-way CA is an NP complete problem, and so far researchers have studied different strategies to compute it, such as greedy algorithms, heuristic search algorithms, and random methods [140].

Recent advances in CIT covered three main areas, as illustrated in Fig. 5: *unconstrained CIT* that consists of generating CIT test suites when the test space is free of constrains, meaning that each possible combination is feasible; *constrained CIT* that consists of generating CIT test suites when not all combinations of parameters are legal, but additional constraints must be satisfied, and *applications* of CIT to real world testing problems.

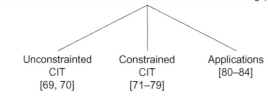

Figure 5 Recent advances in combinatorial interaction testing.

While recent progresses in unconstrained CIT are extension of classic results and have attracted limited attention recently, the research community is particularly active in addressing the problem of generating t-way CA for constrained CIT [71, 73, 75, 77], and in investigating the application of CIT techniques to diverse domains, especially in combination with MBT [80–83].

For a long time, CIT has been applied to the generation of pairwise CA, but recent technical advances demonstrated that the generation of t-way CA with $t > 2$ is feasible and useful [145]. In particular, recent studies confirmed that higher strength combinatorial testing has a high fault revealing capability, therefore CIT should focus on that in the future. In the following sections, we briefly illustrate the key advances in unconstrained CIT, constrained CIT and CIT applications.

6.1 Unconstrained CIT

Unconstrained CIT has been extensively studied in the past and most of the research of the past years has produced incremental extensions to classic approaches [140], without providing clear evidence of the effectiveness of unconstrained CIT compared to random testing [19].

The most relevant progresses in the past years are the definition of Sequence Covering Array and the definition of a greedy algorithm for calculating it [69], and the generation of concrete test cases from test case specifications [70].

Sequence Covering Array (SCA) extends the concept of CA to ordered sequences of events and requires covering every possible t-way permutation of the events, in contrast with parameters in classic CA that do not have an ordering [69]. The problem of turning a test case specification obtained with CIT into a concrete test case springs from the possibility that a combination of parameter values legal in principle might be particularly hard or expensive to be turned into a test case that matches the specification. Blue *et al.* extended CIT with the capability to consider the test data that is already available within an organization to make sure that the resulting test suite will be executable [70]. In particular, they applied CIT to minimize an existing test suite preserving its interaction coverage.

6.2 Constrained CIT

In many applications, parameters can be combined in arbitrary ways, but specific constraints must be taken under consideration. For example given as input parameters browser and operating system, not all combinations of browsers and operating systems can be turned into executable test cases, for instance not all versions of IE are available for Macintosh. Thus, a test case requiring to run IE on Mac would not be executable. In general, generating CIT test suites ignoring constraints might lead to many invalid test cases and waste of effort [140]. Constrained CIT is a particularly active research area that studies how to address the problem of incorporating constraints in CIT. Recent advances in the area covered the definition of the test space, algorithms for handling constraints, and techniques to assess the test suites.

Test Space Definition

Defining the *test space* is a error prone and often labor intensive activity. Omitting an important parameter value or failing to define a constraint can negatively affect the result of the testing process. Segal *et al.* [71, 72] introduced a technique that assists testers during the definition of the test space by visualizing the cartesian product of a subset of the parameters and letting testers introduce restrictions to precisely shape the test space. The technique represents constraints using Binary Decision Diagrams [146] to compactly define large test spaces. Calvagna *et al.* developed CITLAB [73], an extensible framework for CIT that provides a Domain Specific Language for specifying the test space of a combinatorial problem. The framework provides a simple syntax for test space definition that eases the use and adoption of CIT techniques and their fair comparison.

Algorithms

Several techniques have been proposed to generate combinatorial test suites for constrained test spaces. Segall *et al.* proposed an algorithm for generating CAs from a test space described with BDDs [71]. Linbin *et al.* extended the IPOG CIT algorithm [147] to handle constraints using a constrain solver [74]. The algorithm, implemented in the ACTS tool [75], implements multiple optimization strategies to reduce the cost of the generation process. On the same line, Garvin *et al.* [76] adapted and optimized an existing meta-heuristic algorithm [148] to constrained CIT. Finally, Flores *et al.* proposed to use a genetic approach to the generation of 2-way CA [77].

Interestingly, Dumlu *et al.* identified and investigated the masking effect in CIT techniques [78]. A masking effect is the effect of a test failure that may stop the program execution before some relevant behaviors covered by the test case are executed. Dumlu *et al.* addressed this problem for the case of a regression test suite that needs to be executed for multiple configurations of the SUT. Configurations are identified using CIT. The technique works by iteratively generating a CA for SUT configurations, running the test cases, inferring masking effects, and then generating a new CA, until all cases have been covered.

Tes Suite Assessment

CIT test suites are commonly assessed by considering interaction coverage, that is the percentage of t-way interactions that have been covered. Papadakis *et al.* [79] proposed to use mutation analysis as an alternative. The idea is to mutate the model and check if the test cases in the CA violate the mutated model. If the model is violated, the mutant is killed. The higher the mutation score is, the more effective the test suite is. Empirical results suggest that mutation score correlates to fault detection better than interaction coverage.

6.3 CIT Applications

CIT has been applied to many diverse domains, but two domains received specific attention in the past years: testing from finite state machines and testing from feature models.

Finite State Machine

Nguyen *et al.* combined MBT and CIT to generate test cases from FSM models (see also Section 4.2.1) [80]. The idea is to use CIT to generate interesting combinations of values for the parameters of the events in the sequences generated from the FSM, thus augmenting classic structural criteria. Xun *et al.* [81] used CIT to generate test cases, consisting of sequences of events, from a ripped model of the GUI. Since many of the combinations might correspond to infeasible sequences of operations, the technique by Xun *et al.* can benefit from a repair solution that uses a genetic algorithm to turn infeasible test cases into executable test cases [149].

Feature Model

CIT has been also applied to Software Product Lines to generate sets of relevant products for testing. Perrouin *et al.* [82] addressed this problem by automatically transforming a feature model that describes the SPL into a set of Alloy constraints [150], and then using a constraint solver to generate a *t-wise* set of configurations. Along a similar line, Johansen *et al.* [83] generated CA from feature models using a greedy algorithm that, by avoiding redundant computations and exploiting parallelism, is able to scale to large feature models. Finally, Galindo *et al.* used feature models to express the variability of video sequences and generated test cases for video processing routines exploiting CIT techniques [84].

7. CONCLUSIONS

Due to its wide applicability, black-box testing is among the most popular approaches to software testing. In the past few years, we witness relevant progress in automated black-box test case generation in four main areas: random testing, MBT, generation of complex inputs, combinatorial interaction testing. In this chapter, we surveyed the contributions from 2010 to 2014, and we highlighted some interesting trends.

The main recent advances in random testing focus on augmenting random testing with heuristic decisions. The area is pretty lively and we expect researchers to keep addressing the challenge of making random testing more effective for many more years.

The most notable novelties in MBT cluster around the idea of considering models extracted from code and code execution, to reduce the cost of MBT that largely depends on the construction of the models. The main open challenge remains the identification of effective ways for extracting and using complete and consistent models for testing.

In the new area about the generation of complex inputs, which has raised due to the increasing availability of applications that interact with the environment and require real data to be executed, the most notable advances are in the definition of techniques to automatically generate complex syntactically and semantically correct inputs. This is an increasingly relevant area, and the recently defined techniques are likely to seed research towards new more effective approaches.

REFERENCES

[1] G.J. Myers, Art of Software Testing, John Wiley & Sons, Inc, New York, NY, USA, 1979.
[2] S. Anand, E.K. Burke, T.Y. Chen, J. Clark, M.B. Cohen, W. Grieskamp, M. Harman, M.J. Harrold, P. Mcminn, An orchestrated survey of methodologies for automated software test case generation, J. Syst. Softw. 86 (8) (2013) 1978–2001.
[3] V. Massol, T. Husted, JUnit in Action, Manning Publications Co, Greenwich, CT, USA, 2003.
[4] J.W. Duran, S. Ntafos, A report on random testing, in: Proceedings of the International Conference on Software Engineering (ICSE), IEEE, 1981.
[5] T. Ostrand, White-box testing, in: Encyclopedia of Software Engineering, John Wiley & Sons, Inc, New York, NY, USA, 2002.

[6] L.J. Morell, A theory of fault-based testing, IEEE Trans. Softw. Eng. 16 (8) (1990) 844–857.

[7] G. Rothermel, M.J. Harrold, A safe, efficient regression test selection technique, ACM Trans. Softw. Eng. Methodol. 6 (2) (1997) 173–210.

[8] P. Godefroid, N. Klarlund, K. Sen, DART: directed automated random testing, in: Proceedings of the Conference on Programming Language Design and Implementation (PLDI), ACM, 2005.

[9] M. Pezzè, M. Young, Software Testing and Analysis: Process, Principles, and Techniques, John Wiley & Sons, Inc, New York, NY, USA, 2007.

[10] A. Cockburn, Agile Software Development, Addison-Wesley Professional, Boston, MA, USA, 2001.

[11] I. Banerjee, B. Nguyen, V. Garousi, A. Memon, Graphical user interface (GUI) testing: systematic mapping and repository, Inf. Softw. Technol. 55 (10) (2013) 1679–1694.

[12] G. Fraser, A. Arcuri, A large-scale evaluation of automated unit test generation using evosuite, ACM Trans. Softw. Eng. Methodol. 24 (2) (2014) 8:1–8:42.

[13] G. Rothermel, S. Elbaum, A.G. Malishevsky, P. Kallakuri, X. Qiu, On test suite composition and cost-effective regression testing, ACM Trans. Softw. Eng. Methodol. 13 (3) (2004) 277–331.

[14] M. Oriol, Random testing: Evaluation of a law describing the number of faults found, in: Proceedings of the International Conference on Software Testing, Verification and Validation (ICST), IEEE, 2012.

[15] A. Arcuri, M.Z. Iqbal, L. Briand, Formal analysis of the effectiveness and predictability of random testing, in: Proceedings of the International Symposium on Software Testing and Analysis (ISSTA), ACM, 2010.

[16] A. Arcuri, M.Z. Iqbal, L. Briand, Random testing: Theoretical results and practical implications, IEEE Trans. Softw. Eng. 38 (2) (2012) 258–277.

[17] R. Sharma, M. Gligoric, A. Arcuri, G. Fraser, D. Marinov, Testing container classes: Random or systematic? in: Proceedings of the International Conference on Fundamental Approaches to Software Engineering: Part of the Joint European Conferences on Theory and Practice of Software (FASE/ETAPS), Springer, 2011.

[18] M. Böhme, S. Paul, On the efficiency of automated testing, in: Proceedings of the International Symposium on Foundations of Software Engineering (FSE), ACM, 2014.

[19] A. Arcuri, L. Briand, Formal analysis of the probability of interaction fault detection using random testing, IEEE Trans. Softw. Eng. 38 (5) (2012) 1088–1099.

[20] H. Liu, X. Xie, J. Yang, Y. Lu, T.Y. Chen, Adaptive random testing through test profiles, Softw. Pract. Exp. 41 (10) (2011) 1131–1154.

[21] A. Shahbazi, A.F. Tappenden, J. Miller, Centroidal voronoi tessellations–a new approach to random testing, IEEE Trans. Softw. Eng. 39 (2) (2013) 163–183.

[22] Z. Liu, X. Gao, X. Long, Adaptive random testing of mobile application, in: Proceedings of the International Conference on Computer Engineering and Technology (ICCET), IEEE, 2010.

[23] T.Y. Chen, F.-C. Kuo, R.G. Merkel, T.H. Tse, Adaptive random testing: the ART of test case diversity, J. Syst. Softw. 83 (1) (2010) 60–66.

[24] A. Arcuri, L. Briand, Adaptive random testing: an illusion of effectiveness? in: Proceedings of the International Symposium on Software Testing and Analysis (ISSTA), ACM, 2011.

[25] A. Nistor, Q. Luo, M. Pradel, T.R. Gross, D. Marinov, BALLERINA: automatic generation and clustering of efficient random unit tests for multithreaded code, in: Proceedings of the International Conference on Software Engineering (ICSE), IEEE, 2012.

[26] Y. Wei, S. Gebhardt, B. Meyer, M. Oriol, Satisfying test preconditions through guided object selection, in: Proceedings of the International Conference on Software Testing, Verification and Validation (ICST), IEEE, 2010.

[27] A. Groce, C. Zhang, E. Eide, Y. Chen, J. Regehr, Swarm testing, in: Proceedings of the International Symposium on Software Testing and Analysis (ISSTA), ACM, 2012.

[28] M. Ceccato, A. Marchetto, L. Mariani, C.D. Nguyen, P. Tonella, An empirical study about the effectiveness of debugging when random test cases are used, in: Proceedings of the International Conference on Software Engineering (ICSE), IEEE, 2012.

[29] P. Tsankov, M.T. Dashti, D. Basin, SECFUZZ: fuzz-testing security protocols, in: Proceedings of the International Workshop on Automation of Software Test (AST), IEEE, 2012.

[30] P. Tsankov, M.T. Dashti, D. Basin, Semi-valid input coverage for fuzz testing, in: Proceedings of the International Symposium on Software Testing and Analysis (ISSTA), ACM, 2013.

[31] L. Martignoni, R. Paleari, G.F. Roglia, D. Bruschi, Testing system virtual machines, in: Proceedings of the International Symposium on Software Testing and Analysis (ISSTA), ACM, 2010.

[32] A.M. Memon, I. Banerjee, B. Nguyen, B. Robbins, The first decade of GUI ripping: Extensions, applications, and broader impacts, in: Proceedings of The Working Conference on Reverse Engineering (WCRE), IEEE, 2013.

[33] D. Amalfitano, A.R. Fasolino, P. Tramontana, S.D. Carmine, A.M. Memon, Using GUI ripping for automated testing of android applications, in: Proceedings of the International Conference on Automated Software Engineering (ASE), ACM, 2012.

[34] M. Schur, A. Roth, A. Zeller, ProCrawl: mining test models from multi-user web applications, in: Proceedings of the International Symposium on Software Testing and Analysis (ISSTA), ACM, 2014.

[35] A. Mesbah, A. van Deursen, D. Roest, Invariant-based automatic testing of modern web applications, IEEE Trans. Softw. Eng. 38 (1) (2012) 35–53.

[36] S. Thummalapenta, V.K. Lakshmi, S. Sinha, N. Sinha, S. Chandra, Guided test generation for web applications, in: Proceedings of the International Conference on Software Engineering (ICSE), IEEE, 2013.

[37] A. Mesbah, M.R. Prasad, Automated cross-browser compatibility testing, in: Proceedings of the International Conference on Software Engineering (ICSE), ACM, 2011.

[38] S.R. Choudhary, M.R. Prasad, A. Orso, X-PERT: a web application testing tool for cross-browser inconsistency detection, in: Proceedings of the International Symposium on Software Testing and Analysis (ISSTA), ACM, 2014.

[39] C. Hunt, G. Brown, G. Fraser, Automatic testing of natural user interfaces, in: Proceedings of the International Conference on Software Testing, Verification and Validation (ICST), IEEE, 2014.

[40] K. Meinke, M.A. Sindhu, Incremental learning-based testing for reactive systems, in: M. Gogolla, B. Wolff (Eds.), Tests and Proofs, Springer, Berlin, Heidelberg, Germany, 2011, pp. 134–151.

[41] K. Meinke, M.A. Sindhu, LBTest: a learning-based testing tool for reactive systems, in: Proceedings of the International Conference on Software Testing, Verification and Validation (ICST), IEEE, 2013.

[42] K. Meinke, F. Niu, A learning-based approach to unit testing of numerical software, in: Testing Software and Systems, Springer, Berlin, Heidelberg, Germany, 2010, pp. 221–235.

[43] L. Mariani, M. Pezzè, O. Riganelli, M. Santoro, AutoBlackTest: automatic black-box testing of interactive applications, in: Proceedings of the International Conference on Software Testing, Verification and Validation (ICST), IEEE, 2012.

[44] L. Mariani, M. Pezzè, O. Riganelli, M. Santoro, Automatic testing of GUI-based applications, Softw. Test. Verif. Reliab. 24 (5) (2014) 341–366.

[45] J. Hansel, D. Rose, P. Herber, S. Glesner, An evolutionary algorithm for the generation of timed test traces for embedded real-time systems, in: Proceedings of the International Conference on Software Testing, Verification and Validation (ICST), IEEE, 2011.

[46] B.K. Aichernig, H. Brandl, E. Jobstl, W. Krenn, Efficient mutation killers in action, in: Proceedings of the International Conference on Software Testing, Verification and Validation (ICST), IEEE, 2011.

[47] F. Belli, M. Beyazit, T. Takagi, Z. Furukawa, Mutation testing of "go-back" functions based on pushdown automata, in: Proceedings of the International Conference on Software Testing, Verification and Validation (ICST), IEEE, 2011.

[48] P. Tonella, R. Tiella, C.D. Nguyen, Interpolated N-grams for model based testing, in: Proceedings of the International Conference on Software Engineering (ICSE), ACM, 2014.

[49] R.N. Zaeem, M.R. Prasad, S. Khurshid, Automated generation of oracles for testing user-interaction features of mobile apps, in: Proceedings of the International Conference on Software Testing, Verification and Validation (ICST), IEEE, 2014.

[50] N. Li, J. Offutt, An empirical analysis of test oracle strategies for model-based testing, in: Proceedings of the International Conference on Software Testing, Verification and Validation (ICST), IEEE, 2014.

[51] G. Gay, S. Rayadurgam, M.P.E. Heimdahl, Steering model-based oracles to admit real program behaviors, in: Proceedings of the International Conference on Software Engineering (ICSE), NIER Track, ACM, 2014.

[52] A. Chander, D. Dhurjati, K. Sen, D. Yu, Optimal test input sequence generation for finite state models and pushdown systems, in: Proceedings of the International Conference on Software Testing, Verification and Validation (ICST), IEEE, 2011.

[53] H. Hemmati, L. Briand, A. Arcuri, S. Ali, An enhanced test case selection approach for model-based testing: an industrial case study, in: Proceedings of the International Symposium on Foundations of Software Engineering (FSE), ACM, 2010.

[54] H. Hemmati, L. Briand, An industrial investigation of similarity measures for model-based test case selection, in: Proceedings of the International Symposium on Software Reliability Engineering (ISSRE), IEEE, 2010.

[55] H. Dan, R.M. Hierons, Conformance testing from message sequence charts, in: Proceedings of the International Conference on Software Testing, Verification and Validation (ICST), IEEE, 2011.

[56] L. Naslavsky, H. Ziv, D.J. Richardson, MbSRT2: model-based selective regression testing with traceability, in: Proceedings of the International Conference on Software Testing, Verification and Validation (ICST), IEEE, 2010.

[57] D. Sinnig, F. Khendek, P. Chalin, A formal model for generating integrated functional and user interface test cases, in: Proceedings of the International Conference on Software Testing, Verification and Validation (ICST), IEEE, 2010.

[58] A. Arcuri, M.Z. Iqbal, L. Briand, Black-box system testing of real-time embedded systems using random and search-based testing, in: Proceedings of the International Conference on Testing Software and Systems (ICTSS), Springer, 2010.

[59] M.Z. Iqbal, A. Arcuri, L. Briand, Empirical investigation of search algorithms for environment model-based testing of real-time embedded software, in: Proceedings of the International Symposium on Software Testing and Analysis (ISSTA), ACM, 2012.

[60] H. Lackner, M. Thomas, F. Wartenberg, S. Weissleder, Model-based test design of product lines: Raising test design to the product line level, in: Proceedings of the International Conference on Software Testing, Verification and Validation (ICST), IEEE, 2014.

[61] A.B. Sanchez, S. Segura, A. Ruiz-Cortes, A comparison of test case prioritization criteria for software product lines, in: Proceedings of the International Conference on Software Testing, Verification and Validation (ICST), IEEE, 2014.

[62] P.C. Heam, C. Nicaud, Seed: an easy-to-use random generator of recursive data structures for testing, in: Proceedings of the International Conference on Software Testing, Verification and Validation (ICST), IEEE, 2011.

[63] R.N. Zaeem, S. Khurshid, Test input generation using dynamic programming, in: Proceedings of the International Symposium on the Foundations of Software Engineering (FSE), ACM, 2012.

[64] L. Mariani, O. Riganelli, M. Santoro, M. Ali, G-RankTest: regression testing of controller applications, in: Proceedings of the International Workshop on Automation of Software Test (AST), IEEE, 2012.

[65] E. Torlak, Scalable test data generation from multidimensional models, in: Proceedings of the International Symposium on the Foundations of Software Engineering (FSE), ACM, 2012.

[66] L. Mariani, M. Pezzè, O. Riganelli, M. Santoro, Link: exploiting the web of data to generate test inputs, in: Proceedings of the International Symposium on Software Testing and Analysis (ISSTA), ACM, 2014.

[67] M. Bozkurt, M. Harman, Automatically generating realistic test input from web services, in: Proceedings of the International Symposium on Service Oriented System Engineering (SOSE), IEEE, 2011.

[68] M. Shahbaz, P. McMinn, M. Stevenson, Automated discovery of valid test strings from the web using dynamic regular expressions collation and natural language processing, in: Proceedings of the International Conference on Quality Software (QSIC), IEEE, 2012.

[69] D. Kuhn, J. Higdon, J. Lawrence, R. Kacker, Y. Lei, Combinatorial methods for event sequence testing, in: Proceedings of the International Conference on Software Testing, Verification and Validation (ICST), IEEE, 2012.

[70] D. Blue, I. Segall, R. Tzoref-Brill, A. Zlotnick, Interaction-based test-suite minimization, in: Proceedings of the International Conference on Software Engineering (ICSE), IEEE, 2013.

[71] I. Segall, R. Tzoref-Brill, E. Farchi, Using binary decision diagrams for combinatorial test design, in: Proceedings of the International Symposium on Software Testing and Analysis (ISSTA), ACM, 2011.

[72] I. Segall, R. Tzoref-Brill, A. Zlotnick, Simplified modeling of combinatorial test spaces, in: Proceedings of the International Conference on Software Testing, Verification and Validation (ICST), IEEE, 2012.

[73] A. Calvagna, A. Gargantini, P. Vavassori, Combinatorial interaction testing with CITLAB, in: Proceedings of the International Conference on Software Testing, Verification and Validation (ICST), IEEE, 2013.

[74] Y. Linbin, L. Yu, M. Nourozborazjany, R. Kacker, D. Kuhn, An efficient algorithm for constraint handling in combinatorial test generation, in: Proceedings of the International Conference on Software Testing, Verification and Validation (ICST), IEEE, 2013.

[75] Y. Linbin, L. Yu, R. Kacker, D. Kuhn, ACTS: a combinatorial test generation tool, in: Proceedings of the International Conference on Software Testing, Verification and Validation (ICST), IEEE, 2013.

[76] B.J. Garvin, M.B. Cohen, M.B. Dwyer, Evaluating improvements to a meta-heuristic search for constrained interaction testing, Empir. Softw. Eng. 16 (1) (2011) 61–102.

[77] P. Flores, C. Yoonsik, PWiseGen: generating test cases for pairwise testing using genetic algorithms, in: Proceedings of the International Conference on Computer Science and Automation Engineering (CSAE), IEEE, 2011.

[78] E. Dumlu, C. Yilmaz, M.B. Cohen, A. Porter, Feedback driven adaptive combinatorial testing, in: Proceedings of the International Symposium on Software Testing and Analysis (ISSTA), ACM, 2011.

[79] M. Papadakis, C. Henard, leY. Traon, Sampling program inputs with mutation analysis: going beyond combinatorial interaction testing, in: Proceedings of the International Conference on Software Testing, Verification and Validation (ICST), IEEE, 2014.

[80] C.D. Nguyen, A. Marchetto, P. Tonella, Combining model-based and combinatorial testing for effective test case generation, in: Proceedings of the International Symposium on Software Testing and Analysis (ISSTA), ACM, 2012, pp. 100–110.

[81] Y. Xun, M. Cohen, A. Memon, GUI interaction testing: incorporating event context, IEEE Trans. Softw. Eng. 37 (4) (2011) 559–574.

[82] G. Perrouin, S. Sen, J. Klein, B. Baudry, Y. le Traon, Automated and scalable t-wise test case generation strategies for software product lines, in: Proceedings of the International Conference on Software Testing, Verification and Validation (ICST), IEEE, 2010.

[83] M.F. Johansen, O. Haugen, F. Fleurey, An algorithm for generating t-wise covering arrays from large feature models, in: Proceedings of the International Software Product Line Conference (SPLC), ACM, 2012.

[84] J.A. Galindo, M. Alférez, M. Acher, B. Baudry, D. Benavides, A Variability-based testing approach for synthesizing video sequences, in: Proceedings of the International Symposium on Software Testing and Analysis (ISSTA), ACM, 2014.

[85] J.W. Duran, S.C. Ntafos, An evaluation of random testing, IEEE Trans. Softw. Eng. 10 (4) (1984) 438–444.

[86] R. Hamlet, Random testing, in: Encyclopedia of Software Engineering, John Wiley & Sons, Inc, New York, NY, USA, 1994, pp. 970–978.

[87] C. Pacheco, S.K. Lahiri, M.D. Ernst, T. Ball, Feedback-directed random test generation, in: Proceedings of the International Conference on Software Engineering (ICSE), IEEE, 2007.

[88] T.Y. Chen, T.H. Tse, Y.T. Yu, Proportional sampling strategy: a compendium and some insights, J. Syst. Softw. 58 (1) (2001) 65–81.

[89] M.D. Ernst, J. Cockrell, W.G. Griswold, D. Notkin, Dynamically discovering likely program invariants to support program evolution, in: Proceedings of the International Conference on Software Engineering (ICSE), ACM, 1999.

[90] D. Lorenzoli, L. Mariani, M. Pezzè, Automatic generation of software behavioral models, in: Proceedings of the International Conference on Software Engineering (ICSE), ACM, 2008.

[91] V. Dallmeier, C. Lindig, A. Wasylkowski, A. Zeller, Mining object behavior with ADABU, in: Proceedings of the International Workshop on Dynamic Systems Analysis (WODA), ACM, 2006.

[92] C. Pacheco, M.D. Ernst, Eclat: automatic generation and classification of test inputs, in: Proceedings of the European Conference on Object-Oriented Programming (ECOOP), Springer, 2005.

[93] L. Mariani, S. Papagiannakis, M. Pezzè, Compatibility and regression testing of COTS-component-based software, in: Proceedings of the International Conference on Software Engineering (ICSE), IEEE, 2007.

[94] X. Yuan, A.M. Memon, Generating event sequence-based test cases using GUI runtime state feedback, IEEE Trans. Softw. Eng. 36 (1) (2010) 81–95.

[95] N. Li, F. Li, J. Offutt, Better algorithms to minimize the cost of test paths, in: Proceedings of the International Conference on Software Testing, Verification and Validation (ICST), IEEE, 2012.

[96] C. Boyapati, S. Khurshid, D. Marinov, Korat: automated testing based on java predicates, in: Proceedings of the International Symposium on Software Testing and Analysis (ISSTA), ACM, 2002.

[97] R. Mandl, Orthogonal latin squares: an application of experiment design to compiler testing, Commun. ACM 28 (10) (1985) 1054–1058.

[98] R. Brownlie, J. Prowse, M. Phadke, Robust testing of AT&T PMX/StarMdl using OATS, AT&T Techn. J. 71 (3) (1992) 41–47.

[99] D.M. Cohen, S.R. Dalal, A. Kajla, G.C. Patton, The automatic efficient test generator (AETG) system, in: Proceedings of the International Symposium on Software Reliability Engineering (ISSRE), IEEE, 1994.

[100] P. Ammann, J.C. Knight, Data diversity: an approach to software fault tolerance, IEEE Trans. Comput. 37 (4) (1988) 418–425.

[101] P.G. Bishop, The variation of software survival time for different operational input profiles (or why you can wait a long time for a big bug to fail), in: Proceedings of the International Symposium on Fault-Tolerant Computing (FTCS), IEEE, 1993.

[102] P. Oehlert, Violating assumptions with fuzzing, IEEE Secur. Priv. 3 (2) (2005) 58–62.

[103] W. Visser, C.S. Păsăreanu, R. Pelánek, Test input generation for java containers using state matching, in: Proceedings of the International Symposium on Software Testing and Analysis (ISSTA), ACM, 2006.

[104] J. Mayer, C. Schneckenburger, An empirical analysis and comparison of random testing techniques, in: Proceedings of the International Symposium on Empirical Software Engineering (ISESE), ACM, 2006.

[105] T.Y. Chen, R. Merkel, An upper bound on software testing effectiveness, ACM Trans. Softw. Eng. Methodol. 17 (3) (2008) 16:1–16:27.

[106] M. Utting, A. Pretschner, B. Legeard, A taxonomy of model-based testing approaches, Softw. Test. Verif. Reliab. 22 (5) (2012) 297–312.

[107] A.C.D. Neto, R. Subramanyan, M. Vieira, G.H. Travassos, A survey on model-based testing approaches: a systematic review, in: Proceedings of the International Workshop on Empirical Assessment of Software Engineering Languages and Technologies: Held in Conjunction with the International Conference on Automated Software Engineering (ASE), ACM, 2007.

[108] E.T. Barr, M. Harman, P. McMinn, M. Shahbaz, S. Yoo, The oracle problem in software testing: a survey, IEEE Trans. Softw. Eng. 41 (5) (2015) 507–525.

[109] A.M. Memon, Q. Xie, Studying the fault-detection effectiveness of GUI test cases for rapidly evolving software, IEEE Trans. Softw. Eng. 31 (10) (2005).

[110] J. Botella, F. Bouquet, J.-F. Capuron, F. Lebeau, B. Legeard, F. Schadle, Model-based testing of cryptographic components–lessons learned from experience, in: Proceedings of the International Conference on Software Testing, Verification and Validation (ICST), IEEE, 2013.

[111] S. Ali, H. Hemmati, Model-based testing of video conferencing systems: challenges, lessons learnt, and results, in: Proceedings of the International Conference on Software Testing, Verification and Validation (ICST), IEEE, 2014.

[112] S. Weissleder, H. Schlingloff, An evaluation of model-based testing in embedded applications, in: Proceedings of the International Conference on Software Testing, Verification and Validation (ICST), IEEE, 2014.

[113] T. Takala, M. Katara, J. Harty, Experiences of system-level model-based GUI testing of an android application, in: Proceedings of the International Conference on Software Testing, Verification and Validation (ICST), IEEE, 2011.

[114] Conformiq, http://www.conformiq.com.

[115] Smartesting, http://www.smartesting.com.

[116] B. Legeard, A. Bouzy, Smartesting CertifyIt: model-based testing for enterprise IT, in: Proceedings of the International Conference on Software Testing, Verification and Validation (ICST), IEEE, 2013.

[117] Spec Explorer, http://www.specexplorer.net.

[118] C. Schulze, D. Ganesan, M. Lindvall, R. Cleaveland, D. Goldman, Assessing model-based testing: an empirical study conducted in industry, in: Proceedings of the International Conference on Software Engineering (ICSE), ACM, 2014.

[119] H. Heiskanen, A. Jääskeläinen, M. Katara, Debug support for model-based GUI testing, in: Proceedings of the International Conference on Software Testing, Verification and Validation (ICST), IEEE, 2010.

[120] A. Mesbah, E. Bozdag, A. van Deursen, Crawling AJAX by inferring user interface state changes, in: Proceedings of the International Conference on Web Engineering (ICWE), ACM, 2008.

[121] M. Mirzaaghaei, A. Mesbah, DOM-based test adequacy criteria for web applications, in: Proceedings of the International Symposium on Software Testing and Analysis (ISSTA), ACM, 2014.

[122] R.S. Sutton, A.G. Barto, Introduction to Reinforcement Learning, first, MIT Press, Cambridge, MA, USA, 1998.

[123] D. Lee, M. Yannakakis, Principles and methods of testing finite state machines–a survey, Proc. IEEE 84 (8) (1996) 1090–1123.

[124] S. Sandberg, M. Krichen, H. Bjorklund, A. Gargantini, Testing of finite state machines, in: Model-Based Testing of Reactive Systems, Springer, Berlin, Heidelberg, Germany, 2005, pp. 5–116.

[125] S. Fujiwara, G. Bochmann, F. Khendek, M. Amalou, A. Ghedamsi, Test selection based on finite state models, IEEE Trans. Softw. Eng. 17 (6) (1991) 591–603.

[126] A. Gotlieb, D. Marijan, FLOWER: optimal test suite reduction as a network maximum flow, in: Proceedings of the International Symposium on Software Testing and Analysis (ISSTA), ACM, 2014.

[127] OMG, UML, http://www.uml.org.

[128] F. Paterno, Model-Based Design and Evaluation of Interactive Applications, first, Springer, London, UK, 1999.

[129] K. Kang, S. Cohen, J. Hess, W. Novak, S.A. Peterson, Feature-oriented domain analysis (FODA) feasibility study, tech. rep., Software Engineering Institute, Carnegie Mellon University, Pittsburgh, PA, 1990. URL, http://resources.sei.cmu.edu/library/assetview.cfm?AssetID=11231.

[130] K. Pohl, G. Böckle, F.J.v.d. Linden, Software Product Line Engineering: Foundations, Principles and Techniques, Springer, Secaucus, NJ, USA, 2005.

[131] C. Boyapati, S. Khurshid, D. Marinov, Korat: automated testing based on java predicates, SIGSOFT Softw. Eng. Notes 27 (4) (2002) 123–133.

[132] D. Marinov, S. Khurshid, TestEra: a novel framework for automated testing of Java programs, in: Proceedings of the Annual International Conference on Automated Software Engineering (ASE), ACM, 2001.

[133] B. Daniel, D. Dig, K. Garcia, D. Marinov, Automated testing of refactoring engines, in: Proceedings of the Joint Meeting of the European Software Engineering Conference and the Symposium on The Foundations of Software Engineering (ESEC/FSE), ACM, 2007.

[134] D. Coppit, J. Lian, Yagg: an easy-to-use generator for structured test inputs, in: Proceedings of the International Conference on Automated Software Engineering (ASE), ACM, 2005.

[135] A. Nijenhuis, H.S. Wilf, Combinatorial Algorithms for Computers and Calculators, second, Academic Press, Orlando, FL, USA, 1978.

[136] T.T. Cormen, C.E. Leiserson, R.L. Rivest, Introduction to Algorithms, MIT Press, Cambridge, MA, 1990.

[137] N.F. Noy, D.L. Mcguinness, Ontology development 101: a guide to creating your first ontology, tech. rep., Knowledge Systems Laboratory Stanford University, 2001.

[138] C. Bizer, T. Heath, T. Berners-Lee, Linked data–the story so far, Int. J. Semant. Web Inform. Syst. 5 (3) (2009) 1–22.
[139] D. Brickley, R.V. Guha, RDF vocabulary description language 1.0: RDF schema, W3C, 2004, W3C Recommendation.
[140] C. Nie, H. Leung, A survey of combinatorial testing, ACM Comput. Surv. 43 (2) (2011) 11:1–11:29.
[141] D.M. Cohen, S.R. Dalal, M.L. Fredman, G.C. Patton, The AETG system: an approach to testing based on combinatiorial design, IEEE Trans. Softw. Eng. 23 (7) (1997) 437–444.
[142] D. Kuhn, M. Reilly, An investigation of the applicability of design of experiments to software testing, in: Proceedings of the Software Engineering Workshop (NASA), IEEE, 2002.
[143] D.R. Kuhn, D.R. Wallace, A.M. Gallo Jr, Software Fault Interactions and Implications for Software Testing, IEEE Trans. Softw. Eng. 30 (6) (2004) 418–421.
[144] Z. Wang, B. Xu, L. Chen, L. Xu, Adaptive interaction fault location based on combinatorial testing, in: Proceedings of the International Conference on Quality Software (QSIC), IEEE, 2010.
[145] J. Petke, S. Yoo, M.B. Cohen, M. Harman, Efficiency and early fault detection with lower and higher strength combinatorial interaction testing, in: Proceedings of the Joint Meeting on Foundations of Software Engineering (ESEC/FSE), ACM, 2013.
[146] R.E. Bryant, Graph-based algorithms for boolean function manipulation, IEEE Trans. Comput. C-35 (8) (1986) 677–691.
[147] Y. Lei, R. Kacker, D.R. Kuhn, V. Okun, J. Lawrence, IPOG: a general strategy for t-way software testing, in: Proceedings of the International Conference and Workshops on the Engineering of Computer-Based Systems (ECBS), IEEE, 2007.
[148] M.B. Cohen, M.B. Dwyer, J. Shi, Interaction testing of highly-configurable systems in the presence of constraints, in: Proceedings of the International Symposium on Software Testing and Analysis (ISSTA), ACM, 2007.
[149] H. Si, M. Cohen, A. Memon, Repairing GUI test suites using a genetic algorithm, in: Proceedings of the International Conference on Software Testing, Verification and Validation (ICST), IEEE, 2010.
[150] Alloy Community, http://alloy.mit.edu.

ABOUT THE AUTHORS

Leonardo Mariani is an Associate Professor at the University of Milano Bicocca. He holds a Ph.D. in Computer Science received from the same university in 2005.

His research interests include software engineering, in particular software testing, static and dynamic analysis, automated debugging, and self-repairing systems.

He has been awarded with the ERC Consolidator Grant 2014 and he is currently active in several European and National projects. He is regularly involved in the organizing and program committees of major software engineering conferences.

Mauro Pezzè is a Professor of Software Engineering at the University of Milano Bicocca and the University of Lugano.

His general research interests are in the areas of software testing and analysis, autonomic computing, and self-healing software systems. Prior to joining the University of Milan Bicocca and the University of Lugano as full professor, he was an assistant and an associate professor at the Politecnico di Milano, and a visiting researcher at the University of Edinburgh and the University of California, Irvine. He is an associate editor of the IEEE Transactions on Software Engineering and member of the steering committee of the ACM International Conference on Software Testing and Analysis (ISSTA).

He has been an associate editor of ACM Transactions on Software Engineering and Methodology from 2006 to 2013 and member of the steering committee of the International Conference on Software Engineering (ICSE) from 2009 to 2014. He is coauthor of the book "Software Testing and Analysis, Process, Principles and Techniques" (John Wiley, 2008) and he is the author or coauthor of more than 120 refereed journal and conference papers. He is a senior member of the IEEE and a member of the IEEE Computer Society.

Daniele Zuddas is a Ph.D. student at Università della Svizzera italiana, Faculty of Informatics, Lugano, Switzerland, working in the Software Testing and Analysis Research group (STAR) led by prof. Mauro Pezzè. He has received a M.Sc. in Computer Science from the University of Milano Bicocca in March 2014. His main research interest is system testing of interactive applications.

CHAPTER FIVE

Inroads in Testing Access Control

Tejeddine Mouelhi*, Donia El Kateb†, Yves Le Traon†
*itrust consulting, Berbourg, Luxembourg
†Interdisciplinary Research Centre, SnT, University of Luxembourg, Kirchberg, Luxembourg

Contents

Abstract

In the last few years, a plethora of research has addressed security testing issues. Several commercial tools have emerged to provide security testing services. Software security testing goes beyond functional testing to reveal flaws and vulnerabilities in software design and behavior. Access control is a major pillar in computer security. This chapter pursues the goal of describing the landscape in the research area of access control testing. We provide an outline of the different existing research over the literature according to the taxonomy reflecting the different phases of common software testing processes

Advances in Computers, Volume 99
ISSN 0065-2458
http://dx.doi.org/10.1016/bs.adcom.2015.04.003
195

(generation, selection, prioritization, quality assessment, regression). We also provide an outline of some existing initiatives that support usage control besides access control by testing obligation policies. Finally, we point out future research directions that emerge from the current research study. Through this work, we aim at providing useful guidelines for software testers to improve the current trends in access control testing.

1. INTRODUCTION

Software security is one major concern that is required to build trustworthy software systems. In the last decades, we have witnessed an increasing interest in the security testing research area. Several researchers have explored this topic by providing new solutions in terms of security modeling, security features development, and the specification and implementation of the security mechanisms that have to be embedded in software systems. In parallel to the emergence of security concerns, security testing has also gained a considerable interest as it has to be developed conjointly to software security hardening. As a matter of fact, it is crucial to guarantee that the security mechanisms that are in place are correctly implemented. Testing these security mechanisms is very important in order to avoid ending up with security flaws inside the system or the application.

Access control is one of the major and the most critical security mechanisms. It ensures that only eligible users are able to access protected resources in a given system. This book chapter explores the landscape of access control testing and shows advances in access control testing approaches.

We start by providing recent advances in access control testing by surveying recent contributions in this research domain. We present the research contributions according to how they fit in a given research process. In a nutshell, the process of testing access control implemented in a given system or application follows the different steps highlighted in Fig. 1. The first and the most important step aims at *generating* a set of test cases that have to be exercised on the system under test.

Based on real-world applications, a large number of test cases are generated. Due to budget, time, and resources constraints, testers have to choose the tests that have to be run among all the generated tests. The subset of test cases to be run is defined based on business-related criteria according to available budget, computing resources, and the time allocated to testing. Commonly, there are two options, either *selecting* a fixed number of tests

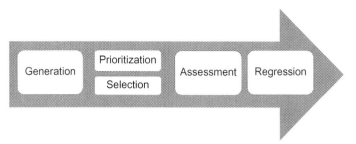

Figure 1 Testing process in a nutshell.

or ordering (*prioritizing*) tests. When *prioritizing* tests, the tests that have highest priority are executed first until the resources that are available for testing such as time or budget are consumed. Finally, once tests are executed and their verdict is checked, we need to assess the quality of these tests to provide guarantee that the test suite is of high quality. Tests assessment enables also to evaluate the fault-detection capability of tests cases. This book chapter goes first through the overall testing process by providing a detailed description of existing research contributions that aim at *generating*, *selecting*, *prioritizing*, and *assessing* test cases. Second, we provide an overall view of international projects which tackled security testing and the emerging commercial products for security testing.

Third, we describe ongoing research that extends the work on access control testing to encompass usage control testing.

We conclude this chapter by discussing the main security testing challenges that are worth exploring in the near future. The remainder of this chapter is organized as follows. In Section 2, we give an overview about access control concepts and mechanisms by focusing on the XACML policy model. In Section 3, we go through the different approaches for access control testing according to a classification according to test targets. Section 4 outlines the research proposals in each step of common testing processes. Section 5 gives an overview about usage control testing. Section 6 discusses future research challenges and finally Section 7 concludes this work.

2. ACCESS CONTROL

In the last few years, XACML (eXtensible Access Control Markup Language) has gained momentum as a standard to develop security solutions. In this section, we introduce key concepts related to access control, XACML architecture, and policy language.

2.1 Access Control as a Security Concept

Unauthorized access to sensitive data is one of the main challenging issues in IT security. Access control is a security mechanism that regulates the actions that users can/cannot perform on system resources. Access control policies are used to manage authorizations in the objective to protect sensitive data. Access control research spans mainly over access control policies models [1], access control policies enforcement mechanisms [2, 3], and access control policies languages definition [4]. Access control policies are defined based on several access control models such as Role-Based Access Control (RBAC) [5], Mandatory Access Control (MAC) [6], Discretionary Access Control (DAC) [7], and Organization-Based Access Control (OrBAC) [8]. Access control policies are specified in various policy specification languages such as the XACML and Enterprise Privacy Authorization Language [9]. An access control policy is composed of authorization rules that regulate the access to data and services. At the decision making time, a request to access a service/resource is evaluated against the rules in the policy. A response is then sent to the user, which authorizes/prohibits her/him to/from access/accessing the requested resource.

2.2 Security Policies

In the last few years, XACML has gained momentum as a standard to develop security solutions. Several commercial and open source solutions have been developed to help build access control systems.

2.2.1 XACML Model

XACML proposes a conceptual model of an access control architecture and defines the interactions between the components in this conceptual model. It also defines an access control policy language and a protocol for access control requests and responses. XACML policy-based systems rely on the separation of concerns, by implementing independently a software system and its associated security policy. Such separation eases policy management and increases the degree of policy interoperability with heterogeneous platforms. It also limits potential risks arising from incorrect policy implementation or maintenance when the policy is hard-coded inside the business logic. In the context of policy-based systems, a Policy Enforcement Point (PEP) is located inside an application's code (i.e., business logic of the system). Business logic describes functional algorithms to govern information exchange between access control decision logic and a user interface (i.e., presentation). To determine whether a user can access which resources, a request is formulated from a PEP located in an application code. Given a request, a Policy Decision Point (PDP) evaluates the request against an access control policy and returns its access decision (i.e., permit or deny) to the PEP.

XACML architecture is based on the following components:

- Policy Administration Point (PAP): It is the policy repository which sends policies to the PDP.
- PDP: The PDP is responsible for making decisions based on the collected information from other actors.
- PEP: It receives an access request whenever a service which is regulated by a security policy is called, sends a request in an XACML format to the PDP and enforces the decision sent by the PDP.
- Policy Information Point (PIP): The PIP retrieves necessary attributes from external resources (i.e., LDAP).
- Context Handler: It transforms requests/responses in an XACML format.

Figure 2 presents the interactions between the different components to handle an access control request: (1) Policies are written and managed in the

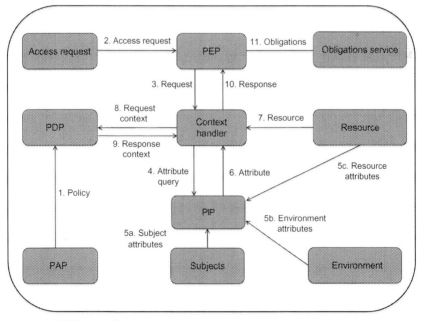

Figure 2 XACML data flow.

PAP. The PDP will fetch the policies in the PAP in each access control request evaluation. (2) The PEP is triggered whenever a service which is regulated by a security policy is called. (3) The PEP sends the request to a context handler that transforms the native format of the request into an XACML format. (4) The context handler sends a request to the PIP to collect attributes. (5) The PIP obtains the requested attributes from subject, resource, and environment. (6) The PIP sends the attributes to the context handler. (7) The context handler may include the resource in the context. (8) The context handler sends an XACML request to the PDP for evaluation. (9) The request is evaluated against the policies in the PAP. (10) The context handler returns the response to the PEP in a format that can be interpreted by the PEP. (11) If some obligations are returned with the decision, the PEP has to discharge those obligations.

2.2.2 XACML Policies

XACML policy has a hierarchical structure as shown in Fig. 3. On the top level of the this structure, a *policy set* can contain one (or more) *policy set*(s) or *policy* elements. A *policy set* (a *policy*) consists of a target, a set of rules, and a rule combining algorithm. The target specifies the subjects, resources, actions, and environments on which a policy can be applied. If a request satisfies the target of the *policy set* (*policy*), then the set of rules of the *policy set*

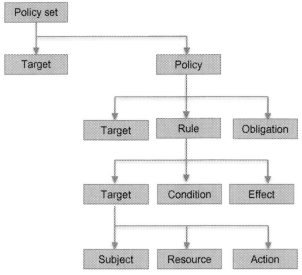

Figure 3 XACML policy structure.

(*policy*) is checked, else the *policy set* (*policy*) is skipped. A rule is composed by a target, which specifies the constraints of the request that are applicable to the rule, and a condition, which is a boolean function evaluated when the request is applicable to the rule. If the condition is evaluated to true, the result of the rule evaluation is the rule effect (*Permit* or *Deny*); otherwise, a *NotApplicable* result is given. If an error occurs during the application of a request to the policy, *Indeterminate* is returned. The rule combining algorithm enables to resolve conflicts when there is more than one rule that can be applicable to a given request. For instance, if the *permit-overrides* algorithm is used:

- If there is one single rule that is evaluated to permit, the permit decision takes precedence regardless of the result of the evaluation of other rules.
- If one rule is evaluated to Deny and all other rules are evaluated to NotApplicable, the final decision is Deny.
- If there is an error in the evaluation of a rule with Permit effect and the other policy rules with Permit effect are not applicable, the Indeterminate result is given.

The access decision is given by considering all attribute and element values describing the subject, resource, action, and environment of an access request and comparing them with the attribute and element values of the policy. An XACML request is composed of four elements: a subject, a resource, an action, and an environment. The values and types of these four elements should be among the values and types defined by the policy rules or targets. Listing 1 illustrates an XACML policy with one rule. The rule (lines 26–58) states that a student can borrow and return books from the library. Listing 2 illustrates an XACML request in which a student requests to borrow a book.

2.3 Beyond Access Control: Usage Control

Usage control extends the notion of access control to consider what can happen to the data in the future [10]. A security policy reflects usage control concepts [11] when it includes some actions that have to be carried out before the access (i.e., the user has to authenticate before accessing a Web site), during the access (i.e., the user has to keep an open window while he is accessing a Web site), or after access (i.e., the user has to submit a form after his access).

In security policies paradigm, those actions are usually referred to as (pre, ongoing, post) obligations [12, 13]. They accurately allow to extend the

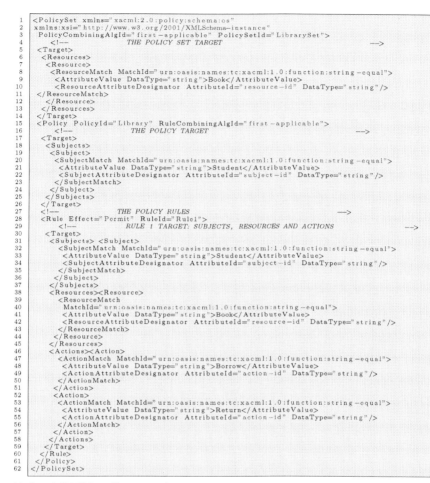

```
1  <PolicySet xmlns="xacml:2.0:policy:schema:os"
2   xmlns:xsi="http://www.w3.org/2001/XMLSchema-instance"
3   PolicyCombiningAlgId="first-applicable" PolicySetId="LibrarySet">
4       <!--                THE POLICY SET TARGET                   -->
5   <Target>
6     <Resources>
7      <Resource>
8       <ResourceMatch MatchId="urn:oasis:names:tc:xacml:1.0:function:string-equal">
9         <AttributeValue DataType="string">Book</AttributeValue>
10        <ResourceAttributeDesignator AttributeId="resource-id" DataType="string"/>
11     </ResourceMatch>
12     </Resource>
13     </Resources>
14   </Target>
15   <Policy PolicyId="Library" RuleCombiningAlgId="first-applicable">
16       <!--                THE POLICY TARGET                       -->
17    <Target>
18     <Subjects>
19      <Subject>
20       <SubjectMatch MatchId="urn:oasis:names:tc:xacml:1.0:function:string-equal">
21         <AttributeValue DataType="string">Student</AttributeValue>
22         <SubjectAttributeDesignator AttributeId="subject-id" DataType="string"/>
23       </SubjectMatch>
24      </Subject>
25     </Subjects>
26    </Target>
27    <!--             THE POLICY RULES                              -->
28    <Rule Effect="Permit" RuleId="Rule1">
29        <!--         RULE 1 TARGET: SUBJECTS, RESOURCES AND ACTIONS       -->
30     <Target>
31      <Subjects> <Subject>
32        <SubjectMatch MatchId="urn:oasis:names:tc:xacml:1.0:function:string-equal">
33         <AttributeValue DataType="string">Student</AttributeValue>
34         <SubjectAttributeDesignator AttributeId="subject-id" DataType="string"/>
35        </SubjectMatch>
36      </Subject>
37      </Subjects>
38      <Resources><Resource>
39       <ResourceMatch
40        MatchId="urn:oasis:names:tc:xacml:1.0:function:string-equal">
41        <AttributeValue DataType="string">Book</AttributeValue>
42        <ResourceAttributeDesignator AttributeId="resource-id" DataType="string"/>
43       </ResourceMatch>
44      </Resource>
45      </Resources>
46      <Actions><Action>
47       <ActionMatch MatchId="urn:oasis:names:tc:xacml:1.0:function:string-equal">
48        <AttributeValue DataType="string">Borrow</AttributeValue>
49        <ActionAttributeDesignator AttributeId="action-id" DataType="string"/>
50       </ActionMatch>
51      </Action>
52      <Action>
53       <ActionMatch MatchId="urn:oasis:names:tc:xacml:1.0:function:string-equal">
54        <AttributeValue DataType="string">Return</AttributeValue>
55        <ActionAttributeDesignator AttributeId="action-id" DataType="string"/>
56       </ActionMatch>
57      </Action>
58      </Actions>
59     </Target>
60    </Rule>
61   </Policy>
62  </PolicySet>
```

Listing 1 XACML policy example.

```
1  <?xml version="1.0" encoding="UTF-8"?>
2  <Request>
3       <Subject>
4           <Attribute AttributeId="subject-id" DataType="XMLSchema#string">
5               <AttributeValue>Student</AttributeValue>
6           </Attribute>
7       </Subject>
8       <Resource>
9           <Attribute AttributeId="resource-id"
10              DataType="XMLSchema#string">
11              <AttributeValue>Book</AttributeValue>
12          </Attribute>
13      </Resource>
14      <Action>
15          <Attribute AttributeId="action-id"
16              DataType="XMLSchema#string">
17              <AttributeValue>Borrow</AttributeValue>
18          </Attribute>
19      </Action>
20      <Environment/>
21  </Request>
```

Listing 2 XACML request example.

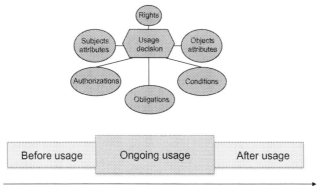

Mutability of attributes, continuity of decision

Figure 4 UCON model.

notion of access rights with related duties, called obligations. Obligations, which have been introduced in Ref. [14], are considered as an important research direction in the domain of usage control [15].

A complete security policy should encompass both rights and duties, both access authorizations and obligations. Usage control model (UCON) [16–18] is a popular model that is built based on the following concepts that we illustrate in Fig. 4:

• *Continuity of decision:* Access control is verified before and during the access. Access to resources can be revoked after it has been granted due to a change of some object or subject attributes.
• *Mutability of attributes:* Subject's or object's attributes can be mutable (i.e., subject name) or immutable (i.e., resource cost). Immutable attributes can be updated before, during, or after the access.

The model is based on a mapping of subjects and objects to access rights. Rights are evaluated based on (1) authorizations which are predicates on subject and object attributes, (2) conditions which represent predicates on environmental attributes, and (3) obligations which represent actions that have to be performed before or during access.

3. TEST TARGETS WHEN TESTING ACCESS CONTROL

XACML policy specification language defines access control policies in an XML format and defines a standardized way to exchange requests/responses. It relies on an abstract architecture consisting of abstract components interacting with each other to handle a decision making process. XACML relies on a standardized encoding since it enables to encode a policy independently from the underlying platform, to make it thus interoperable with heterogeneous platforms. In XACML architecture, the policy is externalized from the application code and from the decision engine. This eases the maintenance of software systems since the update of the policy, usually a frequent task, can be done without changing the system's implementation.

The main components in the access control architecture are the policy, the evaluation engine that evaluates the policy against access control requests, and the underlying implementation. A comprehensive access control framework has to cover these three main components. The massive body of research in access control testing can be classified according to the aforementioned main components. In what follows, we survey the research contributions that have targeted each element in an access control architecture.

3.1 Testing the Policy

The domain of testing security enables to verify that the policy has to behave as expected. Testing XACML access control policies is complex due to the verbosity of the language, the recursive structure of XACML policies and the combining algorithms.

In Ref. [19], Martin has proposed an approach for policy testing based on the analysis of access control responses. Access control requests are triggered and a policy specification error is detected in the policy specification if the access control response related to the triggered request is different from the expected response.

3.2 Testing the Implementation

In most cases, PEPs are implemented manually, which can introduce errors in policy enforcement and lead to security vulnerabilities. To systematically test and validate the correct enforcement of access control policies in policy-based system, Mouelhi et al. [20] have used mutation analysis to verify the correct policy enforcement.

3.3 Testing the Evaluation Engine

Assuming that the policy specification is correct, Daoudagh et al. [21] evaluate a given policy evaluation engine like Sun's XACML implementation[1]

---

[1] http://sunxacml.sourceforge.net/.

by comparing expected responses to the real access control responses that result from the evaluation of requests against the policy. The approach has not identified any error in the evaluation engine in their conducted evaluation; however, the approach can be used to test any policy evaluation engine.

4. ACCESS CONTROL TESTING

Access control testing [22] is based on the evaluation of actual access control responses against expected responses. Tests inputs are access control requests that are evaluated by the PDP against the access control policy. The test outputs are the authorization responses that testers compare against what they expect in terms of authorization response. In what follows, we revisit recent advances in the main building blocks of access control testing by starting with test qualification, then test generation, selection, prioritization, and finally regression testing.

4.1 Access Control Test Qualification

Mutation is widely known and used technique in software testing in general. The aim is to evaluate the test quality in terms of fault detection. A good test suite should be able to detect all faults in a given program. As shown in Fig. 5, to evaluate the effectiveness of the tests, faults are seeded in the program. A unique fault is seeded each time, leading to create a faulty version of the program that we call mutant. Then, tests are executed against these mutants to detect the seeded faults. A good test suite should detect all seeded

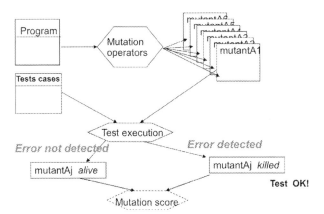

Figure 5 Mutation analysis process.

faults. In some particular cases, the mutated program is semantically equivalent to the original program. In this case, it behaves like the original program and tests cannot differentiate it from the original. These so-called equivalent mutants should be detected and removed. Finally, a mutation score is computed to evaluate the effectiveness of the test suite. Usually, faults are seeded using what we call mutation operators, which seed a very specific fault.

Mutation analysis was adapted and applied in the context of access control testing [23–25]. In this chapter, we present how it was applied to XACML policies. Martin and Xie [23] proposed a first approach to mutating XACML policies. This work was later extended by Bertolino *et al.* [25] with additional mutation operators by including the operators proposed in Ref. [24]. They also performed a better assessment of the proposed mutation operators.

The mutation process for access control testing is described in Fig. 6. Instead of mutating directly the program, the strategy in this case is to mutate the access control policy. Then, since the policy is included inside the code and used to evaluate the requests, the objective of the security test cases will be to detect seeded faults in the policy. A good test suite should be able to detect all faults seeded in the access control policy rules. It is important to highlight the fact that mutation should be applied only to the security part,

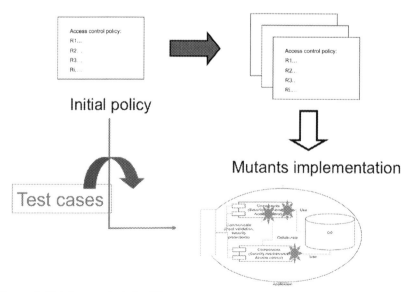

Figure 6 Mutation analysis for AC process.

in this case the XACML policy by mutating the rules. In fact, mutating the application code will not provide useful faults from the access control point of view because we are not testing the system' functionality but rather the implementation of the policy.

The mutation operators are specific to the XACML language and target the modification of the rules and the way response is computed. The list of these operators and their description is shown in Table 1. Most of these operators change the rules, for instance, by impacting the rule effect (inverting deny into permit and vice versa) or changing policy or rule combining algorithm. An interesting operator is definitely the Add New Rule (ANR) operator, which changes the policy by adding a new rule. This operator is an interesting one because it is difficult to detect. Indeed, in order to detect that the policy contains an additional rule, we need to create a test case that checks this added rule. Therefore, the test request should contain the values included in that added rule.

Table 1 XACML Mutation Operators [25]

ID	Description
PSTT, PSTF	Policy Set Target True/False
PTT, PTF	Policy Target True/False
RTT, RTF	Rule Target True/False
RCT, RCF	Rule Condition True/False
CPC, CRC	Change Policy/Rule Combining Algorithm
CRE	Change Rule Effect
RPT	Rule Type is replaced with another one
ANR	Add a New Rule
RER	Remove an Existing Rule
AUF, RUF	Add/Remove Uniqueness Function
CNOF	Change N-OF Function
CLF	Change Logical Function
ANF, RNF	Add/Remove Not Function
CCF	Change Comparison Function
FPR, FDR	First the Rules having a *Permit/Deny* effect

4.2 Access Control Test Generation

In the last few years, Model-Driven Engineering (MDE) [26] has appeared as a paradigm that promotes models as the central key element of all the phases of software development. MDE enables to build an abstraction layer to handle complex software systems and to automate various tasks. Model-Driven Architecture (MDA) illustrates a normalization of MDE that has been proposed in 2000 by OMG (Object Management Group) [27]. MDA offers several techniques that allow denying families of languages and supporting tools. MDE has introduced a new vision to the testing activities which are considered as a core activity in the software development cycle. This vision is illustrated through model-based testing [28] which refers to the automatic generation of test cases based on requirements models. Model-based testing requires to invest effort on building models that can be used to derive test cases. However, this effort is repaid through automation and easiness in capturing the changes in the model.

Model-based testing has been used in the context of security testing. In Ref. [29], Pretschner *et al.* have used the policy model to generate tests. Abstract test cases are derived from all the rules in the policy by a combination of roles, permissions, and contexts. Concrete test cases are derived from abstract test cases. The whole process for security testing is presented in Ref. [30]. The authors use requirements elicitation to build a security model from the application. This model is transformed into platform-specific security code that is woven using aspect-oriented programming [31] into running code. The security tests are derived from the requirements to test the code. A model-based approach based on Petri nets has been proposed by Xu *et al.* in Ref. [32]. The authors have introduced contracts and access control rules into Petri nets and generated access control test cases from Petri nets models. A MIM (Model-Implementation Mapping) description is used to map the model elements into executable tests.

To facilitate the task of test generation to test firewall policies, Hwang *et al.* [33] have defined four techniques for packets generation. The first technique is based on packet generation and aims at generating entities within a given specific domain. The second and the third techniques are based on local and global constraint solving. The local constraint technique generates packets to maximize the satisfaction of constraints defined at the rules level, while the global constraint technique aims at maximizing the satisfaction of the constraints defined at the policy level. The fourth technique automatically generates test cases based on boundary values.

In Refs. [34, 35], Martin *et al.* have proposed a framework to automate tests generation for access control policies. The framework takes as input different policy versions and uses a change impact analysis tool to derive policy portions that are syntactically different. For two different policy versions, a request is generated that provides different responses when evaluated with two policies versions. Requests are finally reduced by identifying the minimal set of test cases that covers all the requirements that have to be satisfied to reach a defined policy coverage criteria.

In Ref. [36], the authors have proposed a model-based testing approach to test PolPA authorizations systems. PolPA authorizations systems are based on a process-algebraic language to specify policies according to UCON [17]. The policy is transformed into a tree structure and the tests are derived from a depth-first exploration of the tree.

In the context of XACML policies testing, Bertolino *et al.* [37] have proposed the X-CREATE tool which proposes two strategies for XACML request generation. The first strategy is called XPT and is based on XACML context schema analysis. Requests are generated with the respect to border values of the different elements in the XACML context schema. The combinatorial strategy is based on pairwise, three-wise, and four-wise combinations of subject, resource, action, and environment elements in the XACML policy.

In Refs. [38, 39], Mallouli *et al.* have proposed a framework for security tests generation that they have applied on a Weblog system. The generated tests check the conformance of the policy specification with the business logic. The business model is expressed through an extended finite-state machine (EFSM). Prohibitions, permissions, and obligations are added to the EFSM as transition or restriction predicates. The authors have developed the SIRIUS test generation tool to derive tests automatically from the system model.

In Ref. [40], Masood *et al.* have proposed approaches to reduce tests that are generated from finite-state models. The approaches are based on heuristics and random selection of paths in the policy model. First-order mutation has been used to evaluate the fault detection capability of the selected test cases.

In Ref. [41], Brucker *et al.* have used the HOL-TESTGEN tool to transform high-level requirements into a formal specification that is encoded in higher-order logic (HOL) and convertible into sequence of test cases.

4.3 Access Control Test Selection

The selection of relevant tests among a test suite is a very challenging task. A selection process usually is based on effectiveness criteria such as performance, execution cost, fault detection, or coverage. Bertolino *et al.* [42] have proposed an approach for XACML test selection based on coverage criteria. The XACML rule coverage criterion is based on selecting tests that match the Rule Target Sets. The Rule Target Set is the union of the target of the rule, and all enclosing policy and policy sets targets.

ALGORITHM 1 Coverage-Based Selection of Test Cases [42]

```
 1:  input: S = {Req₁,...,Reqₙ}              ▷Unordered set of n XACML
         requests
 2:  input: P                                ▷The XACML policy
 3:  output: Result       ▷List of m selected XACML requests with m ¡ n
 4:  Result ← {}
 5:  TargetsConds ← computeAllRulesTargetsConds(P)
 6:  i ← 0
 7:  while i < TargetsConds.size() do
 8:     ContainsReq ← False
 9:     j ← 0
10:     while !ContainsReq do
11:        ReqTargetⱼ ← extractReqTarget(Reqⱼ)
12:        if containsReq(TargetCondᵢ, ReqTargetⱼ) then
13:           Result ← Result ∪ {Reqⱼ}
14:           ContainsReq ← True
15:        end if
16:        j ← j + 1
17:        if then j == n
18:           Break loop
19:        end if
20:     end while
21:     i ← i + 1
22:  end while
23:  return Result
```

According to the XACML specification, in order to match the rule target, requests must first match the enclosing policy and policy sets targets (note that there could be several enclosing policy sets). Here are the different configurations in terms of rule target matching.

- If a rule R_1 contains no condition and if it has a target containing the elements {Subject₁,Action₁,Resource₁} and the policy and policy set targets related to the rule are both empty, then in order to match R_1, a request should contain the same values of {Subject$_1$,Action$_1$, Resource$_1$}.

- If a rule R_1 contains no condition and if the rule target has several subjects, resources, actions, and environments and the enclosing policy and policy set targets are empty, the request should include a subject contained in target subjects set, a resource contained in the target resources set, an action contained in the target actions set, and an environment contained in the target environments set in order to cover the rule target.
- Finally, if the Rule Target Set of a rule R_1 is empty and its condition is evaluated to True or False, all requests are covering the rule R_1.

Algorithm 1 is used for test cases selection. The algorithm takes as input the Rule Target Sets and a set of access requests. Then, it iterates through the requests and selects the ones that match one Rule Target Set according to the aforementioned configurations. However, the coverage criteria that have been defined in Ref. [42] do not take into consideration the combining algorithms, which play an important role when it comes to selecting which rule applies in case of conflicts. The impact of combining algorithms on the quality of the selected test cases in terms of fault detection effectiveness has to be explored. This impact can be investigated by using policies that contain conflicting rules.

In the context of access control tests selection, Mouelhi *et al.* [20] select security tests among the set of functional tests by tracking the test cases that are impacted by security rules. Basically, the authors mutate each rule in the policy for instance by inverting the prohibition rule to a permission rule or vice versa and they identify the tests that kill the mutants. Those tests are considered as security tests.

4.4 Access Control Test Prioritization

Test prioritization is a very important task in the testing process. Indeed, usually projects have limited and strict budget and time resources and since exhaustive testing is practically impossible, it is important to order the tests cases and run the first tests until the resources are exhausted. This is exactly what prioritizing tests is about, ordering test cases in terms of a given testing criteria, for instance fault detection. If for a given policy, there are let us assume 10K test cases and only the first 100 tests can be executed and checked manually due to time constraint, and then it is important to choose the first 100 tests, which achieve the highest fault detection capability. To measure the fault detection capability, it is possible to rely on mutation analysis and then we are able to compare a given prioritization approach to the random prioritization, considered as baseline.

This section presents in details the work done recently by Bertolino *et al.* [43]. It shows the approach in a nutshell and then presents the formal description of the algorithms that were used to order the test cases. Finally, it shows the main limitation and potential improvements.

4.4.1 The Similarity-Based Prioritization Strategy

For XACML policies, there is a recent work from Bertolino *et al.* [43], which proposes a novel approach for prioritizing test cases based on similarity. The main idea of this work boils down to ordering the tests by considering the test cases, which are different from each other, putting first the most different test cases, since a request in XACML contains usually a subject, an action, a resource, and an environment. The objective is to choose the combinations containing different values. Concretely, a distance is computed between each given test case and the others; then, test cases having the largest distance with the other test cases are selected and put first in the list. Then, the process continues for the remaining tests by calculating again the distances and selecting the most interesting test cases in terms of distance.

It is important to highlight the fact that the way the distance is computed has an important impact on the resulting order. Indeed, the distance computation algorithm could include the notion of coverage in order to give priority to test cases, which increase the policy coverage. This way, the tests will trigger the rules defined inside the policy instead of triggering the default rule effect or a rule that is not defined in the policy.

Bertolino *et al.* proposed two criteria to perform similarity-based prioritization in the context of XACML testing, namely the simple similarity and the XACML similarity.

The simple similarity

The simple similarity is straightforward. Given two requests, the distance is equal to 0, when the four values of the two requests (the subject, the action, the resource, and the environment) match. This is the case, when the two requests are identical. If all request values do not match, then the distance value is 4. In the other cases, when corresponding values match partly the distance can vary between 1 and 3. Therefore, the distance value is computed simply by comparing one to one each of the two requests attributes.

XACML similarity

For each request, an applicability matrix is computed. The size of this matrix is $5 \times n$ (n is the number of rules). The five rows contain values related to applicability of the request to subject, action, resource, environment, and the full rule. A request is applicable when it matches the given element (subject, action, etc.). In addition to this matrix, a priority value is computed for all pairs of requests and contains applicability value of the two rules combined. Finally, the distance matrix is computed by adding all values in applicability matrix to the priority value and simple similarity value. If the simple similarity equals to 0, then the value is set to 0; otherwise, it is computed as stated before.

4.4.2 Assessment of the Approach

Assessment of this proposed approach was performed on real work case studies. A set of real world access control policies written in XACML were used in addition to mutation analysis in order to evaluate the effectiveness of the proposed criteria and compare them to the random prioritization, which involves ordering the test cases randomly. The random ordering is considered as a baseline. In addition, the prioritization is compared to the near-optimal heuristic, computed *a posteriori* based on mutation results. In their paper [43], the authors applied the experiment on six policies. In this book chapter, we show two interesting results for the policy with the relatively smallest number of rules and the one with the largest number of rules.

Figure 7 shows the obtained results for continue-a policy, which includes 398 rules, while Fig. 8 presents the results for pluto which contains only 21 rules. Clearly, for both policies the XACML similarity is outperforming the random prioritization and is very close to the near-optimal heuristic.

4.4.3 Limitations and Potential Improvements

The main limitation of this prioritization approach is related to the fact that combining algorithms are ignored and not considered during the prioritization process. Indeed, combining algorithms might play an important role in case the policy contains many conflicting rules. In that case, the proposed strategies to order test cases might not be effective. This claim is yet to be checked by performing more experiments involving policies with several conflicting rules. This future work was mentioned by the authors in their paper [43] and is yet to be done.

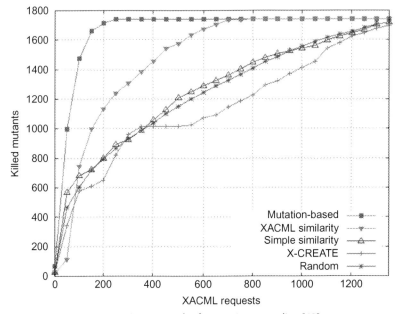

Figure 7 Prioritization experiment results for continue-a policy [43].

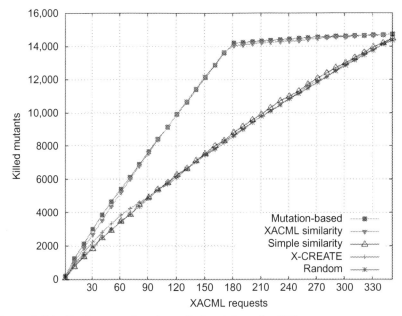

Figure 8 Prioritization experiment results for pluto policy [43].

4.5 Regression Testing

Regression testing [44] aims at verifying that the modified parts of the software are correct. Regression test selection aims at reducing the costs inherent from rerunning all the test cases by selecting the test cases that maximize the fault detection capabilities of the modified version of the software. In Ref. [45], a regression test selection approach has been applied in the context of the policy evolution. A regression test selection process in the context of security policy evolution is illustrated in Fig. 9. The authors have proposed three techniques for regression test selection that reveal implementation faults when the policy evolves. The three techniques are summarized as follows:

- *Mutation-based technique:* This technique establishes a mapping between test cases and rules by exercising tests for a normal policy and a mutated one. The mutated policy has a flip in one of its rules. When a test case presents a different result with a normal policy and a mutated one, a test case is thus mapped to the rule. The second step considers an initial policy and a policy that has been evolved, identifies the different rules in the two policy versions, and uses the correlation step to identify the test regression test selection set.

- *Coverage-based technique:* This technique uses two steps similar to the first technique; however, the mapping step uses coverage analysis instead of mutation analysis. The coverage step aims at tracking the impacted rules when a test executes.

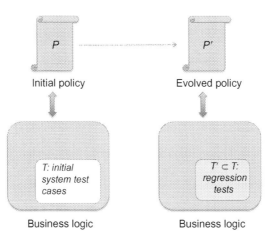

Figure 9 Regression testing in the context of policy evolution.

- *Request evaluation-based technique:* This technique is more efficient than the two previous techniques in terms of execution time since it does not require a mapping step. This technique analyzes requests results at runtime and selects test cases that have different evaluations with an initial policy and its evolved version.

5. USAGE CONTROL TESTING

Even though the research in access control testing has been quite active in the last few years. There is still a major effort to improve usage control testing. Rubab *et al.* [46] have initiated this effort by developing a model-based approach for usage control testing. Their approach is based on an obligations profile that extends the concepts of UML Class and State Machine Diagrams. They have used the Object Constraint Language to define constraints on the obligations profile. The profile completeness has been validated through the modeling of 47 different obligations for four different systems. They have developed the tool to generate executable test cases from UML class diagrams and UML state machines. The quality of the generated test cases has been assessed using mutation analysis. Rubab *et al.* have used the mutation operators that have been defined in the work of Elrakaiby *et al.* [47]. The mutation analysis results showed that on average the generated test cases have been able to kill 75% of the mutants.

6. DISCUSSION

Even though the domain of access testing has been widely explored in the last few years, there is still big room for research to tackle the current limitations and challenges in this research area. These limitations and challenges are the following:

Lack of benchmarking policies and access control implementations

XACML is based on an Attribute-Based Access Control Model (ABAC) that captures several access control scenarios. The lack of benchmarks in XACML access control policies and underlying implementations makes it difficult to define access control testing frameworks that are able to capture all XACML features (i.e., delegation, obligations, combining algorithms). A benchmark for distributed environment such as the cloud environment that illustrates for instance how resources can be regulated for different tenants [48] would provide a room for more challenging testing issues.

Lack of interaction between academia and research

There has always been a lack of communication and collaboration between researchers and industry in general in the software testing and even in software engineering. For access control testing, this lack of collaboration is flagrant and questions the usefulness of the academic research in this area. The vast majority of papers cited in this book chapter were done without any collaboration with industry partners. Even more, some research done in this area is probably not applicable in an industrial setting simply because the case studies that were considered are toy systems or small policies. Therefore, the community should put more effort in bringing the research ideas, approaches, and prototypes to industry by setting more collaborations and more partnerships with companies, specially those involved in building tools for specifying, deploying, and verifying the XACML language like IBM, Oracle, and Axiomatics. Furthermore, the research community should be actively involved in the standardization process. Indeed, as shown on the OASIS XACML technical committee Web page,[2] all members contributing to the XACML standard are from industry. Researchers should be involved and added to the list of contributing members.

Automation challenges

Building automated frameworks for test generation, selection, prioritization, and assessment is still an area of active research. With the growing complexity of policy-based systems, there is a need to develop automated tools that are able to test properties satisfaction and to scale. Moreover, one major challenge that automation has to face is the interoperability issues. In most of the cases, the testing tool is developed based on a specific application and a specific access control model. Subsequently, its usage with a different target application or with a different access control model may require to use specific adapters.

7. CONCLUSION

This book chapter presented a detailed summary of existing approaches tackling access control testing. It has focused on testing the

---

[2] https://www.oasis-open.org/committees/membership.php?wg_abbrev=xacml.

XACML policies and showed the different components of XACML policies testing, namely, the automated test generation approaches, test selection and prioritization approaches, and finally test qualification and assessment based on mutation analysis. This area of research has been very active during the last decade and researchers made significant progress and proposed very effective contributions, in terms of testing strategies and also in terms of tools implementing the proposed ideas.

On the other hand, the area of usage control testing is not as mature and substantial research work in this area is yet to be done. We believe that the work in this area is still in its early phases and there is much to be done for instance, to target testing XACML policies, which include usage control rules.

ACKNOWLEDGMENTS

We would like to thank itrust consulting staff for their help in proofreading this book chapter and their help in providing feedback and comments specially in the discussion part.

In addition, we would like to thank the members of the SerVal research group, from the University of Luxembourg, for their help, comments, and interesting inputs that helped us in improving the contents of this book chapter.

REFERENCES

[1] P. Samarati, S. de Capitani di Vimercati, Access control: policies, models, and mechanisms, in: Foundations of Security Analysis and Design: Tutorial Lectures, 2001, pp. 137–196.
[2] F. Siewe, A. Cau, Z. Hussein, A compositional framework for access control policies enforcement, in: Proceedings of the 2003 ACM Workshop on Formal Methods in Security Engineering (FMSE '03), ACM, New York, NY, USA, 2003, pp. 32–42.
[3] J. Ligatti, L. Bauer, D. Walker, Edit automata: enforcement mechanisms for run-time security policies, Int. J. Inf. Secur. 4 (1–2) (2005) 2–16.
[4] N. Damianou, N. Dulay, E. Lupu, M. Sloman, The ponder policy specification language, in: Policies for Distributed Systems and Networks, Springer, Berlin Heidelberg, 2001, pp. 18–38.
[5] D.F. Ferraiolo, R.S. Sandhu, S.I. Gavrila, D.R. Kuhn, R. Chandramouli, Proposed NIST standard for role-based access control, ACM Trans. Inf. Syst. Secur. 4 (3) (2001) 224–274.
[6] D.E. Bell, L.J. La Padula, Secure Computer System: Unified Exposition and Multics Interpretation (No. MTR-2997-REV-1), MITRE Corp, Bedford MA, 1976.
[7] B. Lampson, Protection, in: Proceedings of the 5th Princeton Conference on Information Sciences and Systems, 1971.
[8] A.A.E. Kalam, S. Benferhat, A. Miège, R.E. Baida, F. Cuppens, C. Saurel, P. Balbiani, Y. Deswarte, G. Trouessin, Organization based access control, in: Proceedings of 10th IEEE International Conference on Policies for Distributed Systems and Networks, 2003, pp. 120–131.
[9] P. Ashley, S. Hada, G. Karjoth, C. Powers, M. Schunter, 2003, Enterprise privacy authorization language (EPAL 1.2), Submission to W3C, p. 1.
[10] A. Pretschner, M. Hilty, D.A. Basin, Distributed usage control, Commun. ACM 49 (2006) 39–44.

[11] J. Park, R. Sandhu, Towards usage control models: beyond traditional access control, in: Proceedings of the Seventh ACM Symposium on Access Control Models and Technologies, SACMAT'02, 2002, pp. 57–64.

[12] M. Hilty, D.A. Basin, A. Pretschner, On obligations, in: ESORICS, 2005, pp. 98–117.

[13] X. Zhang, Formal model and analysis of usage control, Ph.D. thesis, 2006.

[14] N.H. Minsky, A.D. Lockman, Ensuring integrity by adding obligations to privileges, in: Proceedings of the 8th International Conference on Software Engineering, ICSE'85, 1985, pp. 92–102.

[15] K. Irwin, T. Yu, W.H. Winsborough, On the modeling and analysis of obligations, in: Proceedings of the 13th ACM Conference on Computer and Communications Security, CCS'06, 2006, pp. 134–143.

[16] J. Park, R. Sandhu, Towards usage control models: beyond traditional access control, in: Proceedings of the Seventh ACM Symposium on Access Control Models and Technologies, ACM, 2002, pp. 57–64.

[17] J. Park, R. Sandhu, The UCON ABC usage control model, ACM Trans. Inf. Syst. Secur. 7 (1) (2004) 128–174.

[18] C. Danwei, H. Xiuli, R. Xunyi, Access control of cloud service based on ucon, in: Cloud Computing, Springer, Berlin Heidelberg, 2009, pp. 559–564.

[19] E. Martin, Testing and analysis of access control policies, in: Companion to the Proceedings of the 29th International Conference on Software Engineering, IEEE Computer Society, 2007, pp. 75–76.

[20] T. Mouelhi, Y. Le Traon, B. Baudry, Transforming and selecting functional test cases for security policy testing, in: Software Testing Verification and Validation, 2009. ICST'09. International Conference on, IEEE, 2009, pp. 171–180.

[21] S. Daoudagh, D. El Kateb, F. Lonetti, E. Marchetti, T. Mouelhi, A toolchain for model-based design and testing of access control systems, in: MODELSWARD, 2015.

[22] J.H. Hwang, E. Martin, T. Xie, et al., Testing access control policies, in: Encyclopedia of Software Engineering, 2010, pp. 673–683.

[23] E. Martin, T. Xie, A fault model and mutation testing of access control policies, in: Proceedings of the 16th International Conference on World Wide Web, ACM, 2007, pp. 667–676.

[24] T. Mouelhi, Y. Le Traon, B. Baudry, Mutation analysis for security tests qualification, in: Testing: Academic and Industrial Conference Practice and Research Techniques—MUTATION, 2007, TAICPART-MUTATION 2007, IEEE, 2007, pp. 233–242.

[25] A. Bertolino, S. Daoudagh, F. Lonetti, E. Marchetti, Xacmut: Xacml 2.0 mutants generator, in: Software Testing, Verification and Validation Workshops (ICSTW), 2013 IEEE Sixth International Conference on, IEEE, 2013, pp. 28–33.

[26] A. Bertolino, S. Daoudagh, F. Lonetti, E. Marchetti, The X-CREATE framework—a comparison of XACML policy testing strategies, in: WEBIST, 2012, pp. 155–160.

[27] R. Soley, Model driven architecture, OMG White Paper 308 (2000) 308.

[28] L. Apfelbaum, J. Doyle, Model based testing, in: Software Quality Week Conference, 1997, pp. 296–300.

[29] A. Pretschner, T. Mouelhi, Y. Le Traon, Model-based tests for access control policies, in: Software Testing, Verification, and Validation, 2008 1st International Conference on, IEEE, 2008, pp. 338–347.

[30] T. Mouelhi, F. Fleurey, B. Baudry, Y. Le Traon, A model-based framework for security policy specification, deployment and testing, in: Model Driven Engineering Languages and Systems, Springer, Berlin Heidelberg, 2008, pp. 537–552.

[31] G. Kiczales, J. Lamping, A. Mendhekar, C. Maeda, C. Lopes, J.M. Loingtier, J. Irwin, Aspect-oriented programming, Springer, Berlin Heidelberg, 1997, pp. 220–242.

[32] D. Xu, L. Thomas, M. Kent, T. Mouelhi, Y. Le Traon, A model-based approach to automated testing of access control policies, in: Proceedings of the 17th ACM Symposium on Access Control Models and Technologies, ACM, 2012, pp. 209–218.

[33] J. Hwang, T. Xie, F. Chen, A.X. Liu, Systematic structural testing of firewall policies, in: Reliable Distributed Systems, 2008, SRDS'08. IEEE Symposium on, IEEE, 2008, pp. 105–114.

[34] E. Martin, Automated test generation for access control policies, in: Companion to the 21st ACM SIGPLAN Symposium on Object-Oriented Programming Systems, Languages, and Applications, ACM, 2006, pp. 752–753.

[35] E. Martin, T. Xie, Automated test generation for access control policies via change-impact analysis, in: Proceedings of the Third International Workshop on Software Engineering for Secure Systems, IEEE Computer Society, 2007, p. 5.

[36] A. Bertolino, S. Daoudagh, F. Lonetti, E. Marchetti, F. Martinelli, P. Mori, Testing of PolPA authorization systems, in: Proceedings of the 7th International Workshop on Automation of Software Test, IEEE Press, Zurich, Switzerland, 2012, June, pp. 8–14.

[37] A. Bertolino, S. Daoudagh, F. Lonetti, E. Marchetti, The X-CREATE framework—a comparison of XACML policy testing strategies, in: WEBIST, 2012, pp. 155–160.

[38] W. Mallouli, A. Cavalli, Testing security rules with decomposable activities, in: High Assurance Systems Engineering Symposium, 2007, HASE'07, 10th IEEE, IEEE, 2007, pp. 149–155.

[39] W. Mallouli, J.-M. Orset, A. Cavalli, N. Cuppens, F. Cuppens, A formal approach for testing security rules, in: Proceedings of the 12th ACM Symposium on Access Control Models and Technologies, ACM, 2007, pp. 127–132.

[40] A. Masood, R. Bhatti, A. Ghafoor, A.P. Mathur, Scalable and effective test generation for role-based access control systems, IEEE Trans. Softw. Eng. 35 (5) (2009) 654–668.

[41] A.D. Brucker, L. Brügger, P. Kearney, B. Wolff, An approach to modular and testable security models of real-world health-care applications, in: Proceedings of the 16th ACM Symposium on Access Control Models and Technologies, ACM, 2011, pp. 133–142.

[42] A. Bertolino, Y.L. Traon, F. Lonetti, E. Marchetti, T. Mouelhi, Coverage-based test cases selection for XACML policies, in: Software Testing, Verification and Validation Workshops (ICSTW), 2014 IEEE Seventh International Conference on, IEEE, 2014, pp. 12–21.

[43] A. Bertolino, S. Daoudagh, D. El Kateb, C. Henard, Y. Le Traon, F. Lonetti, E. Marchetti, T. Mouelhi, M. Papadakis, Similarity testing for access control, Inf. Softw. Technol. 58 (2015) 355–372.

[44] G. Rothermel, M.J. Harrold, Analyzing regression test selection techniques, IEEE Trans. Softw. Eng. 22 (8) (1996) 529–551.

[45] J. Hwang, T. Xie, D. El Kateb, T. Mouelhi, Y. Le Traon, Selection of regression system tests for security policy evolution, in: Proceedings of the 27th IEEE/ACM International Conference on Automated Software Engineering, ACM, 2012, pp. 266–269.

[46] I. Rubab, S. Ali, L. Briand, Y.L. Traon, Model-based testing of obligations, in: Quality Software (QSIC), 2014 14th International Conference on, IEEE, 2014, pp. 1–10.

[47] Y. Elrakaiby, T. Mouelhi, Y. Le Traon, Testing obligation policy enforcement using mutation analysis, in: Software Testing, Verification and Validation (ICST), 2012 IEEE Fifth International Conference on, IEEE, 2012, pp. 673–680.

[48] J.M.A. Calero, N. Edwards, J. Kirschnick, L. Wilcock, M. Wray, Toward a multi-tenancy authorization system for cloud services, IEEE Secur. Priv. 8 (6) (2010) 48–55.

ABOUT THE AUTHORS

Dr. Tejeddine Mouelhi is a currently a senior security researcher at itrust consulting. Prior to that, he was a research associate at the University of Luxembourg for 4 years. He was involved in the Dynosoar project, focusing on access control testing and modeling. He holds a PhD degree in Computer Science. His PhD subject was about "Testing and Modeling Security Mechanisms in Web Applications."

Prof. Dr. Yves Le Traon is a professor at University of Luxembourg, in the Faculty of Science, Technology and Communication (FSTC). His domains of expertise are related software engineering and software security, with a focus on software testing and model-driven engineering. He received his engineering degree and his PhD in Computer Science at the "Institut National Polytechnique" in Grenoble, France, in 1997. From 1998 to 2004, he was an associate professor at the University of Rennes, in Brittany, France. During this period, Professor Le Traon studied design for testability techniques, validation, and diagnosis of object-oriented programs and component-based systems. From 2004 to 2006, he was an expert in Model-Driven Architecture and Validation in the EXA team (Requirements Engineering and Applications) at "France Télécom R&D" company. In 2006, he became professor at Telecom Bretagne (Ecole Nationale des Télécommunications de Bretagne) where he pioneered the application of testing for security assessment of Web applications, P2P systems, and the promotion of intrusion detection systems using contract-based techniques.

He is currently the head of the Computer Science Research Unit at University of Luxembourg. He is a member of the Interdisciplinary Centre for Security, Reliability and Trust (SnT), where he leads the research group SERVAL (SEcurity Reasoning and VALidation). His research interests include software testing, model-driven engineering, model-based testing, evolutionary algorithms, software security, security policies, and Android security. The current key topics he explores are related to Internet of Things (IoT) and Cyber-Physical Systems (CPS), Big Data (stress testing, multi-objective optimization, analytics, models@run.time), and mobile security and reliability. He is author of more than 140 publications in international peer-reviewed conferences and journals.

Dr. Donia El Kateb is a research associate in the Interdisciplinary Centre for Security, Reliability and Trust (SnT). She obtained her Computer Science Engineering degree at ENSI (National School of Computer Sciences) in Tunisia in 2005. She worked 4 years at the National Digital Certification Agency in Tunisia as a security engineer. She received her PhD in Computer Science at the University of Luxembourg in 2015. Her research interests span over multiobjective optimization, software engineering, and security.

AUTHOR INDEX

Note: Page numbers followed by "*f*" indicate figures, "*t*" indicate tables, and "*np*" indicate footnotes.

SUBJECT INDEX

Note: Page numbers followed by "*f*" indicate figures and "*t*" indicate tables.

CONTENTS OF VOLUMES IN THIS SERIES

Volume 71

Volume 72

Volume 73

Volume 74

Volume 75

Volume 76

Volume 82

Volume 83

Volume 84

Volume 85

Volume 86

Volume 87

Printed in the United States
By Bookmasters